THE LAWYER'S GUIDE TO
Microsoft® Word 2013

BEN M. SCHORR

ABA LAW
PRACTICE
DIVISION
The Business of Practicing Law

Dedication

For Denise Constantine and her team at LP Division Books. Thanks for being gentle with the whip when I missed deadlines getting this book done. Hope it was worth waiting for!

Contents

Chapter 3
Creating a Basic Document   71

Chapter 4
Formatting 87

Chapter 5
Stuff Lawyers Use 117

Chapter 6
Collaboration   135

Chapter 7
Working with Other Programs   157

Chapter 8
Automating Word   173

Chapter 9
Managing and Maintaining Word 2013   189

Chapter 10
Troubleshooting 217

Chapter 11
Mistakes Lawyers Make with Microsoft Word   231

Chapter 12
Tricks to Impress Your Law School Classmates   245

Chapter 13
Keyboard Shortcuts   **261**

Acknowledgments

I'd like to give some special recognition to the following people:

At Microsoft, Jensen Harris, Jamie Sloan, Ed Hickey, and the Microsoft Word team in Redmond for being terrific and accessible and giving so much of their time to help me understand how the product works.

Beth Melton, Stephanie Krieger, and Shauna Kelly: great ladies who've forgotten more about Microsoft Word than most people will ever know. Adriana Linares and Barron Henley for reminding me of things I forgot to include in the first draft.

My business partner, Matti Raihala, and the rest of the Roland Schorr & Tower team for keeping things running smoothly so I could spend all this time banging out yet another book.

Sharon Nelson and John Simek for their support and friendship. Sharon's unending faith and enthusiasm and John's steady whip-cracking are what got me to finish this book and only be six months late.

And last, but most definitely not least, to my beautiful Carrie Rae who came along at exactly the right time and brought with her hope and happiness. Thank you for giving me a new reason to achieve.

About the Author

Ben M. Schorr is a technologist and Chief Executive Officer for Roland Schorr & Tower, a professional consulting firm headquartered in Flagstaff, Arizona, with offices in Astoria, Oregon, and Honolulu, Hawaii. In that capacity he consults with a wide variety of organizations, including many law firms. He is frequently sought as a writer, teacher, and speaker for groups as diverse as the Hawaii Visitor and Convention Bureau, Microsoft, the Association of Legal Administrators (ALA), the International Legal Technology Association (ILTA), and the American Bar Association. More than 18 years ago, Microsoft named him as an MVP in their Outlook product group, and he has been supporting Outlook, Exchange, Office 365, and, most recently, OneNote ever since.

Prior to cofounding Roland Schorr, Schorr was the Director of Information Services for Damon Key Leong Kupchak Hastert, a large Honolulu law firm, for almost eight years.

Schorr has been a technical editor or contributor on a number of other books over the years. For several years he was half of the "Ask the Exchange Pros" team for *Windows Server System* magazine. He is the author of several books on Microsoft Office that are published by the American Bar Association and a contributing author to two books on Microsoft Office 2013 published by O'Reilly.

Schorr has been named by the Pacific Technology Foundation as one of the Top 50 Technology Leaders in Hawaii. He's a member of the Institute of Electrical and Electronics Engineers' (IEEE) Computer Society, the American Bar Association, The American Football Coaches Association, and the United States Naval Institute.

He has been a presenter at ABA TECHSHOW for nine consecutive years, including three years on the planning board for that event, and has presented at the ILTA, ALA, and LegalTech as well.

In his free time Schorr enjoys coaching football, reading, and cooking and is a marathoner and Ironman triathlete. He currently lives in Flagstaff with his wife, Carrie, their rescue dog, Sampson, and the cats who keep them around.

You can reach him at bens@rolandschorr.com.

Introduction

Microsoft Word is one of the most venerable elements of the **Microsoft Office** suite—there are few applications more fundamental than putting words on paper—and it's one of the most important applications in the practice of law. No matter what area of law you practice, you probably have to put words on paper on an almost daily basis.

"One of the hardest things in life is having words in your heart that you can't utter."
—*James Earl Jones*

This new version of Word, however, is a little different from any version you've used before. First, Microsoft has painted it with the new Windows 8-style interface, and that alone is going to take some experienced Word users aback. Second, Word, like the rest of the **Office 2013** suite, is embracing the move toward tablets and touch computing by adding some new features to make these applications more touch friendly. Third, a lot of nice little touches for improved collaboration have been sprinkled throughout the product; we'll see a lot of these as we go through this book.

What's So Special about Word Processing?

We all use Word, and it seems like typing, saving, and printing are relatively simple tasks. So why do you need a book to explain how to do it? Because the documents we create are complex and important: your law practice depends, to some degree, upon the quality of the documents you produce and the efficiency with which you can produce them. In this book,

I'm going to try to help you do it more productively, more efficiently, and more enjoyably. Since this is a book aimed at lawyers and law firms, I'm going to skim over the features I don't think are very useful to lawyers and try to focus more on those tools that you actually use. For example, I don't think most lawyers care much about SmartArt so I'll not waste a lot of time on it in here. I could easily do 700 pages on **Microsoft Word 2013** if I tried to cover every feature and option in depth. I'll save your time (and mine) and try to keep my emphasis on those features and capabilities that will matter to law firms. If you really want a large comprehensive work on Microsoft Word 2013, there are some excellent general books on the market—anything with Beth Melton or Stephanie Krieger's name on it is undoubtedly worth reading if that's what you're after.

Those Who Love Software or the Law Should Not Watch Either Being Made

I thought a quick exploration of how the Office 2013 suite was made would be enlightening here. The story really begins with **Office 2003**. Since Office 2003, whenever you installed Microsoft Office (and now, pretty much any Microsoft product), you get invited to participate in something called the Customer Experience Improvement Program (CEIP). This program sends a lot of non-identifiable data back to Microsoft about how you actually use their software. Don't worry; it doesn't send any actual documents or e-mail addresses or anything like that. Instead it's primarily concerned with *how* you use the software—what buttons you click, how many documents you have open, how many sub-folders you create, how long you spend in each program (that's how we know that **Outlook** stays open longer than any other Office application). The reason for this data (known internally at Microsoft as SQM or Service Quality Monitoring data) is entirely focused on making the next version of Microsoft Office better by gathering historical usage data.

> "Designing Microsoft Office is like ordering pizza for 400 million people."
> –Steven Sinofsky

Prior to the CEIP, boxes of dry erase markers were used in brainstorming sessions. Huge quantities of Chinese food were consumed behind one-way mirrors in the usability labs, and survey after survey after survey was analyzed, all in the name of trying to figure out how users actually used the products. The results of all of that work became **Office XP**, the immediate predecessor to Office 2003. Clearly a better way was needed, and the CEIP is it. Microsoft receives a mind-boggling volume of data from the CEIP; in fact they receive *billions* of sessions of Microsoft Office usage. That data taught a lot of interesting, useful, and surprising lessons, and it is of tremendous help in designing Microsoft

▼

The most commonly clicked toolbar button in Microsoft Word 2003—and it's not even close—was **Paste**, followed, in order by **Save**, **Copy**, **Undo**, and **Bold**.

Office today. As a result, Office 2013 has been built with volumes of direct feedback from real end-users in real-life situations.

Those results can be seen in several areas, most notably in the user interface (UI). **Outlook 2007** replaced the old **File**, **Edit**, and **View** menu structure with what is called the **Ribbon** (see Figure 1.1). The Ribbon is intended to be a more discoverable interface where every feature in the product is easy to find and use, and it was developed using CEIP data. CEIP data was also used was to find out what desirable features—features that users asked for—were rarely used, indicating that they were too hard to find.

FIGURE 1.1 Microsoft's Ribbon

One key indicator that Office needed a new UI was clear from requests received from Word 2003 users. Four of the top ten requests received were for features that were already in the product. People just didn't know how to find them! According to Jensen Harris, Director of Windows User Experience (he was the lead dog on the team that designed the new UI), features like adding a watermark to Word documents were so hard to find that many users had to ask how to use them or didn't even realize they were there. With Word 2007, the watermark was prominently placed on the **Design** tab, and Jensen had a lot of users comment on the "great new feature."

More Bits for Power Users

Office 2010 was the first version of Microsoft Office to be offered in both 32-bit and 64-bit versions and Office 2013 is offered that way too. Understanding the technical details of that distinction is not that important. All you really need to know is that as computers have evolved, the number of bits they can handle at one time has grown. When I first started in law office technology, the migration from 8-bit to 16-bit computers was just starting. For most of the last fifteen years or so, 32-bit computers have dominated the landscape. In the last few years, 64-bit computers started to become more commonplace, and today it's pretty hard to buy a new computer that isn't 64-bit.

Microsoft introduced its first 64-bit operating system for workstations with Windows XP 64-bit. Never heard of it? Almost nobody used it. **Windows Vista** came in a 64-bit flavor too, and it was a little more adopted than Windows XP 64-bit did, but not much. With **Windows 7**, the 64-bit market truly matured. It was almost always a better choice to buy Windows 7 in the 64-bit flavor. Why? I'll give you two reasons.

1. For all practical purposes, 32-bit operating systems are limited to 4GB of RAM (the memory that the computer uses for active processes). That sounds like a lot, but history has shown that RAM usage tends to increase as programs become larger and more powerful, and as the price of RAM has fallen dramatically. As a general rule the more RAM you have, the faster and more stable your computer will be. It's hard to find a new computer with less than 2GB of RAM these days, and we usually recommend clients start at 4GB and consider 6GB or 8GB if the budget allows. The 64-bit operating systems make that possible.

2. **Windows 8** may be the last version of Windows that Microsoft makes that is even available in 32-bit. It's fairly universally accepted that the 32-bit platform is on the luge ride to obsolescence. It makes no sense to invest in a new 32-bit system at this stage *unless* you have key legacy hardware or software that demands it. And if you do have such legacy hardware or software, you should be thinking hard about your ongoing commitment to that gear.

Most 32-bit software will work just fine with a 64-bit operating system.

When it comes to Microsoft Office, however, I'm going to temper that advice slightly. As of this writing the 32-bit version of Office is still the wiser choice for most firms. The reason: few people really need a 64-bit version of Microsoft Office, and a number of add-ins and other pieces of software just don't work properly with the 64-bit version of Office (even though they run fine on the 64-bit version of Windows). Confused? Hopefully by the time you're reading this book, those problems have faded into the past, but as I sit here writing it, there are still some issues.

So Why *Would* I Want 64-bit Office?

The 64-bit version of Office is good for power users who are using *extremely* large files. The advantage, primarily more speed and stability, shows itself mostly on very large Excel workbooks and very large Microsoft Outlook mailboxes. Other than that, you probably won't see a lot of difference between the 32-bit and 64-bit versions of Office. Except, of course, that your add-ins will probably work better in the 32-bit version.

Making the Choice

Luckily making the choice between 32-bit and 64-bit versions of Office is pretty easy—in fact *both* versions are in the box when you buy Office (or available as a download when you subscribe to Office). You just have to decide—when you install—which version you want. Office 2013 requires Windows 7 or newer, so you won't be installing it on a terribly old computer. If you have the 32-bit version of Windows 7, you're going to be forced into the 32-bit version of Office anyhow. If you're installing on a 64-bit operating system, then you'll have the option to install the 64-bit version of Office.

    If, down the road, the 64-bit version becomes desirable and viable for you, you can always reinstall Office and choose the 64-bit version at that time.

> **So to Be Clear**
>
> We recommend most of our clients who are getting new machines opt for Windows 8 Pro 64-bit and Microsoft Office 2013 32-bit.

Getting Office 2013

How you get Microsoft Office is changing quite a bit in the new versions. Historically either you probably bought Office in a box at a retail store, or you paid a little extra for your new computer and it came pre-installed with Microsoft Office. You'll still have those options with Office 2013, though the pricing and terms have become a little less attractive because now Microsoft wants to encourage you to subscribe to Microsoft Office instead.

    For a monthly fee ($12.00 as of this writing) you can get Microsoft Office Professional Plus, which includes Outlook, Word, **OneNote**, **Excel**, **PowerPoint**, **Access**, **Publisher**, and **Lync**. On the surface the price seems OK. At $12 per month it would take more than two years to spend as much as you would buying the same package at retail. The subscription system has two big advantages though:

1. Updates are both more frequent and included. The days of the major Office release every three years are numbered. The Office team plans to start making far more frequent (perhaps as often as

quarterly) and somewhat more incremental updates to the applications. Rather than an entirely new version of Word every three years, you'll just get a new feature or three every few months. If you bought a retail box of Office, you might not get these updates or might get them less frequently. If you're a subscriber, these updates will just appear at no extra charge—though you will be able to hit snooze if the update timing is inconvenient for you.

2. The subscription license lets you install Office 2013 on up to five devices. Perhaps you have a desktop computer at the office, a laptop in your bag, and another desktop at the house. You can install the same license of Office on all three—and still be able to install it on two more if you want. And if that desktop at home happens to be a Mac, you're still covered—you can use one of your licenses to install Microsoft Office 2011 for Mac. When you look at it that way, the subscription plan could work out to be as cheap as $2.40 per month, per device . . . and that's an awful lot cheaper than what you've traditionally paid for Office.

Also if you're an Office 365 subscriber, you may have an Office 365 plan that already includes Office 2013—or you may be able to upgrade to one for somewhat less than $12 per month.

Microsoft sometimes refers to Office by subscription as being "streamed" from the Internet, which leads to a bit of confusion. Let me take a moment to clarify the important points.

First, these applications *are* installed locally, just like the traditional installs of Office. These are not web apps (though there are also web apps for Outlook, Word, Excel, PowerPoint, and OneNote included in Office 365); these are the full, locally installed versions of Office, just like what you're used to. Microsoft is referring to the method of installation when it says they're "streamed"; you don't have to get a DVD or download a huge file to install from. They install from an Internet server. Also the subscription-based version of Office 2013 checks more frequently for updates in the background.

Second, you do not have to be constantly connected to the Internet for this version of Office 2013 to work. Yes, it does check in with Microsoft's servers often, both for updates and to confirm you're still maintaining the subscription, but you can actually go thirty days with no connection at all, and the software will continue to work just fine. These days it would be pretty extraordinary for a business user to not connect to the Internet at all for more than thirty days, so I doubt anybody is going to trip over the problem of not connecting to the Internet in a couple of months and having Microsoft Office go into "reduced functionality" mode (aka Read-Only).

And Now, by Popular Demand . . .

Since you've probably already bought Word 2013 (seeing as how you're reading a book on it) I'm not going to try to sell you on why you should go get it. Let me just briefly highlight some of the key new features of Word 2013 that lawyers are going to love. I'll explain them in more detail later in the book but here's the teaser . . .

1. **New Ribbon**. It's a little cleaner in Office 2013 and more customizable too.
2. **PDF Reflow**. Word has the ability to pull **Adobe Acrobat** files into Word to edit them.
3. **Functional Improvements**. These include many display improvements: smoother typing, smoother searches, and smoother navigation.
4. **Spelling Task Pane**. This feature replaces the old dialog box for easier spelling reviews.
5. **Improved Navigation Pane**. Navigating long documents is easier and quicker. The navigation pane follows you through the document.
6. **Collapsible Headings**. These allow you to work more easily in large documents while focusing on the sections you want to see.
7. **Return to Last Edit**. Reopen a document you were working on, and Word will offer to take you back to the last place you were in the document—handy if you left off editing on page forty-two of a seventy-one–page document.
8. **Roaming Settings and Preferences**. If you use **Microsoft Account** (formerly known as Live ID), some settings and preferences will roam to other machines you use.
9. **Contextual Menus**. Pop-out menus help you format and work with things you select.
10. **Insert Online Pictures**. You can search Bing for images.
11. **Better Tables**. Adding and removing content is easier. Now you can insert rows or columns with a single click, and use the border painter to draw in the lines.
12. **The Design Tab**. You can more easily design the way your document looks.
13. **Track Changes**. New, cleaner markup views are available as are threaded comments, which allow better collaboration.
14. **New Reading Mode**. This mode is cleaner and resizes dynamically. It hides commands you don't need to see when you're just reading a document.

There are many more new features that will really excite your consultant or IT person but might be a tad esoteric for you. I'll mention them throughout the book, but mostly I want to focus on the features and tools that you're really going to use and care about in your daily practice.

So, let's get right into it. Turn the page for Chapter 2, A Quick Tour.

A Quick Tour

2

While many of the Fluent elements from Word 2010—like the Ribbon and the **Quick Access Toolbar** (QAT)—remain, the new Metro-style look gives Word 2013 a very different feel from past versions and may give new users pause. Once you get past the dramatic new styling, the Word 2013 interface isn't *that* much different from Word 2010.

In this chapter we're going to try to help you feel comfortable with the interface and confident that you know where to find everything you need. In subsequent chapters we'll go into how you use what you need.

Backstage

In Office 2007 Microsoft replaced the **File** menu with the **Office Button**, a round button at the top left corner of the screen. Unfortunately many people didn't realize that actually *was* a button, believing it to be mere decoration, and so they never thought to click on it. Equally unfortunate was the fact that many key features of the product, such as **Print**, **Open**, and **Save** were located in the menu that was accessed by clicking the button. Thus people were rather confused about how they were supposed to print or save when there weren't any obvious buttons for that.

Lesson learned. In Office 2010 the File menu was back . . . sort of. Office 2010 introduced a nifty new way to handle your documents called **Backstage**. It's cleverly located behind the File tab of the Ribbon.

Word 2013 retains Backstage and enhances it quite a bit with a nicer navigation pane and more features. Click the **File** tab and you'll see **Backstage**, as you do in Figure 2.1.

FIGURE 2.1 Backstage

▼▼▼▼▼
Every Frustrated Actor's Lament . . . How Do I Get *OUT* of Backstage?
Since Backstage doesn't really look like a tab the way the rest of the Ribbon tabs do, it's not entirely obvious how to get back to your document once you're in Backstage. I've seen a lot of users actually close Word just trying to get back to their document. Word 2013 actually makes it easier than Word 2010 did; in Word 2013 just click the back arrow icon at the top left of the **Navigation Pane**.

Info

The first command you'll find backstage is **Info**, and that's default backstage screen (see Figure 2.1) when you're working in a document. It'll show you a lot of interesting information (and some not-so-interesting information) about the current document.

The first thing it's going to show you right under Info is the name of the document and below that, the full path to the document. Don't underestimate the value of the full path—I occasionally have to be reminded whether the document I'm working on is on my C: drive, a network share, or our SharePoint site.

Along the right side of the window you'll find a list of other metadata about your document including:

- **Size**. This tells you how large the document is on disk. Handy if you're considering e-mailing it to somebody or storing it on a space-constrained media like a USB drive.
- **Pages**. A straight page count.
- **Words**. Wow, there are a lot of words in this book!
- **Total Editing Time**. Useful if this is a billable work . . . but beware, it can include time the document was merely open as the primary document in Word, including the time you left it open while you went to lunch.
- **Title**, **Tags**, **and Comments**. These are shown only if you're using any of those things.

Below that information you can find some interesting date-related information like the last time the document was modified or printed and who created and last modified the document.

The Info group also gives you access to some tools that let you do things with the current document. Specifically which tools are displayed depends a bit upon the document you've opened and whether or not you've saved it yet. We'll talk about some of these tools in more depth later; I'll just introduce them here.

- **Protect Document**. This tool lets you encrypt the document with a password securing it (sort of) from prying eyes, mark the document as final, digitally sign it, or set up the **Information Rights Management** (IRM).

  > Word's password protection feature is like a grocery-store padlock. Good enough to deter amateurs or casual browsers, but will barely slow down a determined or experienced intruder.

- **Inspect Document**. Click the **Check for Issues** button and Word launches a tool that can clean metadata and check for compatibility issues with older versions of Word. More on metadata in Chapter 11.
- **Versions**. One handy feature of Word is the ability to manage multiple versions. That feature is improved in Word 2013, and our discussion of it is improved in Chapter 6.

New

The **New** group gives you a bunch of options for creating a new document. As you can see in Figure 2.2 it's pretty heavy on encouraging you to use

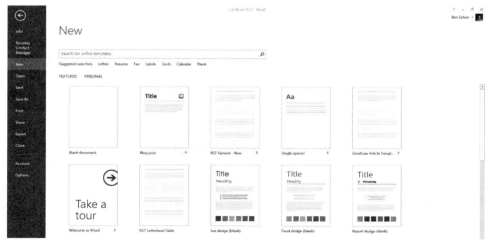

FIGURE 2.2 Creating a New Document

a template to start your new document. Here you can select from any number of templates that you've created or that you have downloaded from other sources. We'll introduce templates in Chapter 4 and get a little friendlier with them in Chapter 8.

Just click the template you want to start with (including **Blank document**) to get started.

Open

Open gives you a way to open a document or file from a storage location (hard drive, flash drive, network drive, SharePoint, OneDrive, etc.). Figure 2.3 shows you how that looks. Click **Open** and you'll be presented with a dialog box that lets you select the file (or files, see Chapter 12) that you want to open. If you used an older version of Word, you'll notice that the Open dialog has been updated rather considerably.

FIGURE 2.3 File > Open in Word 2013

Now the Open dialog first gives you choices of places where your document might be. In Figure 2.3 you'll see that it's offering me the following options:

- **Recent Documents**. This option is a handy list of the last bunch of documents you've opened. By default it shows you the last twenty-five, but you can modify that (I'll show you how in Chapter 9). The most recently used documents appear at the top and as you work on different documents, older documents will scroll off the bottom. If you have a document there that you want to *always* be at the top of this list and never scroll off, just click the pushpin icon on the right side of the document.
- **Roland Schorr Tower**. This option happens to be my company's SharePoint server, which is hosted in Microsoft Office 365. If I click that choice, Word will show me a list of document libraries and documents in our SharePoint site that I can open. SharePoint integration is one area in which Word 2013 is noticeably better than its predecessor.
- **Ben Schorr's OneDrive**. A focus of the Office 2013 suite is closer connectivity with Microsoft's **OneDrive** service (formerly known as **SkyDrive**). That includes making it easier to save and open documents from it. If I select that source, I'll see a list of folders and documents in my OneDrive site that I can edit.
- **Other Web Locations**. This option gives me access to any other miscellaneous web locations I may have configured for documents. Truth be told, I rarely use this option, and I doubt you will either.
- **Computer**. This is the source you're probably most familiar with in Word; it gives you the option to open documents from your local computer's C: drive or other fixed, network, or removable drive.
- **Add a Place**. This option lets you add an additional Office 365 SharePoint site or OneDrive account to the list.

Each of the options (except Recent Documents and Add a Place) gives you a **Recent Folders** list (see Figure 2.3) and a **Browse** button that lets you look in folders that might not be on your Recent Folders list. As with the recent documents you can click the pushpin that appears to the right of a recent folder name when you highlight it to pin that folder to the top of the recent list.

Click **Browse** and you'll get the traditional Open dialog box that you're probably familiar with from past versions of Word (see in Figure 2.4). One handy feature of the Open dialog box in Office 2013 is the **Search** box at the top right corner. If you have a folder with a lot of documents in it, you can very quickly navigate to any of those documents by typing the name in the search box. *Especially* interesting: if you have Windows Desktop Search

FIGURE 2.4 The Open Dialog Box

installed (and you almost certainly do), that search box will search the text *inside* the documents too. So you aren't just relying upon the names of the documents—you can search for a text string that appears inside the document too. Just click in the search box and type.

Save

Save does exactly what you'd expect it to do; it saves the current document in its current format and in its current location. In other words if you're editing \My Documents\resume.docx it will save it as *resume.docx* in the My Documents folder. If you're editing \marketing\great letter.docx then it will save it as *great letter.docx* in the marketing folder. Easy as that. If you're editing a document that never has been saved before, then Save will behave exactly as Save As does. And that means . . .

Save As

Save As is a little more flexible. Save As lets you save a brand new copy of this document leaving the original document (if there is one) unaffected. When you click Save As, Word will ask where you'd like to save the document, prompt you to give the document a name, and give you the option to change the format (from Word 2002 .DOC format to Word 2013 .DOCX format, for example), and the location (to any folder or other accessible storage location) if you wish. Figure 2.5 shows the location options. Figure 2.6 shows your save as options.

FIGURE 2.5 Where Do You Want to Save?

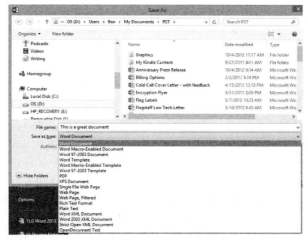

FIGURE 2.6 Document Name and Type, Please

Print

Printing is something lawyers do a lot and Word 2013's Print dialog is very much the same as 2010's. The first thing you'll notice when you go to the **Print** tab (see Figure 2.7) is that there is a **Print Preview** right there on the screen. Don't overlook the value of Print Preview; too often I've had clients find out after they printed a document that something didn't line up or paginate properly. Print Preview usually lets you see that *before* you waste the paper to print it. Take a moment to look at the Print Preview before you click Print.

FIGURE 2.7 Print Dialog Box

The rest of the settings in the Print tab should be pretty familiar, and they will vary slightly depending on what kind of printer you're connected to. Among the settings you'll use most often:

- **Copies**. This is right at the top, and it lets you print multiple copies of the document in a single pass.

- **Printer**. If you have more than one printer, you can select which printer you want to use here. Office 2013 adds a couple of virtual printers when you install it including **Send to OneNote 2013** and **Microsoft XPS Document Writer**.

- **Print All Pages**. Hiding under this option are settings to let you print only the current page, or a specific selection (such as only all of the odd numbered pages) as well as the ability to print some metadata reports about the document—such as a print out of all of the markup in the document.

We'll talk a bit more about printing in Chapter 3 so I'm not going to get too deep on it here.

Share

The emphasis from Microsoft Office 2010 around collaboration and sharing has extended into Office 2013. The **Share** group Backstage is a good example of this as you can see in Figure 2.8.

FIGURE 2.8 Sharing Your Document

Within this group there are several sections.

Invite People

This feature is a tad convoluted but essentially what it's going to do is guide you to save your document to **OneDrive** (though the dialog won't force you to save it there) and then prompt you to enter the e-mail addresses of people you'd like to invite to share and collaborate on the document.

E-mail

In the **Send Using Email** section you have up to five different ways to share this document via e-mail (see Figure 2.9).

- **Send as Attachment**. This is the traditional way Word docs are shared. Click this button and Word will start a new e-mail message for you in your default e-mail program (probably Outlook) and attach the document as a .DOCX file. Unless the other party *needs* to be able to edit it, I would avoid sending Word documents in Word format if for no other reason than to minimize the metadata issues (see Chapter 11).
- **Send a Link**. There's a good chance that this option is going to be grayed out for you. Why? Because to send somebody a link, there has to be a shared location for it to link *to*. Documents on shared network drives can be shared with a link. Documents in the **My Documents** folder on your laptop? Probably not.
- **Send as PDF**. I wish this were the first option because it's usually the best. It creates a new e-mail message just like Send as Attachment but instead of attaching a .DOCX file, it creates an Adobe

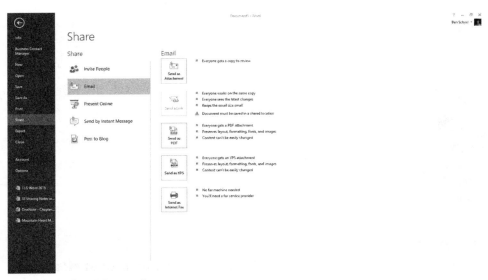

FIGURE 2.9 Share via E-mail

PDF file and attaches that. PDF files are reliably cross-platform. That means your recipient can read it, with high fidelity, on a PC, Mac, iPad, Android tablet, refrigerator, Linux machine . . . well, maybe not a refrigerator. Yet.

- **Send as XPS**. XPS is Microsoft's version of PDF. Do you ever use it? Know anybody who does? Me either, let's move on.
- **Send as Internet Fax**. Faxing is a dying technology as scanning and e-mailing become the predominant way to fill that need. If you still use fax though, and have an account with a fax service provider like **eFax**, you can use this option to send your fax directly from Word.

Present Online

Save to Web offers just one option (See Figure 2.10), but it's an option that has gotten a *lot* more powerful recently—and that's **Microsoft Lync**. Lync is Microsoft's corporate collaboration and communication platform. In Lync you can have secure instant messaging, voice and video calls, conferences, and even webinars. Using the **Present Online** option lets you share this document, in real time, with the Lync meeting you're currently having. And if you're not having one . . . it'll ask if you want to start one.

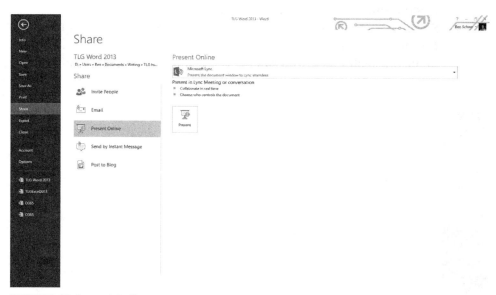

FIGURE 2.10 Present Online

Send by Instant Message

This is a new option in Word 2013. If you click **Send by Instant Message**, you'll get the screen you see in Figure 2.11, which lets you select a contact

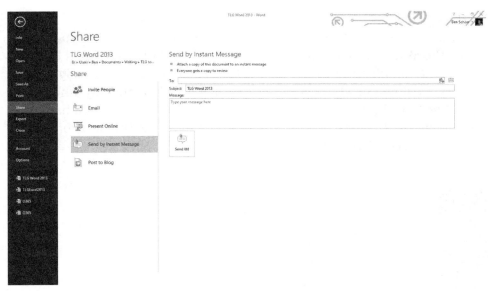

FIGURE 2.11 Send by Instant Message

that you would like to send this document to via instant messenger (such as **Lync** or **Skype**). Of course you must have entered an IM address for that person in your **Contacts** folder, or you'll have to type in the IM address in the **TO** field in order to use it .

Post to Blog

In Word 2007 Microsoft gave folks the chance to use Word to author their blog posts. If your blog is hosted on **WordPress**, **Blogger**, **SharePoint**, **Windows Live Spaces** (which has now been migrated to WordPress), **TypePad**, or a few other popular services, you can use Word 2013 as your blog editing tool. To be honest, I don't know many people who actually *do* use it for that, but you can. I'll talk more about how to do that in Chapter 12.

Export

These next two settings used to be under the **Share** group, but they have been moved into a group all their own.

Create PDF/XPS Document

If you'd like to create a PDF version of your document, and don't have Adobe Acrobat installed, you can do that natively right here. Just click the **Create PDF/XPS document** button (it's the only button on that screen) and the **Save As** dialog will appear with PDF already selected as the default type. (Because you weren't really going to save it as an XPS file, were you?) For creating basic PDF files, this is an excellent solution.

Change File Type

If you have a document that has already been saved in one file type, such as the **Word XML** format that is standard in Word 2013, but you'd like to change it to a different format, this is the place to do that. You might use this feature if you need to share this document with somebody who still uses **Word 2003** (and refuses to install the converters), or if you have a document you'd like to convert to a template to use as the basis of future documents. See Figure 2.12.

FIGURE 2.12 Change File Type

Close

Close puts this document away. If you haven't saved it first, Close will ask you if you want to save before closing.

Account

The **Account** group is where you can configure which account Word is using by default. Why does Word even need an account? Because it's connected tighter than ever with your OneDrive and SharePoint accounts, and Microsoft, like a lot of software companies, is trying to make your settings and documents as portable as possible, so that they'll travel with you from device to device. That requires some sort of account. See Figure 2.13.

Toward the bottom of the left-hand column you'll find the services that Word is currently connected to as well as a button that lets you add a

FIGURE 2.13 Accounts

connection to **Facebook**, **Twitter**, **Flickr**, or additional **OneDrive** or **Share-Point** accounts.

You'll also find settings on this page that let you change the **Office Background**, which is really a piece of decorative fluff across the title bar that you'll barely notice, and the **Office Theme** . . . which lets you choose between white or two shades of gray.

On the right side of the Account screen you'll see some useful information about your application—most notably whether or not it's currently activated. When you first install Microsoft Office, you'll be able to use it twenty-five times without activating it; after that if you still haven't activated, then Office will automatically start in "reduced functionality" mode, which basically means certain important features won't work . . . until you activate. If you got Word through Office 365, it can also go into reduced functionality mode if you haven't connected to the Internet in the last sixty days.

If Word isn't activated, you should get prompted to activate it every time you start the product. Just go thru the wizard, and Word will activate in moments. If you don't see that wizard, or skipped it and went into the product but want to activate

Version 15?

Microsoft uses incremental version numbers internally. The *Office 2013* name is just what the marketing department labels the product. Version 15 is Office 2013, version 14 is Office 2010. Office 2007 was Version 12. Notice they skipped the 13? I was in a meeting with the Microsoft VP who owned Office when 2010 was being developed and he was asked if they were skipping version 13 because Microsoft is superstitious. He smiled and said, "No, but some of our customers are."

anyhow, you can come to the **Account** menu in **Backstage** and where it says **Not Activated**, you'll find a link to the **Activation Wizard** to go ahead and activate it.

Options

The **Options** group is where you configure all sorts of settings that affect how Word works. We have a whole chapter dedicated to this group (Chapter 9) so I'm going to leave it alone for now.

Below the Options group is an area on the navigation pane that is usually blank. But by going to **Options** > **Advanced** > **Display**, you can turn on **Quickly access this number of recent documents . . .** , which will put links in that area to the specified number of your most recently used documents (see Figure 2.14).

FIGURE 2.14 Recently Used Documents

The Ribbon

The most noticeable difference in Word 2013 is the Ribbon. *Ribbon* is the name for the interface at the top of the screen where all of the program commands are found.

The key elements of the Ribbon are the Office **Quick Access Toolbar** (QAT) and a series of Ribbon tabs that contain various commands. The Ribbon is less customizable or variable than the old menu structure was. It will change a bit if certain document elements are selected on-screen, but otherwise it will, by design, remain basically the same. An example of when it changes a bit is when you add a table to your document. In that case, a couple of extra tabs related to tables are added to the Ribbon. The tabs on the Ribbon are made up of groups, which collect the commands.

Some of the groups have a tiny "button" to the right of the group name, which is called a **Dialog Launcher**. I've circled them in Figure 2.15. Clicking a Dialog Launcher opens a larger dialog box containing more commands for working with that family of commands. We'll spend time with the Dialog Launchers as we go thru the book.

One thing to keep in mind with the Ribbon is that it will adapt a bit depending upon the size of your window and your screen resolution. If you don't have Word running full screen and you drag and drop the Word window wider and narrower, you'll notice that the Ribbon changes a bit as you go, so that the various groups compress and expand to fit the available space.

The lack of customization in the Ribbon is by design. When users could heavily customize and move around their toolbars and menus, it became very difficult for help desk personnel to support Office. It was hard to tell people where to go to click something when it could have been moved almost anywhere. Also users would often accidentally turn features on or off, hide toolbars, and make other changes that confused or upset them.

Making the Ribbon more standardized and less customizable (and less easily customizable) results in a much more standard configuration that is easier to support and harder for users to accidentally mess up.

FIGURE 2.15 The Dialog Launchers

To be fair, not all users like the Ribbon. Some have such a long history with the old menu structure that the change to the Ribbon has been uncomfortable. Some have long engrained habits that they'll have to break, and some simply don't like it. It *is* a significant change from the old way. Word 2013 is the third version to incorporate the Ribbon though, and by now, most users do seem to have become accustomed to it.

So let's take a look at the Ribbon in Word 2013.

Home

The **Home** tab (seen in Figure 2.16) on the Ribbon is the default tab and contains the most commonly used editing commands within five groups.

FIGURE 2.16 The Home Tab of the Ribbon

Clipboard

At the far left side you can see the **Clipboard** commands such as **Paste**, which we've learned was the most commonly clicked-on toolbar button in Word 2003.

▼▼▼▼▼
Tricks of the Pros
To display the contents of the Office Clipboard click the **Dialog Launcher** at the right end of the *Clipboard* group label. The Office Clipboard can hold up to twenty-four items at a time, and by exposing it you can select which of the items you want to paste. Unlike pressing **Control+V**, with this method you don't have to paste the last thing you cut or copied to the clipboard.

This is especially handy if you want to paste the same word or phrases in various places of your document without having to recopy them (or worse, retype them). To close the clipboard pane again just click the **X** at the top right corner of that pane.

Font

Next to the Clipboard group you'll find the set of **Font** commands, which include the **typeface** (such as Times New Roman), **font size**, **font color**, **highlighting**, **change case**, and others.

The fonts listed in your document (Times New Roman, Arial, etc.) depend upon the fonts supported by your currently selected printer and the fonts that you have installed on the computer. Change the default printer for the document or system, and the list of fonts may change slightly—though most modern printers support a fairly common set of fonts.

One feature I find very useful is the **Change Case** feature. Occasionally I'll type something, especially a section heading, which I want to have in **Capitalize the First Letter of Each Word** format. In the past you might have had to retype the sentence or at least the first letter of each word. Now just select the sentence, click the **Change Case** button and select that option. Word takes care of the rest. This is one of those great "new features" that has been in Word forever, but many users are just now discovering, thanks to the Ribbon.

Paragraph

Next to the Font group you'll find the **Paragraph** group, which contains buttons for **bulleted or numbered lists**, **justification**, **fill color**, **line spacing**,

borders, **sorting**, and other features. We'll talk more about most of these options in Chapter 4.

Notice that the Paragraph group does have a Dialog Launcher at the bottom right corner. Clicking it will fire up the **Paragraph** dialog box you see in Figure 2.17. In that dialog box you can do some tricky things with **indentation**, **line and page breaks** (notice the tabs at the top of the dialog box?), **line spacing**, and more.

FIGURE 2.17 Paragraph Dialog Box

The last thing I want to call your attention to in the Paragraph dialog box is the **Tabs** button at the bottom left, which launches the dialog box you see in Figure 2.18. This lets you customize your tab stops quite easily. You can create or customize tab stops on the **Ruler**, but I've found that some people have trouble getting the tabs just the way they want them using only the Ruler, so this dialog box may be a little more intuitive for you.

FIGURE 2.18 Customizing Tabs

We'll talk about this in more detail in Chapter 4 as well.

Styles

The next group contains the **Styles Galleries**, which let you apply a style to selected text. It's also easy to modify or create new styles from this part of the Ribbon. Like most of the things on the Home tab, we'll be spending some time with Styles in Chapter 4. This is a nice example, however, of the **Galleries** feature in Word 2013 that gives you WYSIWYWGIYCT (What You See Is What You Will Get If You Click This) capabilities. Despite my doubts that the acronym will catch on, the feature certainly will. If you select some text in your document, then simply hover your mouse over one of the elements in the gallery, such as **Heading 3** for example, the selected text changes temporarily to show you what it will look like if you click. That eliminates the need for trial and error like the old days. Now you can quickly try a bunch of different formats just by moving your mouse thru the gallery.

To see more styles, click the drop-down arrow at the right end of the Styles gallery. Or click the bottom arrow there to see the entire list at once (Figure 2.19), along with a couple of other options . . . which we'll discuss in more depth in Chapter 4.

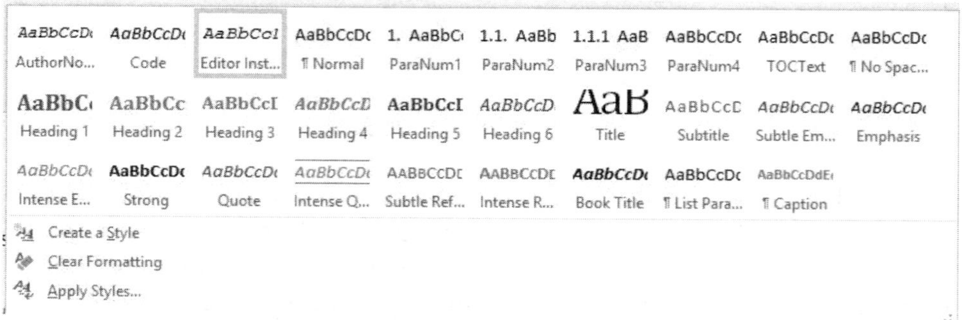

AaBbCcD(	AaBbCcD(	AaBbCcI	AaBbCcD(	1. AaBbC(	1.1. AaBb	1.1.1 AaB	AaBbCcD(	AaBbCcD(	AaBbCcD(
AuthorNo...	Code	Editor Inst...	¶ Normal	ParaNum1	ParaNum2	ParaNum3	ParaNum4	TOCText	¶ No Spac...
AaBbC	**AaBbCc**	AaBbCcI	*AaBbCcD*	**AaBbCcI**	*AaBbCcD*	AaB	AaBbCcD	*AaBbCcD*	*AaBbCcD*
Heading 1	Heading 2	Heading 3	Heading 4	Heading 5	Heading 6	Title	Subtitle	Subtle Em...	Emphasis
AaBbCcD	**AaBbCcD**	*AaBbCcD*	*AaBbCcD*	AABBCCD(	AABBCCD(	**AaBbCcD**	AaBbCcD(	AaBbCcDdE(	
Intense E...	Strong	Quote	Intense Q...	Subtle Ref...	Intense R...	Book Title	¶ List Para...	¶ Caption	

- Create a Style
- Clear Formatting
- Apply Styles...

FIGURE 2.19 Word Styles

Editing

Finally the curiously named **Editing** group contains three buttons: **Find**, **Replace**, and **Select**. These options have changed a bit in Word 2013. Clicking **Find** will take you to the **Navigation Pane** (or open it for you if it's not already open) on the left side of the screen where you can type the text you're searching for in the **Search Document** box. Clicking the drop-down arrow to the right of the Find button will give you several more advanced options for finding and replacing as you can see in Figure 2.20.

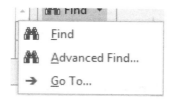

- Find
- Advanced Find...
- Go To...

FIGURE 2.20 The Advanced Find and Replace Context Menu

There are some neat and tricky things you can do with Find, and I'll get into those with a bit more depth in Chapter 3.

Clicking **Replace** opens the dialog box you see in Figure 2.21, and takes you to the Replace tab.

FIGURE 2.21 Replace

Find and Replace are pretty handy tools when you're working with large documents. Find lets you search your document for instances of specific text—a witness name for example. Replace lets you replace something with something else—if you just realized you've been misspelling that witness's name throughout the entire document, it's fast and easy to change the thirty-seven instances of *Smith* to *Smyth*.

> Notice the **Find** tab in Figure 2.21? That's another way to get to the **Advanced Find**. More on that in Chapter 3. Be patient; it's worth it.

The Select tool is one of the most underused tools in Word and, honestly, for good reason. Of the three capabilities it has, two of them are much easier to access in a different way. **Select All** is most easily done by just pressing **Control+A** on the keyboard. **Select Object** is awkward to do with the Select tool, easier just by clicking on the object with your mouse.

The one option in the Select tool that I find marginally useful is the ability to select all text with a similar formatting. Of course, if you're using Styles (as you should be), then you rarely need to do that with the Select tool either. Moving on . . .

Insert

Next up is the **Insert** tab (see Figure 2.22). As you might suspect, it is filled with things you might want to insert into your document: **clip art**, **page breaks**, **Quick Parts**, that sort of thing. Let's take a quick look at each group on this tab.

FIGURE 2.22 The Insert Tab

Pages

The first group you'll find on the Insert tab is the **Pages** group, which includes the **Cover Page** gallery that lets you select from a number of pre-created cover page templates or allows you to create your own cover page to save to the gallery.

The second and third buttons in the Pages group are the **Blank Page** and **Page Break** buttons. The Page Break button inserts a page break at the current cursor location: it forces all of the text after the current cursor location to move down to the next page. Those of you who've used older versions of Word are probably thinking "Wait, doesn't **Control+Enter** do the same thing?" Yes, it does. The **Blank Page** button inserts a blank page into your document at the current cursor location. "Wait, couldn't I just press **Control+Enter** twice?" Yes, you could.

Tables

The next group over on the Insert tab is the little group that could. It has only one button but it's one button that you will want to remember the location of, and that's **Table**. To use it click the button to open the **Insert Table** tool and then just drag your mouse from top left to bottom right to create a table that matches your needs. Everything from 1×1 (which you may also think of as a text box) to 10×8; it's a quick and easy way to create a table that's just the size you need. If you need more columns or rows, there are ways to do that, which we'll talk about in more detail in Chapter 4. For now Figure 2.23 gives you a teaser.

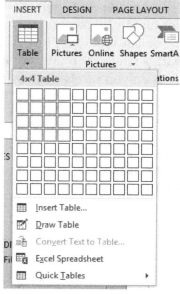

FIGURE 2.23 Creating Tables

Illustrations

The **Illustrations** group gives you a handful of tools to insert all sorts of pretty pictures. From **actual pictures** (photos, scans, or other graphics files) to **clip art, shapes, SmartArt,** or **charts**.

The **Pictures** tool is pretty self-explanatory. You click it and a dialog box opens that lets you browse your storage devices (**hard drives, flash drives, inserted SD cards, CDs or DVDs** . . .) for one or more pictures that you might want to insert into your document. This can be handy if you want to include photos of certain exhibits, properties, or pieces of evidence in your document.

Online Pictures takes this tool a step further, offering you four different web places you can insert pictures from (plus links to Facebook and Flickr) as you can see in Figure 2.24.

- **From SharePoint.** You can select an image that's located in one of your SharePoint libraries.
- **Office.com Clip Art.** This is the traditional clip art repository that Office users are accustomed to, but a little better because it's actually hosted online. So it doesn't require space on your local hard drive, and (in theory) it's continually updated and growing. Clip Art is basically eye candy—small graphics that just add some color and visual elements to a document. They're great in presentations and probably have a role in marketing materials, but you're not going to use them in your legal documents so we won't spend a lot of time on them in this book.
- **Bing Image Search.** This option lets you search the open web for images. Be careful of copyright and licensing issues.
- **OneDrive.** With this option, you can select images from your OneDrive folders. For Windows Phone users this can be especially handy as photos you take with your Windows Phone are probably being automatically updated to your OneDrive.

FIGURE 2.24 Online Pictures

The Clip Art and Bing Image Search are based on keywords. When you find one, you like either double-click it, or drag and drop it to insert it in your document. Again, they're handy for the brochures and the occasional PowerPoint presentation, but not something lawyers use in Word that often. So we'll leave it there.

Shapes, SmartArt, and Charts are not like the fluffy Clip Art. They are tools that might be useful to you in client communications or to illustrate concrete ideas and principles.

- **Shapes** lets you draw figures or simple illustrations in your document.
- **SmartArt** lets you create custom graphics like cycle and process diagrams. Not only does it work in Word 2013 but it works in Excel and PowerPoint as well. I'll give an example of using SmartArt in Chapter 5.
- The **Chart** tool lets you embed a wide variety of charts and graphs into your documents to illustrate comparative data, for instance, revenue over time or relative ownership in a disputed piece of property (shown graphically). If the interface for the tool looks like Excel, that's because it *is* Excel. And you can embed or link to Excel workbooks and/or charts in your Word documents too. We'll talk about that in Chapter 7.

Finally the last button in this group is a handy one . . . **Screenshot**. Screenshot lets you capture the image of any window that you currently have open. There are a few instances where that can be handy; for example, if you're handling a case in which a website that is part of the dispute, you can open the site in your browser, grab a screenshot of it, and paste that screenshot directly into your document.

Apps

The next group on the Insert tab is new to Office 2013: **Apps**. This group is so new, in fact, that many of the Outlook apps require **Exchange 2013** on the back end to work at all. Apps let developers create little add-ins that work with your Office 2013 products to extend their native functionality. For example, there are **Mind Mapping** and **Task List** apps for Word as well as Apps that let you look up things in **Wikipedia** from within Word.

▼

This is going to either intrigue you or anger you (or maybe both) but as of this writing there is a **Free Legal Forms** app available from **LegalZoom** in the Office Apps Store.

Some of the apps are free, others cost money. To be honest, as of this writing, most of the apps I've seen seem like novelty items rather than truly useful extensions, but they are interesting proofs of concept.

To see the list of Apps available for Office 2013 (or manage your existing apps) click the **Apps for Office** button and then click **See All** to get the dialog box you see in Figure 2.25 and the "Find More Apps at the Office Store" link at the bottom left.

FIGURE 2.25 Apps for Office

Media

The **Media** group seems like sort of a waste to me if I'm honest. The **Online Video** button is fine, if you really want to insert a video into a Word document, but it seems like this group should have somehow been combined with the **Illustrations** group because the functionality is so similar. I rather doubt that lawyers are going to insert many videos into their Word documents, so I won't really spend any time on that feature here.

Links

The next group on the Insert tab is the **Links** group. This is a deceptively useful set of tools: the first is the **Hyperlink** tool, which lets you insert a hyperlink into your document. Most people think of this as inserting web links (e.g., http://www.officeforlawyers.com) but you could also use this tool to insert a hyperlink to an internal source like a file on your intranet or a link to a note in OneNote. This feature *does* make your documents highly interactive, but of course you have to keep the ultimate form of the document in mind. If this is a document that is intended to be printed, it doesn't do you any good to insert lots of links—they won't translate to paper in any meaningful way.

Also remember who your audience is. If this document is going to stay electronic but be transmitted outside your organization, it does you no good to create hyperlinks to documents inside your internal systems—the recipients probably won't be able to access those links from their location. By the way, this is a mistake I see made *a lot*. I often receive documents from clients that contain dead hyperlinks because the link points at a location on a private network that I can't access.

Figure 2.26 gives you a look at the Insert Hyperlink dialog box.

FIGURE 2.26 Insert Hyperlink

The next tool in the Links group is one that I use a lot. As you can imagine, I write a lot of long documents (like 300-page books) and I don't usually write them in a single sitting (no matter how many Frappuccinos I drink), so I frequently have to save my place and come back to it later. I also don't tend to write these books sequentially. Right now I'm writing Chapter 2, but I've already written most of Chapter 12 (it's a good one, but wait for it). I can't just press **Control+End** and go to the bottom of the document to pick up where I left off. To make matters even slightly more difficult, I also tend to write multiple chapters at once. Obviously here I am in Chapter 2, but I've also written some of several other chapters. So how do I quickly get back to where I left off and in a particular chapter? Bookmarks.

The **Insert Bookmark** tool (see Figure 2.27) lets you create a new bookmark at your current location, delete an existing bookmark, or go to a bookmark you've already defined in the document. As you can see in Figure 2.27 I currently have at least twelve bookmarks defined. You can have as many as you'd like and sort them either by name or by location. A location sort will place them in the order they appear in the document from page one forward. The way it works is pretty simple; you click in a spot or select a block of text and then go to the **Insert** tab of the Ribbon and choose **Bookmark**. The Bookmark dialog box will appear and you can type a name for your new bookmark. You can't use spaces or many of the punctuation characters (like hyphens) in your bookmark name but you can use underscores (_, as in A_Quick_Tour) to separate words.

FIGURE 2.27 Insert Bookmark

Notice the checkbox for **Hidden bookmarks**? Those are a special case. Word uses them for a variety of purposes—usually without you realizing it. One example is the **Table of Contents**. When you add a Table of Contents to your document and flag an item for inclusion, Word puts a hidden bookmark at that spot so that the hyperlink from the Table of Contents can take you back there when you click it.

The third item in the Links group is the **Cross-Reference** tool. This lets you build links between **text** and **figures**, **pages**, **tables**, and so forth. The key to it is that if the table or figure is moved, the cross-reference can be "automatically" updated. I am a little disappointed to have to put "automatically" in quotes but the reality is that it doesn't quite get automatically updated—you have to initiate the update by pressing **F9**. To update *all* cross-references you just press **Control+A** to select the entire document and then press **F9**.

If you've got a lot of cross-references in a document, and you've been doing some editing, you should make a habit of reconfirming your cross-references by doing a **Control+A**, **F9** before you save and finalize the document. Even small edits could have caused things to move around and repaginate in the document, so it's always a good practice to recalculate tables of contents, indexes, cross-references, and any other similar elements you may have in your document.

Comments

The next group is sort of new to Office 2013. I say "sort of new" because it's not really new . . . but its placement on the Insert tab is. Comments contains just a single button and that button inserts a new comment in the text at the current cursor location. Used to be you had to go to the Review tab to find the button to insert a comment (and you still can) but now you'll find it here as well.

Header & Footer

Next to Comments you'll find the **Header & Footer** group. One of the more straightforward groups, this is where you can add a **Header** or a . . . wait for it . . . **Footer**. A header is the section at the top of a page that frequently might include the name of the firm, the name of the case, or other title information. The footer is the section at the bottom of each page that might include the date, page number, or other information.

Tricks of the Pros

Tired of stacks of outdated letterhead sitting in your supply closet? Got more scratch paper than you can use? A lot of firms have taken to creating templates of their letterhead in Word by using the Header and Footer features for much of the static information, and then printing their letters (including the letterhead template) on blank paper as needed. No more ordering overpriced letterhead, some of which will end up stacked in a back closet when you move to a new office or have turnover among the associates.

The Header & Footer group contains good examples of one of the better features of Word 2013 and those are the galleries. Figure 2.28 shows what happens when you click the drop-down arrow under Header. You're presented with a fairly long gallery of predefined headers you can choose from, and if you don't like any of the predefined ones, you can just choose **Blank** and edit it to create your own header. You can also remove your header from here if you've accidentally added one or just decided you don't want a header on this document after all. Footer works in much the same way. Clicking the drop-down arrow opens a large gallery of predefined footers. We'll talk more about Headers and Footers in Chapter 4.

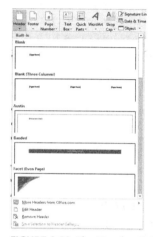

FIGURE 2.28 The Header Gallery

The third feature in the Header & Footer group is **Page Number**, which, when clicked, gives you a number of galleries to view in four different categories.

- **Top of Page** creates a header for you that contains the page number in a variety of formats.
- **Bottom of Page** creates a footer that contains the page number in a variety of formats.
- **Page Margin** creates a page number on the left or right side of the page, depending on the option you choose.
- **Current Position** will let you insert the page number right where you are on the page.

Additionally you can change the format of your page numbers or remove them entirely from the Page Number menu. We'll cover page numbering more in Chapter 4.

Text

The next group you'll find is the **Text** group. It contains a number of items you can add to your document such as **Text Boxes** (graphical boxes that contain text), **Quick Parts**, and others. **WordArt** lets you create text with very stylish graphics while **Drop Caps** are a stylish way to open a paragraph, and they are especially useful in newsletters and other marketing materials. Figure 2.29 shows the WordArt gallery.

FIGURE 2.29 The WordArt Gallery

Quick Parts are where you'll find **AutoText** and the **Building Blocks Organizer**, a *very* useful tool that we'll talk about more extensively in Chapter 8. Pay attention to this one; you'll probably use it a lot once you learn how.

The other things you'll find in Quick Parts are Document Property and Field, which let you automatically populate a document with information like the Author name or a large selection of various formulas. We'll talk a bit more about that when we get to Chapter 8 and discuss automating Word.

There are three more options in the Text group, the first two of which are very useful to lawyers:

- **Signature Line** lets you save and insert a standard signature line for use on letters, contracts, and other documents. It can also insert a digital signature for use in electronic documents.
- **Date & Time** is a feature you'll likely use often; it inserts the current date and/or time in a variety of formats (as you can see in Figure 2.30).

FIGURE 2.30 Insert Date & Time

One option you have with Date & Time is the **Update Automatically** option. If you check this box Word will automatically update the date and time to the current date and time whenever you open this document. This is handy if you're creating a template and want the date to always be today's date. But be careful—if you're creating a letter and you want the original date to be persistent, you should leave this unchecked.

The **Object** feature on the Text group has two options in it, both of which can be very useful for lawyers. The first option is to insert an Object, and that's how you embed items from other applications, as you can see in Figure 2.31. What you're going to see in this window will vary a bit depending upon what applications you have installed. We'll look at some uses of this feature in Chapter 7, and it might make an appearance in Chapter 12 as well. You can either create a new item from that application or insert an item from an existing file.

FIGURE 2.31 Insert Objects

The other option you'll find if you click the arrow next to the Object button is **Text from File**. This is a deceptively helpful feature that will insert all of the text from an existing file. Let's say you have a document on your hard drive and you want to incorporate all of that text into your document, but you don't want to have to retype it, and you don't want to have to open that document separately and do a Copy and Paste. Use **Object** > **Text from File** and Word will just insert all of the text from the file you select at the current insertion point. It's a great way to reuse content from other documents. You may know this feature as **Insert File** from previous versions of Word.

Note that after you insert that text you'll probably have to go through and apply formatting to it for it to look right . . . but after Chapter 4, you'll be using styles anyhow so that should be a breeze.

Symbols

The last group on the Insert tab is the **Symbols** group, which contains two commands. The **Equation** button actually launches a gallery that lets you select from a wide selection of items like **Pythagorean Theorem**, **Quadratic Equation**, and others. Probably not something lawyers are going to use very often, to be honest, but if you have kids over the age of thirteen, they may find it useful in doing their homework. The second command in the group, **Symbol**, is more useful to lawyers, however. Among the more law-useful symbols under this command are Δ, §, and ©. Note also that if you use a symbol from the **More Symbols** list, it will be helpfully added to the initial gallery of symbols so that next time you go to use that symbol, you don't have to click into More Symbols to find it. (See Figure 2.32.)

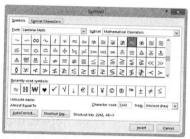

FIGURE 2.32 More Symbols

Design

The **Design** tab (see Figure 2.33) is new to Word 2013. It contains some elements, like **Themes**, that have been moved from other tabs along with a new **Document Formatting** gallery.

FIGURE 2.33 The Design Tab

Document Formatting

This enormous group incorporates the Themes command and some really good (though probably not appropriate for legal documents) built-in collections of style sets.

The first button is a **Themes** gallery that lets you select one of many built-in Themes, manage the currently applied Theme, download additional themes, or even create your own theme.

After the Themes button is a gallery of **Document Formatting** choices. Move your mouse slowly across the gallery to see how your current document would look if you applied that style set. There are some pretty nice options there, and you can even create your own style set there as well. That might have some application for you—if you have a couple of different kinds of documents and you actually do create custom styles for each, you could save those as style sets that you could reuse on future documents.

▼

For the most part I think it's pretty rare that lawyers will ever need to tweak the theme settings. The vast majority of your documents are going to be black text on white paper and with a relatively small number of fonts or "effects." The reality is that many of your documents are mandated to a certain look and feel by the court, and I don't care how liberal your judge is, he or she probably doesn't want a pink or green font on yellow paper. Accordingly we're not going to spend much time on Themes in this book.

The next two options, and one just next to those, are nicely related to the Theme—in fact, they are elements that the Theme controls: **Colors**, **Fonts**, and **Effects**. Each of those buttons launches a gallery that lets you set the text colors, available fonts, and graphical effects that will be used in your document.

A useful button on the Document Formatting group, however, is the **Paragraph Spacing** button. This, as you might surmise, lets you control how much space your document will have between paragraphs. Click to drop down the gallery shown in Figure 2.34, and you'll see that you have some options for your paragraph spacing. People trying to stretch (or compact) a paper to fit page length requirements love this setting.

FIGURE 2.34 Paragraph Spacing Gallery

Finally, clicking **Set as Default** will designate your current style set as the one that all of your new documents will start with (unless you start your new document from a custom template).

Page Background

The **Page Background** group has three commands that affect what goes around and behind the text in your document. For lawyers the first one, Watermark, is generally the most useful.

Watermark, which we talk about in more depth in Chapter 12, lets you create a faded bit of text or image that sits behind your text. It is most often used in law firms to apply words like *DRAFT* or *CONFIDENTIAL* to a printed or digital copy so that the reader is aware of the status of the document. You can see an example of that (which I darkened to make it easier to read for this screenshot) in Figure 2.35.

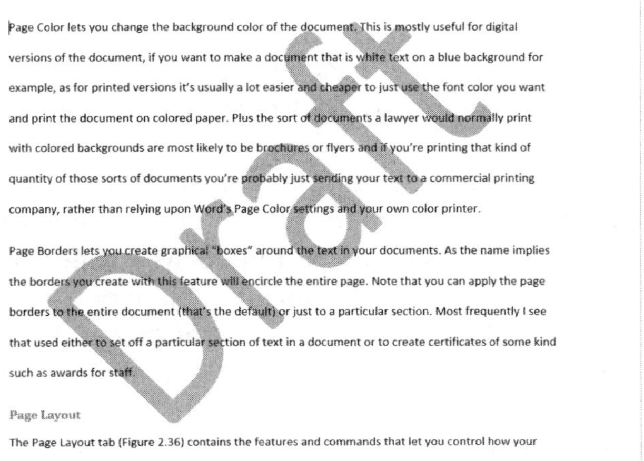
Page Color lets you change the background color of the document. This is mostly useful for digital versions of the document, if you want to make a document that is white text on a blue background for example, as for printed versions it's usually a lot easier and cheaper to just use the font color you want and print the document on colored paper. Plus the sort of documents a lawyer would normally print with colored backgrounds are most likely to be brochures or flyers and if you're printing that kind of quantity of those sorts of documents you're probably just sending your text to a commercial printing company, rather than relying upon Word's Page Color settings and your own color printer.

Page Borders lets you create graphical "boxes" around the text in your documents. As the name implies the borders you create with this feature will encircle the entire page. Note that you can apply the page borders to the entire document (that's the default) or just to a particular section. Most frequently I see that used either to set off a particular section of text in a document or to create certificates of some kind such as awards for staff.

Page Layout

The Page Layout tab (Figure 2.36) contains the features and commands that let you control how your

FIGURE 2.35 A Watermark

Page Color lets you change the background color of the document. This is mostly useful for digital versions of the document if you want to make a document that is white text on a blue background for example. As for printed versions, it's usually a lot easier and cheaper to just use the font color you want and print the document on colored paper. Plus the sort of documents a lawyer would normally print with colored backgrounds are most likely to be brochures or flyers, and if you're printing that kind of quantity of those sorts of documents, you're probably just sending your text to a commercial printing company, rather than relying upon Word's Page Color settings and your own color printer.

Page Borders lets you create graphical "boxes" around the text in your documents. As the name implies the borders you create with this feature will encircle the entire page. Note that you can apply the page borders to the entire document (that's the default) or just to a particular section. Most frequently I see that used either to set off a particular section of text in a document or to create certificates of some kind, such as awards for staff.

Page Layout

The **Page Layout** tab (Figure 2.36) contains the features and commands that let you control how your page will appear on the printed page. Most notably things like **page margins**, **line numbers**, and **indents**.

FIGURE 2.36 The Page Layout Tab

Page Setup

The **Page Setup** group contains commands that let you control the basic layout of the page, most notably things like **margins**, **paper size**, and **columns**.

Margins (Figure 2.37) are a feature that is pretty familiar to folks who work with documents; they control the white space around the edges of your document. Clicking the Margins button opens a gallery of common margins that you can use for your document. If none of those are exactly what you need, you can always click **Custom Margins** at the bottom of the list to create your own. Keep in mind that if this document is going to be printed, your printer almost certainly has an unprintable area. Very few printers can print all the way to the edge of the paper; the vast majority will have some small area, on the sides especially, but also at the top and bottom, that it just can't put ink or toner on. So no matter what you set your margins to in Word, your printer will generally enforce some minimal unprintable area.

FIGURE 2.37 Page Margins

Orientation is fairly simple; there are only two choices there: Portrait or Landscape. **Portrait** is the typical vertical alignment, like this book. **Landscape** is with the page rotated 90 degrees, more like how the typical computer monitor is.

Size lets you set the size of the paper you're going to print on. We're all used to **Letter** (8.5 × 11) and **Legal** (8.5 × 14), but you can also choose from a variety of other sizes like **A4** or **Envelope**, or you can specify a custom paper size.

Columns are a little trickier to work with, and we'll talk about those in more depth in Chapter 4. Clicking the Columns button here, however, drops down the Columns menu like you see in Figure 2.38. You can choose from five default column settings or you can click **More Columns** to set something custom. Generally speaking if you need something other than one of the five default column selections, then you might consider using a Table instead of columns, but there may be occasions when you'll want some sort of fancy custom column arrangement.

FIGURE 2.38 The Columns Menu

The **Breaks** command gives you a number of choices for breaks you can insert. As you can see in Figure 2.39, the menu is actually pleasantly notated. Not only does it give you a graphical hint of what the command will do, but there is some explanatory text as well. That's a big improvement over the old **File**, **Edit**, and **View** menus that never really told you much about what a command was about.

FIGURE 2.39 The Breaks Menu

Page Breaks are probably the most common breaks you'll use, and perhaps **Column Breaks** as well. If you're using sections in your documents, perhaps to separate out exhibits, then you have some choices there as well.

The important thing to remember about **Section Breaks**—so important that I'll probably repeat this in Chapter 4—is the difference between a Next Page and a Continuous break. A **Next Page** break is actually going to create a new page for you and start your section there. A **Continuous** break is going to start your new section right at the point of the page that you place the break. Usually lawyers will want a Next Page section break.

Line Numbers are a very intriguing idea, especially if you have to create your own pleading paper. It's not quite as easy as you might imagine it to be but there *are* ways to do it. Stay tuned—we'll talk about that in more detail in Chapter 5.

Finally, another new addition to the Page Layout tab in Word 2013 is **Hyphenation**, which gives you some control over how Word will (or won't) automatically hyphenate long words for you at the end of a line. By default Word won't hyphenate, which means that those long words will just get bumped down to the next line in their entirety. However, you can turn Hyphenation on so that Word will automatically hyphenate certain words for you, splitting the word across the two lines. You can also set hyphenation to **Manual**; then Word will ask you where (or if) you want certain words hyphenated when necessary.

Paragraph

The **Paragraph** group contains two related sets of commands for controlling your indent and spacing. As you might suspect these settings apply on a paragraph-by-paragraph basis. I'm not going to really get into these here, but we'll discuss them in some depth in Chapter 4. Suffice it to say that these commands on the Ribbon are an example of Direct Formatting, and you'll generally be better served by the indirect formatting provided by Styles. If this is a subject you're passionate about, you'll have to flip to Chapter 4 to enjoy more about it.

Arrange

The **Arrange** group controls how text and items on a page interrelate. This is especially useful when you have a **graphic**, **chart**, **text box**, or other item on the page and you want to be able to control exactly where it appears and how the surrounding text will behave.

Most of the commands in this group will only be active if you have an object (like an inserted image) selected.

The **Position** button opens a gallery that helps you align the object on the page (see Figure 2.40). You can select one of nine default positions on the page, or you can position it so that image appears at the current cursor point and the text wraps around the object. Like all galleries in Word this demonstrates a powerful feature: if you move your mouse over the various gallery options, Word will temporarily alter the display of your document to reflect how the change would look. Saves a lot of time in trial and error for aligning text and objects.

FIGURE 2.40 The Position Gallery

The next command is complementary to the Position button; **Wrap Text** lets you specify how (or if) your text should flow around the object you have selected.

The next two commands (**Bring to Front** and **Send to Back**) demonstrate a surprising capability of Microsoft Word—the ability to have multi-layered documents. There are more options than just having text next to images. You can actually have text in front of (or behind) images, or you can have multiple images stacked on top of each other. You can use the Front/Back commands to arrange the images the way you like them. This really

Tricks of the Pros

One of the rare times I do see lawyers use this feature (or want to) is if they are annotating exhibits. Perhaps you've pasted in a satellite photo of a piece of real estate in dispute and you want to type (or draw) annotations on top of it. Then Bring to Front or Send to Back are features you might want to get cozy with.

isn't a feature lawyers use very often, so I'm not going to spend additional space on it in this book.

The **Selection Pane** solves a common problem with multilayered documents. It can be very hard to manipulate images that are layered together simply because it's hard to select them. Click the Selection Pane icon to turn on the Selection Pane (see Figure 2.41) and you'll find it easier

FIGURE 2.41 The Selection Pane

to handle them. As long as you're in there, rename your images to make them easier to identify on the page.

Figure 2.42 shows the **Align** menu, which lets you finetune how you want to align a selected image (or images) on the page. You can even turn on gridlines for precision text and image layout. Not really a feature lawyers will use very much, so we're not going to spend a lot more time on it here.

FIGURE 2.42 The Align Menu

If you have multiple images that you want to be able to link together, then the **Group** command is for you. With images grouped you can move and format them together. Clicking the group button offers two options: **Group** or **Ungroup**. For reasons that may be obvious, only one of them will be active at a time.

Finally if you insert an image that is not aligned on the page the way you would like it to be, the **Rotate** button gives you the option to rotate or flip the image either left or right.

References

The **References** tab on the Ribbon, see in Figure 2.43 below, is one that can be *very* powerful for lawyers creating complex documents by helping to automate some of the more challenging and time-consuming tasks.

FIGURE 2.43 The References Tab

In Chapter 5 we'll see examples of using many of these features.

Table of Contents

The **Table of Contents** group contains tools that help you create and maintain a Table of Contents. In Word this is primarily accomplished by using the **Header** styles, but you can also use the **Add Text** command to add a current bit of text, such as a custom heading, to your Table of Contents.

Update Table does just what you think it does, making another pass thru your document and updating the Table of Contents with any new headings that you've added since the last update. Also, it will correct for any headers that have moved to a different page, making sure the page numbers on your Table of Contents are always correct. It's important to do this before you finalize a document that has a generated Table of Contents in it.

Footnotes

Lawyers love footnotes. With the **Footnotes** group, you have some powerful tools for creating and maintaining footnotes and endnotes.

Insert Footnote lets you create a footnote at the bottom of the current page. **Insert Endnote** creates a note at the end of the document.

The **Next Footnote** button is a little deceptive. Clicking that button will take you to the next footnote in your document, as you'd expect. Clicking the drop-down arrow next to the button, however, exposes a little menu that includes **Previous Footnote**, **Next Endnote**, and **Previous Endnote**. Handy for navigating through your footnotes and endnotes.

The **Show Notes** feature takes you to the actual notes area. If you're working in a document that has both footnotes *and* endnotes, then Word will politely ask you which one you want to see.

Citations and Bibliography

The **Citations and Bibliography** tool has a lot more than meets the eye. At first glance you may not realize that it helps you maintain a database of sources and insert them, consistently, where and when you need them. The feature is powerful enough and useful enough that we'll devote a little space to it in Chapter 5. For now . . . this is where you find these tools.

Captions

The **Captions** tool is for images or graphics inserted into a document. It should be really useful, and in some cases it probably is, but to be honest, every time I've tried to use the feature, I found it was more in my way than helping me. The problem is the inflexible manner in which the caption is created—you don't have much control over it. Unless you really love the way Word chooses to create the captions, you'll spend a lot more time trying to fix them than if you'd just created the captions manually.

If you do decide to use the captions, I'd advise not applying them until you're nearly done with the document. For example, if you caption images and then reorder the images (or insert one), the caption numbering can sometimes stay in the original order . . . meaning that your *Figure 3-6* may end up after *Figure 3-7*, which is confusing to everybody. Applying the captions last will give you a better chance to get them right.

Index

The **Index** group does for indexes (typically found at the end of your document) what the Table of Contents group does for Tables of Contents (typically found at the beginning). This is a really useful set of tools that lets you create and maintain an Index. You can mark any term or phrase as an entry for the Index, and Word will automatically add it. Best of all, if that text should move to a different page through subsequent editing, simply clicking **Update Index** will correct the page numbers associated with the terms in the Index. As with the Table of Contents it's important to update your Index before finalizing any document that contains one.

Table of Authorities

Lastly **Table of Authorities** employs commands essentially similar to the Table of Contents and Index groups to create and maintain a Table of Authorities. Using this tool is actually pretty easy. When you create a citation in your document that you want to add to the Table of Authorities, you just highlight that text and then click the **Mark Citation** button on the Ribbon. Once you've gone through and marked your citation, just go to the place in the document where you want to place your Table of Authorities and click the **Insert Table of Authorities** button. The table will be nicely created for you.

If you later want to add some more citations to the Table of Authorities, just mark them as the others; then click the **Update Table** button. Yes, we'll also spend more time on this in Chapter 5.

Mailings

The **Mailings** tab on the Ribbon (see Figure 2.44) is primarily concerned with helping you create mail merges, very handy for doing large "personalized" mailings, but it also contains the commands for creating envelopes or mailing labels.

FIGURE 2.44 The Mailings Tab

Create

Creating and printing envelopes using Word is a feature I've always used in Word. I even bought a second paper tray for my printer just to hold envelopes. We'll talk about it more in depth in Chapter 7.

Creating mailing labels is a fairly similar process—clicking the command on the Ribbon launches the **Envelopes and Labels** dialog box to the **Labels** tab. You'll notice right away that it offers you a large field to type the address you want to appear on the label. Less obvious is the tiny **Address Book** icon just above the address field (it looks vaguely like an open book), and you can see it next to the **Use return address** checkbox in Figure 2.45. Clicking the address book icon will let you access your Outlook address books, especially your Contacts folder, so that you can select one or more address from those lists to print on the labels. Yes, that's really handy.

Tricks of the Pros

One of my client firms uses this tool to print a whole page of mailing labels when they open a new file for a client. They know there will be a number of mailings and deliveries to this client, so after adding the client to Outlook, they come into this tool and print a full page of labels, which they then put in the paper file. Anytime they need to send something to the client they can just peel the next label off the sheet, and they're ready to go. If they run out of labels, it's trivial to just print up a new sheet.

FIGURE 2.45 Creating Mailing Labels

Start Mail Merge

Start Mail Merge is the button you'll click to initiate the mail merge. It has a whole collection of options that let you specify what kind of document you're going to merge to. **Select Recipients** and **Edit Recipient List** are tools used to manage the source data for your mail merge. I won't spend much time on these here because we're going to go into mail merge in detail in Chapter 7.

Write & Insert Fields

The **Write & Insert Fields** group contains the tools you'll use to build your merge documents. This is another group we'll spend a lot more time with in Chapter 7. One of the features I do want to point out here, though, is the **Rules** command. This lets you take your mail merges to a whole new level by letting you add some logic to your mail merge. For example, if you know the address of the property in question, you may be able to use a rule to automatically insert the address of the relevant courthouse.

Preview Results

Preview Results is an underappreciated set of tools; these let you see what your merge results are going to be without having to waste paper to do it. Click **Preview Results** to get a test merge on-screen, and then you can use the forward and back arrows to scroll through your merge set and make sure everything looks right before you commit to printing or sending it.

Tip

If you have Adobe Acrobat installed, you may have a **Merge to Adobe PDF** group and button on the right end of the Ribbon. It's just a handy way to create a set of merge files as PDFs instead.

Finish

The **Finish** group seems a little silly because it contains only a single command: **Finish & Merge**. This is the command you'll use when you're confident that your merge is ready to go. Clicking this button will perform the final mail merge of your data and template and create the finished documents for printing, e-mailing, or whatnot.

Review

The **Review** tab contains a number of tools you'll use to collaborate with other parties on documents as well as to review and finalize a work in progress. You can see the tab in Figure 2.46 below.

FIGURE 2.46 The Review Tab

We'll dig into many of these features in Chapter 6, but let's introduce you to them here.

Proofing

The **Proofing** group contains some tools that you can use to check and finalize a document before sending it out. The **Spelling & Grammar** tool is largely active as you type—we've all seen the red squiggly lines that appear beneath text that Word believes is misspelled.

The **Define** tool is a *very* handy piece of kit for making sure that you're using exactly the words you want to use—it helps you check the definitions of words or phrases as well as find alternatives that might be better. Just select the word you want defined and click **Define** on the **Review** tab. See Chapter 12 for a bit more coverage of the Define function.

The **Thesaurus** can help you to find exactly the word you want—showing you synonyms (and antonyms) of the word you select so that you might decide to use something else. To use it just select the word you're interested in; then click **Thesaurus** (aka Lexicon, Vocabulary, Glossary, Phrasebook, Wordlist . . .).

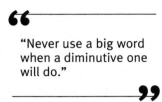

> "Never use a big word when a diminutive one will do."

The last option in the Proofing group is the **Word Count** button. This gives you quick access to a bit of statistical information (more than just the word count) about your document, as you can see in Figure 2.47.

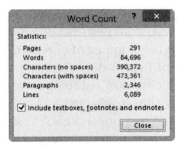

FIGURE 2.47 The Word Count Dialog Counts More Than Words

The Word Count tool shows you how many words, sentences, paragraphs, etcetera that you have in your document, but this isn't the best way to get to this information. Keep reading; later in this chapter we're going to talk about the **Status Bar**, which you'll find is quite powerful.

Language

Translate is one of those features that you won't use often, but when you do need it you'll be happy to have it. Word 2013 has the ability to help you translate text from and to more than a dozen different languages. Is that pretty cool in our very international world? *Creo que si.*

▼▼▼▼▼
CAUTION! (CUIDADO! AVERTIR!)
The Word Translator is not perfect and should not be used as a substitute for a capable human translator. If you use it to translate anything important, you should be sure to have that text proofread by a person who is fluent in the language you're translating to or from.

The **Translation Screen Tip**, which is turned off by default, allows you to highlight a piece of text in your document and Word will pop up a screen tip that shows you information about the word and its translation in one of four languages.

The **Set Language** command lets you specify that a particular piece of text was written in a particular language and that the Spell Checker should treat it accordingly. Word does a pretty good job of automatically detecting what language text is in, but there may be times when you'll need to give it a hand and tell it what language you've used.

▼

Anybody notice that one of the language choices is Hawaiian?

Comments

If you're going to review a document you'll almost certainly want to include **Comments**. You won't believe the number of comments my editors will be inserting in this manuscript before they send it back to me! Comments can be colorful and those colors are automatically assigned to each reviewer through a magical algorithm involving page count, margin size, and the phase of Jupiter . . . OK, I'll be honest; I can't find anybody who knows exactly what the algorithm is, and it really doesn't matter. The bottom line is that you can't readily control what color you're assigned without manually assigning everybody's colors.

The comments (you can see one in Figure 2.48) are identified not just by color but by the name of the reviewer ("Ben Schorr" in my case). You can't easily control the colors but you can easily control the name. Click the **File**, then **Options**, and on the **General** group you'll find a place to specify the user's initials. You'll want to change the initials if you inherited the machine from another user, or if another user you collaborate with frequently shares the same initials you do.

FIGURE 2.48 Comments

Other than being able to add or delete comments there are also buttons here that will help you navigate to the previous or next comments in the document, or turn on/off the display of comments entirely.

Tracking

The **Tracking** group is one of the most important groups on the Ribbon, especially for lawyers. This is one place where you can control track changes and adjust how (or even if) Word displays those changes.

The **Track Changes** button lets you turn tracked changes on or off; under the drop-down arrow on that button you'll find a way to prevent others from turning Track Changes off. Clicking **Lock Tracking** will prompt you to enter a password (twice). Anybody who wants to turn Track Changes off on this docu-

Tip

Be *very* careful with comments. This is one of those document elements that can get you into trouble if you're not careful. Before you finalize any document and prepare it to be sent out of the firm, even to the client, be sure that there are no comments in the document that you wouldn't want to see on the front page of the New York Times.

ment will have to enter that password to do it . . . and if you don't already have Track Changes on, setting Lock Tracking will enable it for you too.

The next two options in the Tracking group are very important, so you may want to read this section twice. In fact, I recommend buying a second copy of this book and opening them side by side just to get the full effect. The first is the **Display for Review** drop-down list, which you can see in Figure 2.49. We'll explain it in more depth in Chapter 6, and I'll mention it again in Chapter 11. More than a mere shameless attempt to reuse content in order to inflate my page count, this really is an important discussion about a feature of Word that lawyers *need* to be aware of. Yes, really. It's no less than the way you display (or hide) markup and metadata in the document.

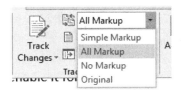

FIGURE 2.49 The Display for Review List

The next option, **Show Markup**, is equally important because it controls what kinds of markup the **All/Original Showing Markup** views will reveal. Figure 2.50 shows what you'll see there. Of particular interest to us are **Comments**, **Insertions**, and **Deletions**.

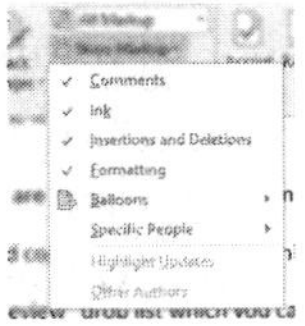

FIGURE 2.50 Show Markup

The **Balloons** menu gives you some options for how (or if) you want Word to use Balloons to show the revisions. You can see an example of a balloon in Figure 2.47. Even though that's a comment balloon, a revision balloon looks basically the same. The primary function of the Balloons button is to let you control if you want your tracked changes to appear inline or off to the side (aka "in balloons"). Generally speaking, I tend to prefer **Show Only Comments and Formatting in Balloons** unless there are so many changes that it makes the document difficult to read. Since this is just a display setting, there's no harm in leaving it set to that and then switching to **Show Revisions in Balloons** later if the inline starts to annoy you. Or vice-versa.

Reviewing Pane lets you turn on (or off) the Reviewing Pane (you can see an example of that in Figure 2.51) and also choose if you want the pane to be vertical (alongside the document) or horizontal (beneath the document). I tend to prefer it vertical, since that's the more efficient way to display the data in it.

FIGURE 2.51 The Reviewing Pane

Most people don't realize that you can actually break the Reviewing Pane off and put it on the right, left, top or bottom. In fact, you can break it off and just let it float anywhere on your screen. Got dual monitors? You can break it off and drag it to your other monitor too.

Changes

The **Changes** group contains tools that you'll use to specify what you want to do with tracked changes made to the document. **Accept** and **Reject** will accept or reject (of course) the currently selected change and then move on to the next change. Note that the Accept and Reject drop-down menus include the ability to accept or reject *all* of the changes in the document in one shot. That can be really handy—especially if you're finalizing and you know that you want to accept all the changes. Accepting the changes, then turning off track changes, and then running the Metadata checker is a good way to finish your document before you send it off.

Generally when I'm reviewing a document, I will reject the changes I know I don't want and leave the other changes alone until I'm done with the review. Once I've completed my review—and I may take multiple passes at it—I assume that all of the remaining, un-rejected, changes are changes I want to accept, so I'll simply Accept All to the remaining changes and go from there.

If you don't want to accept or reject the currently selected change, just click **Previous** or **Next** and it will take you to the previous (or next) change and leave the current change unresolved. I don't think I need to explain those beyond that, do I?

Compare

Compare is another feature that lawyers use *a lot*. We'll demo this a bit in Chapter 6, but these tools were significantly improved in Word 2010. The Compare feature lets you put two documents side by side, and it will show you the differences. It's what we used to call Redline but now seems just as often to be called Blackline. Whatever color you like to call it, that's what this tool does—shows you the two documents side by side, gives you a copy of the documents that merges the changes, and shows you what they are.

Protect

The **Protect** group contains *two* commands: **Block Authors** and **Restrict Editing**.

Block Authors protects a specific section of a document from being edited.

Restrict Editing is an extremely handy way to protect some or all of a document. I'll mention this again in Chapter 6, but just remember that this is how you configure restricted editing and document protection.

▼

Most of you will find the Block Authors button grayed out with no obvious way to enable that functionality. That's because it's only available on documents that are saved to a SharePoint site that supports Workspaces. As Office 365 gains popularity, more and more of you actually have that kind of environment.

Ink

If your machine supports digital ink, you may have a group called **Ink** and a single button called **Start Inking**. That's used to turn on the ink annotation features. When it's turned on, you can select from a small variety of colored "pens" that you can use to draw on or annotate the document.

OneNote

Office 2010 was the first Microsoft Office suite that included Microsoft **OneNote** right in the box. We'll explore this a bit more in Chapter 7; put briefly, if you want to take notes about your document in Microsoft OneNote (as opposed to in the document itself), you could use this feature to link those notes to the document. That can be pretty handy if you want to take notes that you want to be sure are *not* included within the document's metadata itself. It remains to be seen how many lawyers actually avail themselves of that capability.

View

The **View** tab gives you the controls to handle how Word is going to display your document (see Figure 2.52). There are a number of useful commands here, so let's dig in.

FIGURE 2.52 The View Tab

Views

The **Views** group lets you switch between the five basic views that Word offers.

- **Read Mode**. This was a new view in Word 2007 and one that users tend to either love or hate, though it has been considerably improved in Word 2013. When you open a Word document from an e-mail message, for example, Word defaults to showing it to you in Full Screen Reading view. This is a read-only view with no editing allowed by default (see sidebar), so you probably won't choose to use it that often. If you don't like it for viewing received documents, by the way, I'll show you how to turn it off in Chapter 9.
- **Print Layout**. This is the default view that most people use most of the time. It lays out the document on the page more or less how it's going to look if you print it. It's a familiar, comfortable, and capable view, and that's why most people use it. Note that which printer you currently have selected under **File** > **Print** may affect how pages display and paginate in Print Layout view. If you're going to use this view, and I'll bet you are, try to have the printer you're actually going to print on already selected in the print settings in order to reduce the chances of a nasty surprise later.
- **Web Layout**. This view shows how your document will look as a web page. Very few lawyers will use this view; there aren't any

page margins and the pagination and layout may be different from how the document will look when you print it or send it.

- **Outline**. This view is optimized for outlining. There's not much formatting, and switching to Outline view turns on the **Outlining** tab on the Ribbon (see Figure 2.53). It's occasionally useful for highly structured documents (or if you just like to use Word to create outlines), but you should be sure to switch back to Print Layout view to finalize your document formatting and layout.
- **Draft**. The Draft view is a clean look at your document without all the bells and whistles that some find distracting. It can be somewhat faster than Print Layout view because it doesn't do foreground repagination—which is a fancy way of saying that it won't stall you while it tries to do administrative stuff with your long document. Do note, however, that if you have images, charts, or clip art pasted into your document, they won't show up in Draft view. You'll need to switch to one of the other views (Print Layout most likely) to see them.

FIGURE 2.53 Outline View

Show

The next group is the **Show** group, which is just a small collection of checkboxes that turn on and off some common features of Word.

If you'd like to enable editing in the **Full Screen Reading** view, click the **View Options** at the top right corner of the view and choose **Allow Typing**.

- **Ruler**. Turning off the Ruler saves you a tiny bit of space at the top of the document and does give you a slightly cleaner look. I actually do like to turn it off personally, especially since it's so easy to turn it back on for those rare instances when I want or need it.
- **Gridlines**. If you need to do some really precise alignment of elements of your documents, or if you just have an odd fetish for typing on graph paper, you can turn on the gridlines. Primarily this is used when you're doing some more advanced graphic design such as laying out a graphically complex newsletter. I can honestly say that in twenty years of working with lawyers and technology I've never seen a lawyer who turned the gridlines on. And I've never had one ask me if there was a way to turn the gridlines on either.

- Note that on some older documents the gridlines will only appear as "notebook paper" rather than as a full grid and that turning gridlines on will switch you to Print Layout view if you weren't there already.

- **Navigation Pane**. In Word 2007 this was called **Document Map**, and it's been greatly improved in the newer versions. The **Navigation Pane** (see Figure 2.54) is a text-based outline that shows you your document based on the headings, and it helps you navigate readily up and down in a long document. I use it quite often, especially when writing a document like this book. We'll talk about it more in Chapter 12.

FIGURE 2.54 The Navigation Pane

Zoom

The **Zoom** group gives you some quick controls that help you display your document in the most productive way for you. Important to note that *all* of these buttons and settings are basically just presets of various zoom levels. Clicking **Multiple Pages**, for example, sets the Zoom level to a percentage that will show two pages on the screen, side by side, at the same time. **Note**: the Multiple Pages button is ignored in Draft mode.

Clicking the Zoom button will open the Zoom dialog box in Figure 2.55. From there you can more precisely control how your document is zoomed including some of the pre-created zoom options like Text Width or Page Width. What's the difference? **Text Width** excludes the right and left margins; **Page Width** doesn't. **Whole Page** is going to zoom the document so that you see the entire page, top to bottom and left to right on the screen at once (the same as clicking **One Page** on the Ribbon).

FIGURE 2.55 The Zoom Dialog Box

The other buttons in the Zoom group give you quick access to popular zoom options. The **100%** button takes you quickly to the 100% zoom level; **One Page** and **Two Pages** set the zoom to display either one or two pages.

I have to admit that I used to sort of shrug off the Zoom settings, but as I've gotten older, I find that it's actually kind of nice to work with my document zoomed to about 130%. I encourage you to fiddle with the Zoom settings a bit and see if you can find a setting that is more pleasant for you as well.

> Want to get to the Zoom dialog box without having to go to the View tab on the Ribbon? Just click the percentage indicator on the Zoom Slider on the Status Bar at the bottom right of the document window.

Window

Word has always allowed you to work with multiple documents at once in multiple windows.

If you already have a document open, clicking **New Window** might surprise you just slightly . . . rather than opening a new, blank Word window, it actually opens a second copy of your open document in the new window. That can be really handy if you're copying and pasting text from one part of your document to another, or if you're using cut and paste to move text from one part to the other and you want to be able to see both bits of the document at the same time.

Once you have opened one or more **New Windows**, you can use the **Arrange All** command to lay those windows out side by side (actually one on top of the other, stacked vertically) on the screen. This will arrange *all* Word windows for you, by the way, not just windows you open using the New Window command. Most of the time if you have multiple instances of Word running, it's because you opened multiple documents from your document management system, from Windows Explorer, or by just starting another instance of Word from the operating system—as opposed to using the New Window command.

Naturally if you have only one instance of Word open, you can click **Arrange All** as often as you like, and it won't really do anything other than make your one window of Word full screen.

▼▼▼▼▼

CAUTION

If you use multiple monitors be aware that Arrange All isn't going to respect your current settings. If you have some or all of your documents on a second monitor, Arrange All is going to move them to the first monitor. That can be a minor annoyance as you have to start dragging them back to your preferred screen.

Another tool that lets you see multiple parts of your document at the same time is the **Split Window** tool. When you click it, you'll get a horizontal line you can place anywhere on the screen. When you place it, Word will split the screen at that point. You'll get two sections of the window, each with the same document (see Figure 2.56).

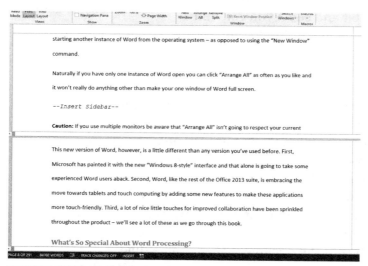

FIGURE 2.56 The Split Window

You can scroll up or down in either window to compare, copy, or paste text. When you're done with the split, just click **Remove Split** to turn it off. Really this is just another way to view two bits of the same document side by side (actually one above the other). You could also do it with New Window; using Split just does it within a single window.

Word 2013 provides you with a lot of tools to compare documents, and one of them is the **View Side by Side** option. In this regard, they really heard the feedback from the users because this feature has been asked for a lot. And they even gave it a couple of nice bells and whistles. This button is only enabled if you have two or more documents open.

Click **View Side by Side** and if you have more than two documents open, Word will ask you which of the other documents you want to view side by side with the current document.

Clicking the **Synchronous Scrolling** command (which only works if you have View Side by Side enabled) sets the two Word windows to scroll in lock step. So if you scroll up or down in one, the other will follow. This is a great feature when you're trying to compare two documents as it makes it easy to make sure you're always in sync.

If you happen to move or resize your documents when they're in Side by Side mode and want to restore them to be equally sized and side by side, you can click the **Reset Window Position** button, and it'll put your Word windows back the way they were when you first viewed side by side.

The **Switch Windows** command (see Figure 2.57) is reasonably self-explanatory—clicking it will let you choose among all of the Word windows you have open. You can do the same thing on the Windows task bar, and I invariably do.

FIGURE 2.57 Switch Windows

Macros

The final group on the View tab is the **Macros** group and it contains just one command. Clicking the Macros button will give you the options to record or manage Word macros. I suspect they put this command here because . . . well . . . they didn't really know where else to put it (see next section). We're going to talk more about Macros in Chapter 8.

Developer

I know what you're thinking . . . . "Developer tab? *What* Developer tab?" Well . . . the **Developer** tab is sort of an odd hybrid tab. There are some tabs that are standard: Home, Insert, Page Layout, and so on. There are some tabs that are contextual: the Table or Drawing Tools tabs only appear when you have a table or when you have a drawing selected. There are tabs that will appear only if you have certain software installed—for instance Adobe Acrobat adds a tab if you have Acrobat installed. But the Developer tab is a slightly different animal—it's a tab that you can turn on and off in the **Word Options** (see Figure 2.58). By default it's turned off, so

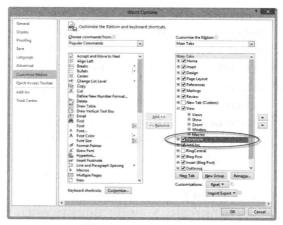

FIGURE 2.58 Enable the Developer Tab

if you're one of the few folks who want it on, you'll have to hit **File**, then click **Options**, and on the **Customize Ribbon** group you can check the box to enable the **Developer** tab.

Once you've turned it on (see Figure 2.59), however, you get a number of features that are interesting to people who want to extend Word with some custom code. We'll touch on this a bit in Chapter 8, but since most lawyers don't have a lot of interest in programming Word, we're not going to spend a lot of time on it. If **Visual Basic for Applications** fascinates you and you really want to develop your own elaborate Word extensions, there are a number of books and resources out there for you. I'll list a few of those in Chapter 8, but for now, let's just take a cursory run around the tab so you know what's on it and why.

FIGURE 2.59 The Developer Tab

Code

The **Code** group contains the starting points for developing custom Word solutions. The **Visual Basic** button is going to launch the Microsoft **Visual Basic Editor**, which you can see in Figure 2.60. From here a talented programmer can make all sorts of magic happen. And even a total amateur can probably stumble around and, with just a little time and effort, at least create a program that inserts "Hello World" into a document over and over again.

The **Macros** button launches the Macros dialog box you see in Figure 2.61. From here, you can also launch the aforementioned Visual

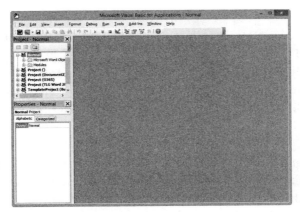

FIGURE 2.60 The Visual Basic Editor

FIGURE 2.61 The Macros Dialog Box

Basic Editor to create or edit Macro code, or you can manage (read: Delete) your Macros.

For most of you, the more useful option here is actually going to be the **Record Macro** command, which lets you create a custom macro simply by starting the recording, performing a set of tasks, then stopping the recording, and saving that result as a Macro. Anytime you want to do that set of tasks again, simply "play" the Macro. Cool, huh? If that concept has your juices flowing, then I suggest you hurry up and get to Chapter 8 because we'll go over it in more detail there. If that idea doesn't interest you at all, then maybe you'll skip straight to Chapter 9. It's fun too.

The final option of the Code group actually doesn't have a lot to do with creating code and has a lot more to do with securing Word against other people's code. Clicking the **Macro Security** command will open the **Trust Center** dialog of Word Options and let you control how Word handles a document it encounters that has macros in it. The default setting is to **Disable with Notification**, which I recommend you leave as is. That will *not* allow macros in a document you receive to run, but will tell you there are macros in the document, just in case you didn't know, and give you the option to enable them. Continue with Chapter 9 if you want to learn more about these settings.

Add-Ins

The **Add-Ins** group offers two controls that help you determine which Templates and COM Add-Ins are currently installed in Word. We'll talk about these a little more in Chapter 9 but as a general rule you should leave these settings alone. Some of the crashes and instability we see in Word can be directly traced to misbehaving or misconfigured add-ins.

Controls

The **Controls** group gives you a tribe of little controls you can use to insert things like **date pickers**, **drop-down lists**, and such into your document. Mostly these are used when creating custom document templates that include some level of automation in them. Chapter 8 will mention these further and give a little demonstration on their use.

Mapping

If you're an XML guru and really want set up XML mappings to content controls in Word, then the **XML Mapping Pane** is your friend. Not interested in that at all? Then you're pretty normal; let's move on.

Protect

The **Protect** group may look familiar—that's because it's identical to the one you found on the **Review** tab. Same buttons, same purpose, same function. I guess anything worth doing is worth doing twice.

Templates

The **Templates** group rounds out our tour of the Ribbon and does so in style. It's one of those groups that is actually pretty useful if you're doing Word development (and if you're not, why are you on the Developer tab?). From here, you can manage your templates and document information panels.

We'll talk more about templates throughout the book, most notably in Chapters 5, 8, 11, and 12. But keep your eyes open, you never know where the little fellas might turn up.

Document Information Panels are a little different animal, however. They give you access to some of the basic metadata about the document in a handy panel.

From this panel you can see and edit information such as the document's **Title**, **Keywords**, **Author** and even add **Comments** about the document. You can manually display the panel by clicking **File** and then **Properties**. Don't see properties? It's subtle—at the top right of the Info panel (see Figure 2.62). And you can see a sample panel in Figure 2.63.

Clicking the **Document Panel** button in the **Templates** group, however, will present you with the **Document Information Panel Options** dialog box that you see in Figure 2.64.

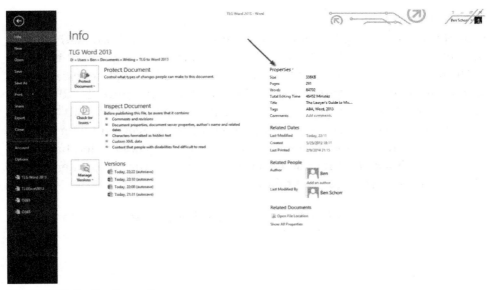

FIGURE 2.62 Finding Properties

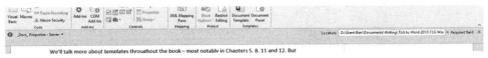

We'll talk more about templates throughout the book – most notably in Chapters 5, 8, 11 and 12. But

FIGURE 2.63 A Sample Document Panel

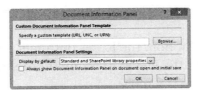

FIGURE 2.64 The Document Information Panel Options Dialog Box

Here you can specify a custom Document Information Panel if you want to, or simply select different settings to have displayed by default. Most significantly, though, you can choose to have the panel automatically displayed when a document is opened or saved for the first time. This is a great way to remind you what the document is about and to prompt you to add information (like the aforementioned Comments, Title, Subject, Keywords, etc.) to a document when you save it.

Those of you who are using document management systems, like **DocsOpen** or **iManage**, which prompt you for a document profile, are familiar with the concept already. If you are using a document management system like that, then you probably don't need to use the Word Document Panel much.

Customizing the Ribbon

One of the things people complained about the most in Word 2007 was the inability to customize the Ribbon. That was somewhat addressed in Word 2010, and those improvements continue in Word 2013. Right-click anywhere on the Ribbon, and you'll get the option to customize the Ribbon (See Figure 2.65). In this dialog box you can turn on or off any tab (but not Backstage), any group, or any icon of the Ribbon or even add your own custom tabs and groups. You can also add features from the left-hand column (click **Choose Commands From** to see more features) to an existing Ribbon tab or to your custom tab(s).

FIGURE 2.65 Customize the Ribbon

If you've made a hash of your Ribbon, the **Reset** button is here to rescue you; it'll put the Ribbon back to the way it looks out of the box.

Quick Access Toolbar

On the Word 2013 title bar you'll find the **Quick Access Toolbar** (QAT), which was added in the Office 2007 days as a concession to those who wanted to retain some customizability to the interface. You can add or remove commands that you use often from the QAT. In Figure 2.66, you might notice that I've added the **Insert Horizontal Line**, **Quick Print**, and **Insert Address** buttons to the QAT. To add something to the QAT click the downward chevron button immediately to the right of the

FIGURE 2.66 The Quick Access Toolbar (QAT)

QAT or right-click (almost) anywhere on the Ribbon. You can add a few standard elements (like Save) to the QAT or click the **More Commands** option to select from a list of every command or macro in the program. You can also add any button on the Ribbon to the QAT simply by right-clicking it and selecting **Add to Quick Access Toolbar**. That can save you a little time if you often have to click away to a different tab to access a frequently used command.

With some time and patience you can actually build out the QAT to be a powerful personalized toolbar of commands.

There is another command on the Customize Quick Access Toolbar menu that you will want to get to know:

Show Below the Ribbon. This will move the Quick Access Toolbar to a line of its own at the bottom of the Ribbon. This gives you a lot more space to work with, handy if you're adding a lot of commands to the QAT. It also reduces the distance you have to move your mouse to get to the QAT by an inch or two. Word 2013, you'll find, has made a few efforts to reduce the amount of mileage you put on your mouse to reach your commonly used commands.

The Status Bar

At the bottom of the Word window is the new and improved **Status Bar**. This is one of the underappreciated features of Word and it's an area that lawyers can really get a lot of value from. On the left end of the Status Bar, you'll (usually) find the page count (e.g., Page 9 of 30), which tells you which page you're on and how many total pages you've got. The tricky thing about this item is that it's also a button—if you click it, you'll get the **Navigation Pane** we discussed previously that lets you go immediately to any heading, lets you search for text, and even lets you reorder headings.

The reason I said "usually" is that this Status Bar is very configurable. Right-click the bar and you can choose a number of things to add to the Status Bar (see Figure 2.67). Among the choices you'll have:

- **Formatted Page Number**. This shows you the number of the page you're currently on. I usually don't bother with this one because I like the **Page Number** option (below) better, and I find them redundant.
- **Section**. If you're using section breaks, this will tell you which section you're currently in. In my experience, most firms don't use sections as often as they should so it will almost always be Section 1 for you.

FIGURE 2.67 Controlling the Status Bar

- **Page Number**. This is on by default, and it tells you which page you're on and how many total pages you have, for example, Page 53 of 125.
- **Line Number**. Many documents prepared for courts have very specific line number requirements, so it can be handy to know which line number you're on.
- **Column**. This field is a little deceptive. When you first see it you might think, as I did, that it refers to columns like newspaper columns. Legal documents frequently have multiple "columns" especially in the headers. So you might expect that Column was going to tell you if you were in column 1, 2, or 3. But that's not what it is at all. In fact **Column** in this context refers to the horizontal cursor position. In other words, when your cursor is all the way on the left end of the line, the Column will read "1." As you move across the line from left to right that number will increase incrementally. Usually it's not that handy, but if you need to align two words or characters vertically, it can be useful to know that both of them are, for example, at Column 17. Those of you who ever used an IBM Selectric typewriter might remember a similar thing with the little arrow that increased incrementally from left to right as you typed.
- **Word Count**. Right next to the page number you'll find **Word Count**, which tells you how many total words you have in the document at the moment. And yes, it updates live. Oooh, there's 18,043 for me. 18,046. 18,047. If you happen to select one or more words, this item will tell you how many words you've selected. Selecting that previous sentence told me I had "19/18,066" for example.

- **Track Changes**. A *very* handy tool that I recommend *all* lawyers turn on; this will tell you at a glance if Track Changes is currently on or off for this document. (It's on.)
- **Overtype**. This item tells you if you're in **Insert** mode or **Overtype** mode.

▼▼▼▼▼

Insert mode lets you place your cursor somewhere on the screen, **between** two characters for example, and whatever you type will be inserted, moving any content to the right of your insertion point to the right. **Overtype** mode will replace the content to the right of your insertion point with whatever you happen to type. If you typed "Farrah Majors" and want to add the "Fawcette," you'd make sure you were in **Insert** mode, click in front of *Majors* and type "Fawcette" to get "Farrah Fawcette Majors." If you typed "John Cougar" and you want to change it to "John Mellencamp" (without having to release another album) you'd place your insertion point to the left of the *C* in *Cougar*, make sure you were in **Overtype** mode, and type "Mellencamp" to replace "Cougar."

Typically changing modes involves simply pressing the **Insert** key on your keyboard—it's a toggle that switches back and forth. In Word 2013 you can also just left-click on the **Insert** (or **Overtype**) on the Status Bar to switch back and forth between them. There are no features in Word 2013 that let you disable obscure 80s pop culture references, however.

Just to the right of the Status Bar you'll find some controls that affect how Word displays your documents.

First up are buttons that let you select from three of the five document views that we discussed above.

- **Read Mode**
- **Print Layout**
- **Web Layout**

Next up is a **Zoom Slider** that you can drag right or left to zoom in or out of your document. At the right of that is the **Zoom Level Indicator** to tell you what level of zoom you're currently at. These are great if you're like me and your eyes aren't quite what they used to be, or if you have an especially large monitor and want to pull back to see more of the page at once.

All of the settings on the Status Bar, even the Zoom settings on the right end, can be turned on or off quite quickly and easily in the **Customize Status Bar** dialog we talked about previously.

Collapse the Ribbon

One of the first things people said when they first saw the Ribbon in Word 2010 was "Wow, that takes up a lot of screen." In Word 2013, by default, the Ribbon starts out minimized to take up less space. Click on any of the tabs and it will expand, momentarily, to let you select a command.

You can restore (or collapse) the Ribbon by double-clicking on any tab on the Ribbon, or by right-clicking any tab or the QAT and selecting **Collapse the Ribbon** on the resultant context menu. You can also restore the Ribbon by clicking the tab to temporarily expand the Ribbon, and then click the pushpin icon at the bottom right corner of the expanded Ribbon to pin it open again. Or press **Control+F1**. Yes, there are a lot of ways to expand or collapse the Ribbon.

Finally Word 2013 offers a new way to control how the Ribbon looks. If you click the **Ribbon View** button at the top right (it's immediately to the right of the Help question mark button) you'll get the menu you see in Figure 2.68. The choices presented are:

FIGURE 2.68 The Ribbon View Button

- **Auto-hide Ribbon**. This puts Word in sort of a full screen mode where the Ribbon is hidden unless you click at the top of the screen to unhide it. Note than when the Ribbon is hidden, the Status Bar at the bottom is hidden too. This is new to Word 2013.
- **Show Tabs**. This is the same as Collapse the Ribbon.
- **Show Tabs and Commands**. This is the conventional view of the Ribbon.

Mini Toolbar

Word 2013 has another little time-saver in store for you. When you select some text in Word using your mouse, a small floating toolbar will appear that contains some of the most common functions that people do with selected text, for instance, **Bold**, **Font size**, **Font color**, or even **Format Painter**. If you want to use one of these functions, just click the button on the floating toolbar and you're done. This saves you from having to mouse all the way to the top of the screen and possibly having to change to a different tab on the Ribbon to find the command you want.

The Mini Toolbar will appear automatically any time you use the mouse to select text in Word, and it will go away automatically if you ignore it—it only persists if you actually move the mouse to it and use it. It can take a little practice to get good at the Mini Toolbar; it appears and fades away like

▼

The **Mini Toolbar,** like many Office functions, has gone thru several names internally at Microsoft. At one point it was called the Minibar. At another point it was called the Floatie. Mercifully they ultimately settled on Mini Toolbar.

a mischievous puppy hiding behind the couch. Once you've mastered the art of mousing with the Mini Toolbar, however, I think you'll find it quite handy. If not, you can easily turn it off; just click **File**, go to **Options**, and the very first option on the very first tab is to turn on or off the display of the Mini Toolbar.

Summary

Word 2013 is a very nice update to Word 2010. The Fluent interface has been refined and updated to improve on some of the changes made in Word 2010. The new color schemes do take a bit of getting used to but in time you'll adapt and they won't be quite so glaring.

Other features of the new interface include the more sophisticated, useful, and configurable Status Bar and the handy little Mini Toolbar that appears when needed to save you time in performing common formatting tasks.

Creating a Basic Document 3

At some level, creating a basic document is just that: basic. If you know how to navigate the program, it becomes a matter of using the basic tools. In this chapter I'll try to familiarize you with those tools and give you some tips for using them more effectively.

Start from Scratch

We'll talk about using templates in Chapter 4, but for now let's look at how you can use Word to start from a totally blank sheet of paper. To get a clean sheet of "paper" go **Backstage** by clicking **File**, then click **New**.

The New Document window will appear (see Figure 3.1), and Blank Document should be the first template offered. Click it once and you'll get a new blank sheet of paper in Word that's ready to type in.

Another option for creating a new document is from **My Computer** (aka **Windows Explorer**, aka **File Explorer**). Right-click in the folder you want to locate the new document in, and choose **New** > **Microsoft Office Word Document** (see Figure 3.2). This will create a blank document in the folder, which you can then double-click to open it in Word. Take note that when you first create the document this way, Windows will have the name highlighted so you can change it. Presuming you don't really want to call it "New Microsoft

Office Word Document.docx," you should change it. But don't change the .docx extension, or Windows won't know what to do with it anymore.

FIGURE 3.1 The New Document Window

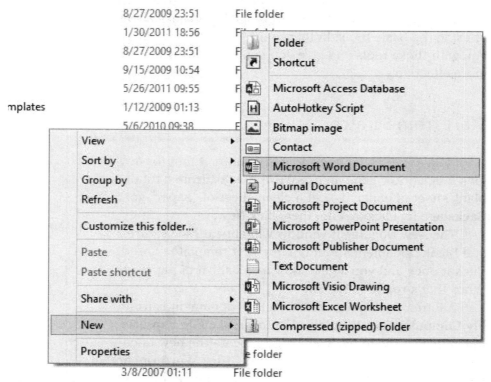

FIGURE 3.2 The Create New Document Context Menu

Adding and Editing Text

Adding text in Word is quite easy—just point and click the mouse to place the insertion point where you want to put the text and start typing.

The ability to click anywhere on the page and just start typing was actually introduced in Word 2003—it eliminates the need to insert a lot of carriage returns (**Enters**) and Tabs to get your cursor to a particular place on the page.

▼

If for some reason you don't like **Click and Type,** you can turn that off under **File** ----> **Options** ----> **Advanced**. I've never seen anybody intentionally turn it off yet.

Selecting Text

Frequently when working in Word you'll want to select a word, sentence, or paragraph so that you can delete it, move it, or apply formatting. (In Chapter 4, I will caution you about using Direct Formatting too much.) Word provides some handy tricks for quickly selecting text.

- Click once to place the cursor on the page.
- Click twice to select the word you're pointing at.
- Click three times to select the paragraph you're pointing at.
- Hold down **Control** and click once to select the sentence you're pointing at.
- Hold down **Control** and double-click to select an additional word, for example, if you want to select two words that are not contiguous. If I wanted to select *additional* and *example* in the previous sentence, I could do that by double-clicking on *additional* then holding down **Control** and double-clicking on *example*.
- To select a part of your document click at the starting point of your selection, then hold down **Shift**, and click at the end point of your selection. Try it.
- To select your entire document press **Control+A**.
- To cancel any selection, just single-click anywhere on the page.

Find and Replace

Have you ever typed an entire document, and then discovered that you repeatedly misspelled the defendant's name? Or maybe you're reusing a document from a previous client and only making relevant changes. Well, if you've ever had to search a long document for every instance of a word or phrase with the intention of changing or correcting that word or phrase, then **Find and Replace** (see Figure 3.3) is a feature you're going to adore. It does more or less exactly what the name suggests: you tell it what to find and it will replace that text, either with or without prompting you at each instance, with a different string of text that you specify. Want to change every instance of *Smith* to *Brown*? Simply go to the Editing group on the right end of the **Home** tab of the Ribbon, click **Replace**, then type *Smith* into the **Find What** field and *Brown* into the **Replace With** field. Click **Replace** if you want Word to prompt you on each instance, or **Replace All** if you're confident that you need to change it everywhere. This is also handy if you need to change every instance of *Smith* to *Smyth*.

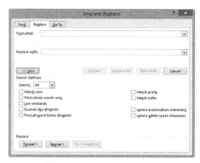

FIGURE 3.3 Find and Replace

Be careful with **Replace All**. There is a famous story of a newspaper that let their computers correct some of the text in one of their news stories and the next day their readers were surprised to discover that the "budget for the State of Massachusetts was back in the Afro-American." It's usually worth letting a human approve the changes—or at least proofread the results.

If you look closely at the options on the **Advanced Find and Replace** dialog (click **More** if you don't see them), you'll notice that you can match case so that only exact matches, case-sensitive, will be affected. That's helpful when John Matter sues Case Tractor Corporation and you want to replace the names but not the words.

There are three other useful options on this tool I want to point out:

- **Use Wildcards**. This option lets you use wildcards in your search terms to search for a broader set of matches. A question mark (?) replaces a single character. *The?* will find *Them* and *They* but not *Their* or *Thessaly*. An asterisk (*) replaces a string of characters. *Tw** will find *Two*, *Twain*, and *Twitter*. An asterisk (*) by itself will find every word in the document, handy if you're just messing around with **Find and Replace**, I guess, and want to see what a document consisting of 53,213 instances of *Pancake* looks like.
- **Sounds Like**. This should be an amazing feature, but as it stands, it's only pretty good. You can type a term and have Word Find (and Replace if you like) words that sound like the word you

specify. That can be a fantastic way to find not only your specified terms but also perhaps misspellings of the word. It's also handy if you're not entirely sure how to spell the word. The downside to it is that it's not that accurate. It often finds words that are similar to your word but really don't sound that much like it. Still . . . a really good effort at this feature and sometimes handy.

- **Find All Word Forms.** This is a great tool because it will find variations on the word. For example, searching for *run* will also find *running* and *ran*. But not *jog*.

Find and Replace has a lot of other nifty uses as well. At the bottom of the Find and Replace dialog are two more buttons of interest.

Format

The **Format** option lets you search for (and replace if you want) different formatting options. In fact, nearly every formatting option in Word can be accessed through this option. Need to change all of your Bold formatted text to Small Caps? Find and Replace can do it. You can remove all highlighting throughout your document. Now before you look at this as the best tool for controlling text formatting in Word, you really should read Chapter 4 where we talk about Styles. But if you need to do something about Direct Formatting, this can be a good tool.

Special

The Special button in Find and Replace lets you find (and replace) special characters. Click the **Special** button and you'll get a list of the characters you can work with like the one you see in Figure 3.4. One character that lawyers are likely to want to find is the section character (§).

> **Tips of the Pros**
>
> Notice that you can also use this tool to remove manual page breaks if you need to. Just do a **Replace**, select **Manual Page Break** from the **Special** menu as the thing to find and leave the Replace field blank.

Spell Check

Microsoft Word 2013 includes a powerful spell checker that is designed to help you with your document creation. I have to confess that I make considerable use of it myself. The nice thing about it is that you don't have to do anything to invoke it; it's running all the time by default (unless you turn it off). If Word thinks you've misspelled a word, it will underline that word with a red squiggly line that indicates Word has identified a possible

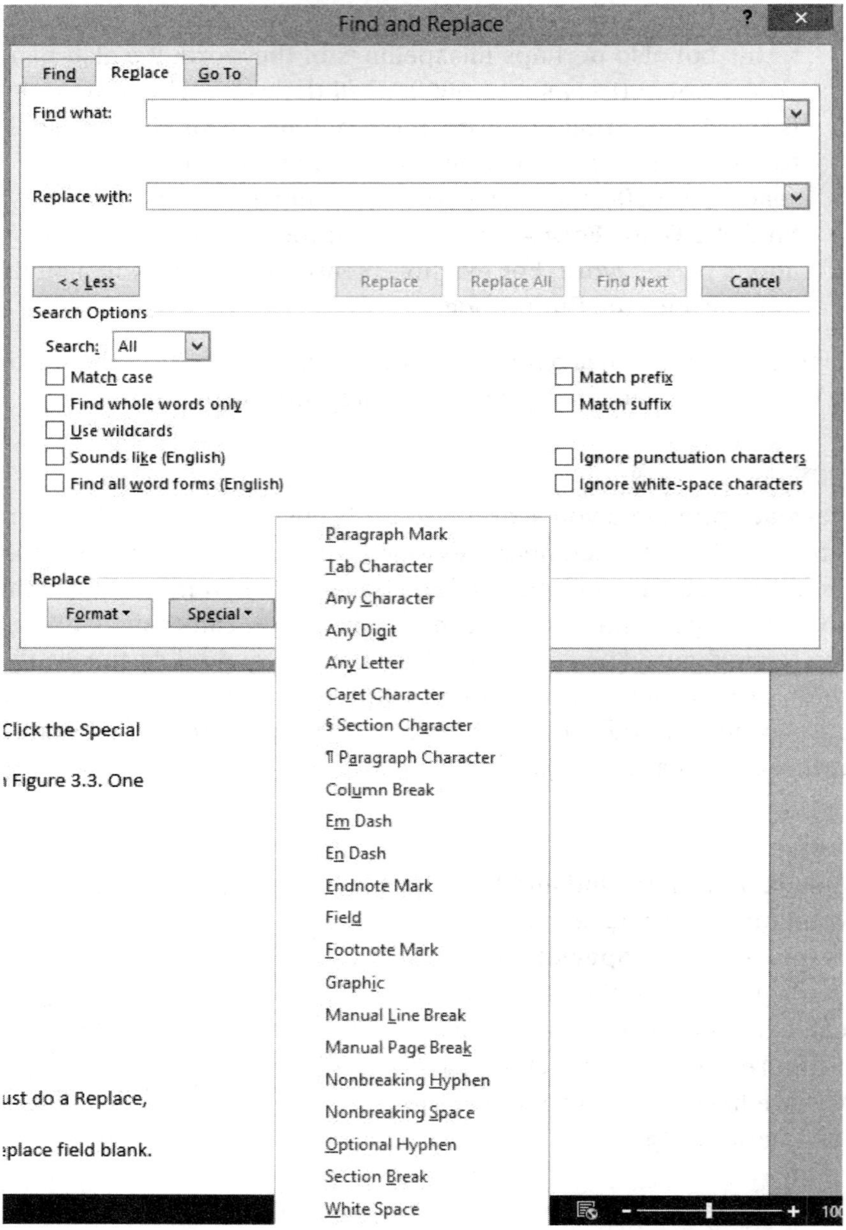

Find and Replace ? ✕

| Find | Replace | Go To |

Find what: ⌄

Replace with: ⌄

<< Less   Replace   Replace All   Find Next   Cancel

Search Options

Search: All ⌄

☐ Match case   ☐ Match prefix
☐ Find whole words only   ☐ Match suffix
☐ Use wildcards
☐ Sounds like (English)   ☐ Ignore punctuation characters
☐ Find all word forms (English)   ☐ Ignore white-space characters

Replace

Format ▾   Special ▾

Paragraph Mark
Tab Character
Any Character
Any Digit
Any Letter
Caret Character
§ Section Character
¶ Paragraph Character
Column Break
Em Dash
En Dash
Endnote Mark
Field
Footnote Mark
Graphic
Manual Line Break
Manual Page Break
Nonbreaking Hyphen
Nonbreaking Space
Optional Hyphen
Section Break
White Space

Click the Special

Figure 3.3. One

ust do a Replace,

place field blank.

FIGURE 3.4 Replacing Special Characters

problem (see Figure 3.5). Right-click the word and Word will offer you some suggested corrections.

If you're confident you have the word spelled correctly but Word thinks otherwise (as it often will for proper names for example), you can add it to Word's dictionary when you right-click the word (see Figure 3.6). Then Word will know what it is when it sees it again in the future.

don't have to do anything to invoke it; it's running all the time by default (unless you turn it off). If Word

thinks you've misspelled a word it will underline that word with a red squigly line that indicates Word

has identified a possible problem (see Figure 3.5). Right-click the word and Word will offer you some

suggested corrections.

FIGURE 3.5 Word Flags Words It Thinks Are Misspelled

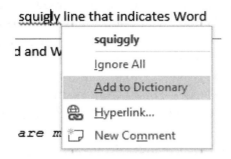

FIGURE 3.6 Add to Word's Dictionary

In Chapter 9, I'll show you how to customize some of the spell check options.

AutoCorrect

AutoCorrect is one of those features of Word that enables you to type quickly and fixes little mistakes for you as you go. Among the things it will do for you is auto-capitalize the first word in a sentence, just in case you forget or just don't want to be bothered with it, and fix common spelling mistakes such as when you type "teh" but mean *the*.

> If you really want to type "teh" one time just click **Undo** or press **Control+Z** after it changes it to *the* and it will change back (like I just did). You may have to click Undo twice.

The AutoCorrect options can be set **Backstage** if you click **File** > **Options**, then go to the **Proofing** group and click the **AutoCorrect Options** button to get the AutoCorrect dialog box you see in Figure 3.7.

FIGURE 3.7 AutoCorrect Options

Grammar Check

A feature that was added to Microsoft Word a few versions back and has slowly improved is the grammar checker. This works in conjunction with the spell checker and will underline any perceived errors of grammar with green squiggly lines. To be honest I find it mostly useless myself; it generally points out sentences it thinks are fragments and not a lot else. As you may have noticed I have a sort of specific writing style, and some of what I write is not grammatically impeccable . . . but I probably wrote it that way for a reason. Somewhere Mrs. Selsor from Walter Reed Jr. High is weeping, but it's just how I write. It's very rare that Word suggests a grammatical correction that I accept, so I usually turn the grammar checker off . . . just to save that tiny bit of performance. Besides, if my grammar were perfect how would my editors earn their keep?

Saving

If you're creating documents you care about, and presumably you are, you will at some point want to save them. Saving a document in Word is pretty simple, you can click the **Save** icon, which is one of the few default icons on the Quick Access Toolbar or you can click **File** > **Save**. The mouse-averse among you can press **Control+S** to save. If it's the first time you've saved the document, Word will prompt you to give the document a name and choose a location (if you want to save it somewhere other than the default location). If you've saved the document before, Word will just quickly and quietly save the document, overwriting the previous version of the document.

▼▼▼▼▼
CAUTION!
One of the biggest mistakes lawyers make with Word (see Chapter 11 where I will beat you over the head with this one again) is reusing an existing document from another client or matter, making changes and then accidentally saving the new edits over the old version. *Be careful!*

Your other basic saving option is to click **File** > **Save As**. What that does is prompt you for a new filename and/or location to save the file. This is great if you want to leave the original file as is (see the sidebar. I know;

read it again) and save this document as a new file. Another reason to use Save As is to save this file in a different format—like **Office 97-2003**, **Rich Text Format**, or maybe it was an older file format to begin with and you want to save it as an **Office 2013 OpenXML** (.DOCX) file. You can also get to this option by pressing **F12** on your keyboard, by the way.

New File Format

Either way that you choose to save your documents, Word 2013 defaults to the same new file format that Word 2007 introduced. Office Open XML is that format, and you can readily identify documents saved in Office Open XML by their file extension .DOCX. It is the default Word extension (replacing the venerable .DOC) and the *X* tells you it's an XML document. The default extension for Word 2013 templates is .DOTX. You might occasionally see .DOCM or .DOTM—those are macro-enabled documents and templates, respectively. They don't necessarily contain macros, but they can (and in practical usage usually do).

The Office Open XML documents have a few notable advantages. First and foremost they are quite a bit smaller than the old .DOC files. These .DOCX files are actually ZIP files—compressed—containing several discrete files. A .DOCX file can actually be as much as 50 percent smaller than the same document in .doc format. That can really pay off if you have a large document library because it can significantly reduce storage space requirements and enable significantly faster backups and faster transfer speeds when e-mailing documents or working with them remotely.

▼▼▼▼▼
CAUTION: Geek Content Ahead!
If you really want to see what's under the hood of a .DOCX file, just rename the file and change the extension to .ZIP. Then open it like you would any other .ZIP file (compressed folder). You'll be able to see the individual files that make up a .DOCX file. Can you add outside files to this ZIP file, rename it back to .DOCX, and use that to sneak files to somebody? Yes, though if anybody tries to open the file, Word 2013 will complain that there is unreadable content in the file and offer to recover it. That might tip off an observer that something's up with the file and prompt them to take a closer look.

Another advantage of the new file format is interoperability. XML is a popular and open file format and is much easier for other vendors to work with than the old, proprietary, binary .DOC files were. Exchanging documents with other applications or working with .DOCX files in other applications (like document management or indexing tools) is much easier in the new format.

.DOCX files are both more resilient and more recoverable than the old format documents were. They're less likely to corrupt or fail, and if they *do* corrupt, you're much more likely to be able to get your data back. That's because rather than being one big file, the .DOCX is actually, as I mentioned above, a compressed file that contains a number of smaller files. Your text is actually stored separately, within the .DOCX file, from the formatting for example. If a bit of your formatting gets corrupted, Word can probably still recover your text by simply deleting the file containing the formatting. You might have to go back through your document and reapply your formatting, but that's a lot better than losing all of your text too. And, frankly, it's pretty unusual that you'd even have to do that with the new formats.

Naming Files

Folks who've used computers for a long time are familiar with the "8 point 3" naming convention. Back in the old days, before flash drives and Wikipedia, we used to have to name our documents things like *jonesbrf.doc* because of the limitations of the File Allocation Table (FAT) file system. But since FAT gave way to FAT32 (the 32-bit version of FAT) and NTFS (NT File System; the preferred file system of Windows XP and its descendants), long filenames became possible and preferable. That means you can use up to 255 characters in a filename, including some symbols. You can now name your documents things like *Moraes v Harmon Memo.docx* or *Letter to Judge Steffey regarding jury selection in Pena matter.docx*.

▼

If there are others in your firm, you should discuss your naming system with them, so that you're all on the same page. Don't restrict the discussion just to partners or lawyers; encourage paralegals and legal secretaries to participate too. Experienced legal secretaries can have some very valuable input to help you come up with the best solution. Plus, if you get them involved from the beginning, you'll make it that much easier to implement whatever policy you come up with.

Especially if you're not using a document management system like **DocsOpen** or **Worldox**, you should implement a sensible naming system for your documents in order to facilitate finding them later. What system you use is up to you, but don't neglect it.

By the way, don't get crazy with the filenames. Just because you *can* use up to 255 characters doesn't mean you should. If you start naming documents *Letter to Amstutz, Huddleston and Malcom requesting electronic production of all documents including but not limited to those documents relating to sales of Widgets in the Northeastern*

and surrounding sales territories during fiscal 2006.docx, then . . . well . . .
just don't. It's excessive, annoying, and ultimately not useful.

Folders

If you're going to use the basic Windows file system to organize your files,
I would encourage you to adopt a thought-out system of folders. Don't just
throw everything into one folder and then hope you can find it. But at the
same time, try not to create an enormous complex of rabbit holes with too
many folders. The system you use is up to you, but I would recommend
something along the lines of:

- Clients
  - Client A
    - Matter 1
    - Matter 2
  - Client B
  - Client C
    - Matter 1
    - Matter 2

- Administrative
  - Accounts Payable
  - Advertising

And so forth. With an intelligent hierarchy of folders it's easier to find
what you need. In this example Client B only has one matter (and isn't
expected to have a second) so there really isn't a need to create any subfolders for that client. Some lawyers I've seen will create subfolders of the
Matter subfolders for different kinds of documents, but generally I think
that just adds a needless layer of complexity. Use the long file names to
specify what kind of document it is, and keep all of those documents in
the single "Matter x" subfolder. Unless there are hundreds of documents,
there really isn't a need to further subdivide the subfolder. In Chapter 12,
I'll mention full text search—that's another tool you can use to help find
files you've stored in subfolders.

Tags

When you save your document, Word will give you the option to apply a
tag to the document. **Tags** can be useful for categorizing your documents
and making them easier to find later. You might tag items with the client
or matter number of the case, or perhaps with a tag that explains what
kind of document it is (memo, brief, etc.). It's tempting to use the Tags feature to include keywords about the document, but you usually shouldn't
bother using keywords that actually appear in the document because

▼

Data about your document, such as keywords, is metadata.

Instant Search will find those documents. Tags are better used for keywords *about* the document that don't actually appear *in* the document. To add a tag, just click the **Tags** field and type in whatever you'd like to add. Separate multiple tags with a comma.

Printing

Before we go too far it only seems appropriate to tell you how to Quick Print. The fastest way to print is by using the Quick Print tool on the **Quick Access Toolbar** (QAT). Don't see it? That's because it's not there by default. Click the little drop-down arrow next to the QAT and select **Quick Print** to add it. Now you can print to it with one mouse click.

There's also another thing you can do . . . if you tap the **Alt** key you'll see a number appear over the icon. On my machine it's "5," but the number you see will depend where on your QAT the icon appears. If you're a keyboarder, once you've added the icon to the QAT, you can Quick Print by simply pressing **Alt+[number]** (whatever number it is that appears over the icon).

In the normal course, most users print Word documents just by clicking the **File** and then **Print**, but Word 2013 has a lot of powerful printing tools that can be extremely useful. You can also press **Control+P** to launch the Print dialog box (see Figure 3.8) just like you have in Word for years.

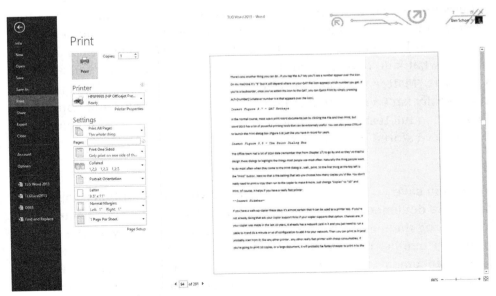

FIGURE 3.8 The Print Dialog Box

The Office team had a lot of SQM data (remember that from Chapter 1?) to go by, so they've tried to design these dialogs to highlight the things most people use most often. Naturally the thing people want to do most often when they come to the Print dialog is . . . well . . . print. So the first thing at the top left is the **Print** button. Next to that is the setting that lets you choose how many copies you'd like. You don't really need to print a copy and then run to the copier to make 9 more. Just change **Copies** to *10* and **Print**. Of course, it helps if you have a really fast printer.

The next option in the dialog box lets you choose which printer you want to print to if you have multiple printers in your firm. Keep in mind that different printers have different features, so which printer you choose will slightly affect the options you have—in fact pretty much everything else within the **Printer Dialog Box** is affected by which printer you have selected. Printing to a color printer will give you color printing options, while printing to a network-attached copier may give you options for duplexing and stapling.

One classic option you may not see that is fairly universal is a **Print to File** checkbox, which sends the print job to a file on disk instead of to the printer. In previous versions of Word it was right out here in the open. In Word 2013 you have to click the **Printer Selection Tool** to drop down the list of printers. You'll find **Print to File** at the bottom. When you select that and click **Print**, it will prompt you for a file name and location (such as your Documents folder or a flash drive), and when you save it, Word will create a .PRN file, which contains all of the printer instructions like fonts, colors, and such that would be needed to print the file later. Typically, you would use that option if you were creating a document, such as a flyer or brochure that you were going to send to a commercial printing company. You'd get it just the way you want it, print it to a file, and send that file to the commercial printer so they could print your brochures or whatnot. Don't use this option to just share a document with another lawyer—that's what Adobe PDF files are for.

Clicking the **Properties** button in the **Printer Dialog Box** will give you access to that printer's properties (just like accessing it through the

---

If you have a walk-up copier these days it's almost certain that it can be used as a printer too. If you're not already doing that, ask your copier support folks if your copier supports that option. Chances are, if your copier was made in the last ten years, it already has a network card in it, and you just need to run a cable to it and do a minute or so of configuration to add it to your network. Then you can print to it (and probably scan from it) like any other printer . . . any other really fast printer with cheap consumables. If you're going to print ten copies, or a large document, it will probably be faster/cheaper to print it to the copier. Plus most of those copiers can collate, staple, duplex and do all those great things *as you print*. Saving you time and effort.

Control Panel > **Printers** tool) so you can make changes for this print job to low-level printer settings. This tool can be completely different from printer to printer so I won't even attempt to explain it here. Your printer documentation will probably cover that fairly adequately.

Pages

You might not always want to print the full document and the **Page** section is there to help you with that. Here you can print a range of pages. That's pretty helpful when you just need to reprint pages 11–14 of a contract because somebody, and I'm not saying who, Kim, accidentally spilled coffee on them. Just type the page range you want in the Pages box. Separate the range with a hyphen (like *11–14* or print noncontiguous pages by separating the page numbers with a comma (like *3,6,11,20*).

If you have a slightly more complex print range in mind, click the **Print All Pages** button to drop down a list of other choices (see Figure 3.9).

FIGURE 3.9 The Pages Dialog Box

Here you can print only the **current page**, print **document properties** (like a list of styles in the document or only the markup on a document you've been collaborating on), or print a **specific selection of text**.

If you'd like to just print one specific paragraph, or some specific bit of a document but not entire pages, you can just select the text you'd like to print with the mouse, then press **Control+P** (or click **File** > **Print**), and choose **Selection** under the **Print All Pages** button.

Zoom

Another option I find helpful when I go to print is the Zoom option. If I'm printing a long document and it's just for internal use, for example, so I can proofread a draft on paper, I'll often choose to save paper by having Word print two or four pages on a single sheet of paper. The end result comes out looking something like Figure 3.10. The text is small, but still readable and, especially if I also use duplexing, I can save an awful lot of paper this way.

FIGURE 3.10 Multiple Pages on a Single Sheet

To do this just click where it says **1 Page Per Sheet** at the bottom of the Print dialog and you'll get a drop-down menu like Figure 3.11. I generally don't go any smaller than four pages per sheet . . . sixteen per sheet would be impossible for humans to read unless they're printing on enormous paper.

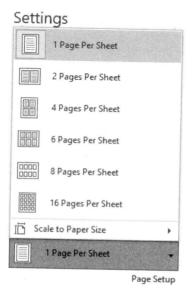

FIGURE 3.11 The Print Zoom Menu

Note: Don't be concerned that your print preview doesn't reflect the change—for some reason changing the number of pages on a sheet doesn't show up in Print Preview.

Another good use for the Zoom section is if you need to resize a document's printing. Let's say you have a document that was initially created for 11 × 17 paper and you decide to print it on 8.5 × 11. Just changing the paper type in Word isn't going to solve the problem by itself—you also need to go into **Zoom** and under **Scale to Paper Size** be sure to select the properly sized paper (*Letter* in this example).

Summary

Creating a basic document in Microsoft Word is a fairly straightforward process. Once you've mastered the basics, learned to use the tools that Word provides such as Spell Check and AutoCorrect, and gotten a handle on the many print options available, you can do some powerful things. In our next chapter we're going to look at how you can make those basic documents look good.

Formatting

4

Word has two basic kinds of formatting: Direct and Indirect. **Direct** formatting is formatting that you apply directly to text, for example, when you select a word, sentence, or paragraph and then click the **Bold** button on the Mini Toolbar or change the font from the Ribbon.

Indirect Formatting is formatting that is applied via a Style. You apply the formatting attributes to the Style, and then you apply the style to your text. Many of the formatting problems you'll encounter with Word come about because of a conflict between an underlying Style and some Direct Formatting applied on top of that Style.

Generally speaking you should use Indirect Formatting (Styles) whenever possible. It'll make your life a *lot* easier (well, at least that part of your life that creates and edits documents in Word).

Styles

A **Style** is a predefined collection of formatting properties: fonts, typefaces, spacing, text colors, and so forth that you can apply to text. There are a lot of good reasons to rely on Styles for most of your formatting needs. Not the least of them are consistency and the ability to modify the formatting of vast amounts of text very easily. You can set a style to have 11-point text, for example, and apply it broadly across your document.

> "There is probably no more important feature for you to learn about Word than Styles."
>
> —*Me*

If you later decide you want to change it to 12-point text, you need only adjust the style, and just like magic, all of the text assigned that style will be updated.

Word 2013 gives you quick and easy access to some commonly used styles right on the **Styles Quick Gallery** on the **Home** tab of the **Ribbon** (Figure 4.1).

FIGURE 4.1 The Styles Gallery

Tricks of the Pros

If you click the **Dialog Launcher** on the **Styles Gallery,** you get a pane that shows you all of the styles available to you in that document. It's a smaller and sometimes more efficient way to apply styles if you're going to be applying a lot of different styles to the document. Bonus: if you grab the top of that Styles pane, you can drag it and drop it somewhere else on the screen or you can even have it float anywhere on the screen. Got dual monitors? You can even drag it to your other monitor and have it float over there.

To apply a style just click on the paragraph you want to apply the style to and click the style you want to apply, simple as that.

Depending upon the style you're applying, that style may persist as you continue to type succeeding paragraphs or it might not. How do you know? Right-click the style you want to apply and choose **Modify**. You'll get the dialog box you see in Figure 4.2. Notice the **Style for Following Paragraph**? That tells you that when you hit **Enter** to create a new paragraph, the next paragraph will be in the designated style. In this example you can see that the *Heading 1* style will be followed by the *Normal* style.

FIGURE 4.2 Modifying Styles

Can you modify that setting? You bet you can. That can be really handy if you want to save yourself a little time and you know that every time you use Heading 2 you want to follow it with a custom subtitle style before you finally move on to Normal body text. Lots of possibilities here.

If you were to look at the **Style for Following Paragraph** setting for the Normal style, you'd find that the following paragraph is set to be automatically . . . Normal. Makes sense, generally you'd be using Normal to bang out paragraph after paragraph of body text.

So what other settings can you modify in a style?

Fonts

A font is the combination of the typeface and other elements like size, pitch, and spacing that determines the shape of the letters in your document. You can take a basic typeface like Times New Roman and apply other characteristics to it like Boldface, 13 point and underlined. One thing

> One of the first modifications most lawyers make in Word is to change the Normal style from the default typeface of Calibri to something more acceptable in your jurisdiction. Often that's Times New Roman.

that can be a little confusing in Microsoft Word is that *font* is sometimes used to refer only to the typeface (like Courier or Times New Roman), and sometimes *font* is used to refer to the typeface *and* the various characteristics applied to it (like Calibri 12 point italic). I wish I had an easy answer for you on that one; you'll just have to try to understand from the context what is being meant. For the purposes of this book I'll try to use *Typeface* when I mean just the typeface (Courier, Arial, etc.) and *Font* when I mean the whole thing.

Paragraph Options

In Word, Paragraph is an important concept. Most of the styles you'll use will be paragraph styles, and most of the formatting applied will be applied on a paragraph level. There are a number of options that apply to a paragraph in Microsoft Word.

Line Spacing

Line spacing refers to the amount of space between lines of text: **Single**, **Double**, etc. You can control your line spacing on a paragraph-by-paragraph basis using Direct Formatting with the **Line Spacing** button on the Ribbon (see Figure 4.3) or (better still) you can modify the line spacing for the style that your text is based on so that the line spacing is consistent across all of

FIGURE 4.3 The Line Spacing Button

your paragraphs assigned to that style. Generally speaking, in legal documents your line spacing is going to be specified by the court anyhow so you probably won't have a lot of discretion in what it should be. But for correspondence, marketing materials, and other personal documents, you can probably make your line spacing whatever you'd like it to be.

Justification

Justification relates to how the text aligns on the page horizontally, from left to right. Typically our text is left justified, which means that it aligns to the left side of the page. As you type your text moves across the page from left to right but it's always in a straight line down the left side of the page. The right end of the line can be somewhat ragged, as mine is here, depending upon the words in the line and how long it actually is.

Right justification aligns the text to the right side of the page. For illustration I'm right-justifying this paragraph and you can see that my text lines up perfectly along the right side . . . but now the left side is a bit ragged depending upon the length of the line.

The next option is center justified, like this paragraph is. Now the lines won't necessarily line up on *either* side but they'll all be perfectly balanced along the horizontal center point of the page.

Finally you have full justification. A line that is full justified will line up both left *and* right, but Microsoft Word will play around with the word spacing in the line to make the line stretch fully across the page unless it's the last line of a paragraph.

Paragraph Spacing

One important concept is the spacing between paragraphs—essentially what happens when you press **Enter** to end a paragraph. If you find yourself hitting Enter more than once to create blank space, then you'd be better off adjusting the Paragraph Spacing in your style so that enough space is automatically added after each paragraph. To do that right-click the **Style** in the style gallery and choose **Modify**, then click the **Increase Space** button (see Figure 4.4) until you get the spacing the way you like it. Once you have that correct, you can delete all those extraneous hard returns you created to artificially make the spacing right.

FIGURE 4.4 Increase Paragraph Space

If you can't get the spacing the way you like it with the Increase Space button, click the **Format** button at the bottom left corner of the **Modify Style** dialog box and choose **Paragraph**. That will open the Paragraph dialog box, and it gives you a number of options including . . . precise control over the spacing **Before** and **After** paragraphs of this style.

Creating Your Own Style

My favorite way is to create a new style is to apply a style that is pretty close to what you want, apply it to some text, use Direct Formatting to make whatever adjustments you need (bigger font, different color, italics, line spacing, whatever), then select your carefully crafted text, click the **More** button (see Figure 4.5), and click **Save Selection as a New Quick Style** . . . at the bottom on the **Styles Gallery** (see Figure 4.6). Word will ask you to name your new style, and then it will appear on the Styles gallery right along with the rest.

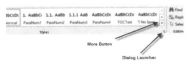

FIGURE 4.5 The More Button Opens the Styles Gallery

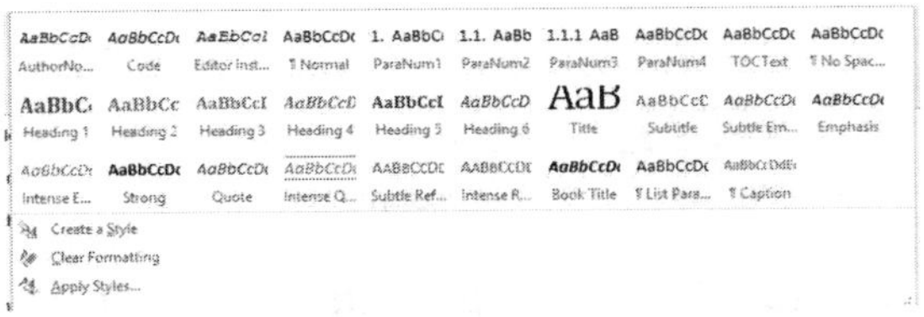

FIGURE 4.6 Creating a New Style

Sharing Styles

It may come to pass that you've created a style that you want to share with others in your firm. Or maybe just copy to another machine that you own or use (like a laptop). Luckily it's not too hard to do that.

The first thing I do, before copying the first styles, is create a new, blank, document called Transfer. I locate it in my Templates directory to make it easy to find. **Note**: you only have to do that once, unless you want multiple transfer documents. I reuse the same transfer file over and over.

Next click the **Dialog Launcher** on the **Styles** group to get the **Styles Task Pane** you see in Figure 4.7. Then click the **Manage Styles** button at the bottom to get the **Manage Styles** dialog box (see Figure 4.8). In the

Manage Styles dialog click the **Import/Export** button to get the **Styles Organizer** you see in Figure 4.9. Click **Close File** on the right side and then **Open File** to select your Transfer document.

FIGURE 4.7 The Styles Task Pane

FIGURE 4.8 The Manage Styles Dialog Box

FIGURE 4.9 The Styles Organizer

Once you have **Transfer** selected on the right side, select the styles you want to copy from the left side and click the **Copy** button to copy them to the Transfer file. When you're done, click **Close**.

Copy that Transfer file to the computer you want to copy the styles to—then repeat the process. Open **Transfer**, go to the **Styles Task Pane** (Figure 4.7 above) > **Manage Styles** > **Import/Export** . . . and now you should see Transfer on the left and Normal on the right. Unless you only want these styles to be available in certain documents/templates go ahead and copy those styles to the Normal template. Done.

Themes

One of the options that Word 2013 offers for formatting is **Themes**. Themes are sort of like the superset of styles—they control the colors and fonts and basic look and feel of the document. I don't think most lawyers are going to take any notice of Themes, so other than observing that they exist in Word 2013 and giving you the heads up about what they do (control the color and font scheme) I'm not going to spend too much time talking about them. The vast majority of what lawyers and law firms do in formatting can be addressed with Direct and Indirect Formatting—especially Styles in the default theme. I seriously doubt many of you will ever care to change the Theme.

Page Options

Just as you have options that apply on a paragraph-by-paragraph basis, there are also options that are relevant on the page level.

Margins

Margins are a concept that's pretty familiar to anybody who has worked with documents in the past—they are the white space on the left, right, top, and bottom of your document. Generally speaking, in your legal documents, your margins are probably going to be pretty standard. For your nonofficial documents, like letters or internal memos, you'll have a lot more leeway, and there are a couple of things to consider when it comes to margins:

1. You almost certainly have to have *some* margins, especially if the document is going to be printed. Very few printers are capable of printing all the way to the edge of the paper, so your printer will probably enforce some minimal margins.
2. If it's a document that is intended to be studied and/or commented upon, you may deliberately want to leave ample margins for note-taking.

▼▼▼▼▼
CAUTION: Geek Content!
Why can't you print all the way to the edge? Pretty simple, actually, your printer needs to have some way to handle the paper. Almost every printer uses rollers to move the paper through the printer, and it can't print on an area of the paper that is under the rollers. Modern printers have gotten pretty good at using very small, or carefully positioned, rollers to minimize that problem but there is still almost always at least a little bit of the page that the printer can't quite reach. Some very high-end printers, used almost exclusively by professionally printing companies, are able to work around this. Few law firms will have (or need) that kind of equipment.

The old dot-matrix printers used to use tractor-feed strips attached to the sides of the paper to allow them to handle the paper and still print all the way to the edge. Tearing those perforated tractor strips off the sides was an unwelcome chore, however.

You control the margins on your page on the **Page Layout** tab of the **Ribbon**. Look for the **Margins** button.

Columns

Columns help to break up the text in your document. You are probably most familiar with columns in the context of a newspaper or magazine. Some legal documents can make use of columns in the headings, for example, pleading headers in many jurisdictions have traditionally been formatted with three columns (the middle column just being a container for a graphical border). They can be quite useful in other cases as well, to help break up large blocks of text for style and readability.

To set up columns in your document go to the **Page Layout** tab of the **Ribbon** and click the **Columns** button to get what you see in Figure 4.10.

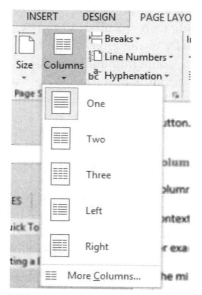

FIGURE 4.10 Setting up Columns

Here you can choose from the gallery to have one, two, three, or more columns. You can also do some unbalanced columns like Left or Right—which are excellent for setting up letterhead by the way.

▼▼▼▼▼
Tricks of the Pros

Preprinted letterhead is just so 1997. These days all the cool kids are printing their letterhead on demand as part of their documents. Just create a template with the margins you want, put your firm header at the top, create a column on the left (or right) to list your addresses, partners, associates . . . all the stuff you've got on your preprinted letterhead now. A good graphic designer or Microsoft Word expert (heck, even a savvy legal assistant) can set up a Word Template for you that looks almost identical to your preprinted letterhead.

Now that you've got that template, create all of your letters and such using that template, and just print on plain blank paper (or bond if you like). It'll look like you printed on preprinted letterhead, but it'll save you a lot of costs both up front and in the future. Tell the truth . . . how many boxes of letterhead do you have in a closet preprinted with the names of lawyers who are no longer with your firm, or featuring the address of your old office? If you're printing your letterhead on demand, from a template, you make a simple change to the template when somebody joins or leaves the firm or when an address or phone number changes and voila . . . your new letterhead is ready. With the .DOCX file formats you can even retroactively change the template applied to previously created documents—so if you ever reprint those documents in the future, they can be printed with the current letterhead template; instead of the template that was in use months or years back when the document was originally created.

Most of the time lawyers are happy with one of those default column choices presented in the gallery. For the rare instance when you need custom columns other than what you see there, just click the **More Columns** command at the bottom of the gallery to get the Columns dialog box you see in Figure 4.11. Here you can set up some extremely specific columns, with custom spacing and everything.

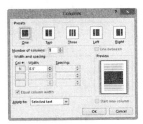

FIGURE 4.11 Create Custom Columns

There are two really useful settings in this dialog box that I some-times use even when I've only created a basic two-column page, for example:

- **Line Between.** This will create a nice vertical line between your columns. Handy in pleading headers and other places where you want a vertical line to separate your columns. No need to create a bogus center column just for a graphical divider in your headings anymore.
- **Apply To.** The default is **Whole Document** but the other option in that box is **This Point Forward**. I'll use that to turn off columns—by setting the columns to **One**—if I only wanted to have two columns for part of a page, or if I want subsequent pages to have a different column layout.

Seriously—think about using Columns instead of Tabs to do those compli-cated page layouts. It can save you a lot of time and aggravation. In a little bit we'll talk about Tables, which are another good way to do complex page layouts in an elegant and reliable fashion.

Page Borders

Page borders sound like margins but they're actually quite different. Borders are a line that you draw around the page. Again, probably not something you'll have the option to use on a legal document, but in some cases, like brochures or certificates, you may want to use them as a styl-ized element of your document. Click the **Page Borders** control on the **Design** tab of the **Ribbon** to get the **Borders and Shading** dialog box you see in Figure 4.12. This dialog box is actually somewhat more powerful than simple page borders, though we'll start there. Here you can set a bor-der around the page, or even have the entire page shaded. The border can be a solid line or a broken line or a dashed line or a . . . you get the idea. And, of course, you can specify the thickness of the line. You can have the border apply to the entire document or just to certain sections of it.

FIGURE 4.12 Page Borders

If you click the **Borders** tab of the **Borders and Shading** dialog box, you can create paragraph borders. For lawyers theses are actually somewhat *more* useful, though not something you'd use in a pleading most likely. They let you enclose a particular paragraph (or more) within a border, setting it off graphically for emphasis.

Horizontal Line

There is another useful tool that you've spent a *lot* of time looking for and that's **Horizontal Line**. When I create training or instructional materials, I sometimes like to divide sections of the page or document with a horizontal line. When I first started using Word 2007, I probably wasted far more time than I needed trying to find out where this command had gone, and

> **Tricks of the Pros**
>
> If you like to insert horizontal lines, you may want to just add this command to the Quick Access Toolbar (QAT). To do that click the drop-down arrow next to the Border command in the Paragraph group, find the Horizontal Line option, right-click it and choose "Add to Quick Access Toolbar."

it took me two or three uses before I remembered that it was now semi-hidden under the **Borders** button in the **Paragraph** group command (see Figure 4.13; I kept looking for it under Insert > Shapes).

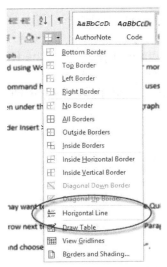

FIGURE 4.13 The Horizontal Line Command Is under Borders

Headers and Footers

Headers and Footers are text elements that appear at the top and bottom of each page. In many cases these may be empty or blank—simply margins. In other cases they can contain highly formatted or dynamic data such as a letterhead masthead in the Header, and page numbering, dates and document titles in the Footer, and so forth.

To create a Header just go to the **Insert** tab of the **Ribbon**, click the **Header** command on the **Header & Footer** group, and you'll get the gallery you see in Figure 4.14 with a number of standard headers you can add. You can use one of those; start with one of those and then modify it; or even start with a blank header and create your own content.

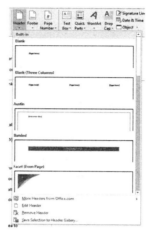

FIGURE 4.14 The Header Gallery

To delete a header from your document just click the **Remove Header** option from the **Header** gallery.

Creating a Footer is essentially the same process but with a slightly different gallery (see Figure 4.15).

FIGURE 4.15 The Footer Gallery

In either case if you build a custom header or footer and think you'll want to use it again in the future, you can simply select your custom header or footer, then pop the appropriate gallery (header or footer) as described above, and then click the **Save Selection to [Header/Footer] Gallery** . . . button. The gallery is stored with the template so any future documents you create with the same template (Normal.dotm, usually) will have your custom header or footer in the gallery for your easy access.

When you have a header or footer in your document and you double-click the header or footer area to edit it, another contextual tab is added to the Ribbon and that's the **Header & Footer Tools: Design** tab as you see in Figure 4.16.

FIGURE 4.16 Header & Footer Design Tools

The **Header & Footer** group contains the same tools that the Header & Footer group on the Insert menu does and those tools, naturally, work the same way here. The Insert group contains four commands that you'll also find on the Insert tab of the Ribbon—these are things you might commonly insert into a header or footer. Honestly I doubt that many lawyers will be inserting too many pictures or bits of clip art into a header or footer (though you could use that to insert a firm logo I suppose), but **Date & Time** would be a pretty common thing to insert and the **Quick Parts** include document properties like **Author** and fields like the document's **Path**, which is quite popular with lawyers. You can also create and save custom Quick Parts like boilerplate text (a disclaimer perhaps?) that you want to reuse again and again.

The **Navigation** group has tools that make it a little easier for you to move around between headers and footers, though I rarely see these commands used by lawyers in practice.

The **Options** group, however, has some *very* useful commands in it; in particular **Different First Page** and **Different Odd & Even Pages**, which lets you create documents that don't have to have the same header and/or footer on every page. That's especially handy if you're creating a document with a cover page (which you might not want the same header or footer on), or if you're creating a book-style document where the even/odd pages will face each other and you want to put unique information on those facing pages. We get a *lot* of requests for omitting the footer from a first page of a document, and Different First Page is the answer.

The **Position** group includes two very useful but confusingly named commands: **Header From Top** and **Footer From Bottom**. These commands actually let you specify the height of the header and footer, respectively. If you have a lot of information you want to fit into your header or footer, you can make it larger, or if you want an especially svelte header or footer, you can make it smaller. These are also handy if you're trying to match up the header or footer to a preprinted form or piece of letterhead.

The third command in the Position group lets you create an **Alignment Tab** in the header or footer. Alignment Tabs were a new feature in Word 2007, and unlike other tabs, which have an absolute position on the page (*at 2.5 inches*, for example), Alignment Tabs are relative to the margins of your page. So if you create an alignment tab that is 2.5 inches from the left margin and you later change the margins, then the alignment tab will move as well. In theory, it's a handy way to align text within your header or footer without having to worry about realigning it if you later change your page margins.

Finally the **Close Header and Footer** button gets you out of the Header and Footer and back to editing your page. You can accomplish the same thing by merely double-clicking anywhere on your page (other than in the header or footer). If you want to get back into the Header or Footer . . . just double-click it.

Page Numbering

Another area we get a lot of Word questions about is how to do page numbering. To start with, click the **Insert** tab of the Ribbon and go to the **Page Number** button. It's not a coincidence that this is located in the **Header & Footer** group. Click the button and you'll get the menu you see in Figure 4.17. Clicking any of the first four options will open a gallery of appropriate choices.

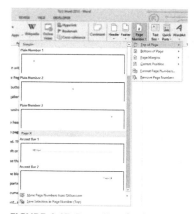

FIGURE 4.17 Page Numbering

Top of Page puts the page number in the header and **Bottom of Page** puts it in the footer. That seems pretty obvious. **Current Position** puts the page number . . . well, where your cursor is right now. That's an intriguing idea, but I've never seen it used. The final option is **Page Margins**, which, interestingly, will create your page number in either the left or the right margin, as an accent bar or other effect. It's actually quite stylish and I've been meaning to use that in a document or article sometime.

Format Page Number lets you make some blanket changes to the page number format, including letting you force the page number to start at a particular value. That's handy if you're creating a document that will be part of a larger document, and you want the page numbering to account for the seventeen pages that came from the other document . . . so you can start your numbering at *18*, for instance.

Sections

There may be times when you want certain parts of your document to have significantly different formatting from the rest: different margins, different page orientation (landscape or portrait), different headers and footers, page numbering, and so on. You could try to do that manually, but it would probably be a nightmare; especially if the document changed in any substantial way and you had to add or remove pages.

The better way to do it is to create a separate section. To create a section you have to insert a **Section Break**—which you'll find on the **Page Layout** tab, cleverly hiding under the Breaks button.

Click **Breaks** and you'll get the menu that you see in Figure 4.18. Below the Page Breaks you'll find the **Section Breaks**.

- **Next Page** starts your new section on the next page. Similar to inserting a page break.
- **Continuous** starts your new section right there where the cursor is. You can actually have more than one section on a page by using Continuous Breaks. This is another good way to have a page where part of the page is in columns and the rest of the page is not, for example.
- **Even Page/Odd Page** starts your new section on the next even or odd page. This is handy if you have chapters broken out as sections and you always want your next chapter to begin on an even (or odd) page.

You can't actually *see* section breaks on your page normally. If you need to delete one (or just be reminded where it is), you'll want to turn on

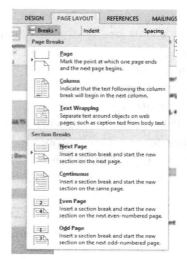

FIGURE 4.18 The Breaks Menu

formatting marks by clicking the **Pilcrow** (¶) on the **Ribbon** or pressing **Control+Shift+8**. The section break looks like what you see in Figure 4.19. Click on it and press Delete if you want to delete it.

FIGURE 4.19 A Section Break

Tabs and Indents

Tabs and Indents are related, but different, concepts. Both are used to align content horizontally on the page but with a subtle difference. **Tabs** set anchor points for you to align text on the current line. **Indents** move the entire current paragraph (or at least the first line). You can have text on either side of a Tab, but the Indent acts like a temporary margin that moves the text inward from the side of the page the specified distance. You can have multiple Tabs across the line, but a given paragraph will have just a single Indent setting (well, one on the left and one on the right if you like).

Controlling how Tabs and Indents are set up in your document can be done one of two main ways:

1. Using **Settings** on the **Horizontal Ruler** at the top of the page.
2. Via the **Paragraph** dialog box seen in Figure 4.20. (You can see the Indent settings in the figure; clicking the **Tabs** button at the bottom left would launch the Tabs dialog box to control the Tab settings.)

FIGURE 4.20 The Paragraph Dialog Box

Personally I prefer the Paragraph dialog box. I know the Ruler is always there, and I've seen people work their magic with a mouse and a few deft strokes, but to be honest, I never quite seem to get the results I want from setting Tabs on the Ruler, and after a few minutes of trying, I usually give up and fall back to the tried and true, well-understood, Paragraph dialog box. In case you really want to use the Ruler to set your Tabs and Indents though, let's take a moment to look at how you do that . . .

Using the Ruler to Set Tabs and Indents

First of all, when you first look at the Word Ruler, you won't see any defined tab stops, but you know (or you will after you finish reading this sentence) that the Normal template in Word includes default tab stops every .5 inches. And you can see that in action if you start at the beginning of a blank line and start pressing the Tab key. The cursor will advance to the right half an inch every time you press the button.

There's a reason that Tabs and Indents are on the Paragraph tab of the Page Layout group—they are assigned to Paragraphs by default. If you set Tabs on a Paragraph and then continue typing the next paragraph, the Tab settings will follow. If you select an existing paragraph in the middle of a bunch of paragraphs, your new Tab settings will only apply to the selected paragraph. Want to apply the Tabs to multiple existing paragraphs? Select them, and then set the Tabs. Want to apply it to the entire document? **Control+A** to select all, and then set your Tabs.

The first step in setting up your Tabs is to place your insertion point in the paragraph that you want these tabs to apply to. For simplicity, we'll assume you're just going to set up some Tabs up to use in the current and future paragraphs.

The next step in setting up your tabs is to click the **Tab Selector** at the left end of the Ruler as you can see in Figure 4.21. By default it looks sort of like a capital *L*.

FIGURE 4.21 Setting Tabs

Each time you click it you'll get a different cryptic little symbol. The first three to be addressed are fairly standard types of Tabs:

- **Left Tab** looks like an *L*, sensibly enough. If you set a Left tab, the text you type starts where you set the tap and will continue as you type, to the right. This is the sort of Tab you're most commonly used to. You can see one in Figure 4.21.

- **Center Tab** looks like an upside-down *T*. Set a center tab, and the text you type will center off that point—in other words, it will adjust left and right from that spot.

- **Right Tab** looks like a backward *L*. Set this tab, and the text will proceed from that point to the left as you type.

> If you don't see the Ruler at the top of your document, you probably have it turned off. Go to the **View** tab of the **Ribbon** and click the **Ruler** checkbox.

The next two tabs are a little different.

- **Decimal Tab** looks like the Center Tab character (the upside-down *T*) but with a decimal point to the right side of it. When you set a decimal tab, the text (which is presumably numbers) will align along the decimal point. This is the way you can align a column of numbers with decimal places so that they align on the decimal just like what you see in Figure 4.22.

FIGURE 4.22 Aligning a Column of Numbers

- **Bar Tab** [Pause for laughter] is a type of tab that is different from the rest in that it's not designed to align text. It creates a vertical line on the page—the sort of thing you might use

> If you're not sure which kind of Tab you're looking at in the Tab Selector, just hover your mouse over the top of it, and you'll get a Tool Tip that tells you.

to create the vertical line in a pleading heading (if you didn't heed my advice to use the **Line Between** setting in **Columns**). When you click the Tab Selector until it looks like a vertical line, that's the Bar Tab. If your waitress starts to look like a vertical line, it's probably a good time to ask for your Bar Tab . . . and call a cab.

After you've clicked through the five kinds of tabs, the Tab Selector button will, curiously, offer you two types of Indent you can set up.

- **First Line Indent**. The first line indent does pretty much you think it does—indents the first line of the paragraph the specified distance. The icon for this one looks like a downward pointing triangle.
- **Hanging Indent.** The hanging indent moves the entire paragraph over the specified amount. This icon looks like a small box.

Once you've selected the type of Tab or Indent that you want to create, click on the Ruler where you'd like the place the Tabs or Indents. You can place as many Tabs as you like (within reason), but only one Indent per paragraph.

Tricks of the Pros

Want to quickly remove a tab you set manually? Just drag the Tab Indicator off the Ribbon using your mouse.

Using the Tabs Dialog to Set Tabs

To get into the Tabs dialog press **Alt+O, T** (or go through the **Paragraph** Dialog Launcher and click **Tabs** as I mentioned above) and you'll get the dialog box you see in Figure 4.23. Here you can type in the placement of the tab stops you want, and you can select what type of tab alignment you want.

FIGURE 4.23 The Tabs Dialog Launcher

The other setting you can select here that's interesting is the **Leader** setting. By default there's none, but if you want dots, a dashed line, or an underline (i.e., a "leader" across the blank area) between the tab and the text that follows it, you can select that here.

▼▼▼▼▼

Tricks of the Pros

One question I get asked sometimes is "How can I have some text on a line that's right aligned and other text on the same line that's left aligned?" We often see that in a header, for example. I've seen people muddle around trying to do it manually, but there's a *much* easier way. All you need to do is create a right-aligned tab, and set it all the way against the right margin. To do that, click the **Tab Selector** to change it from Left tab to **Right Tab**, then click on the **Ruler** near the right margin to place that Right tab. Now gently drag it from where you placed it, to the right until it's directly on the right margin. Now . . . just type your left-aligned text on the line. It'll naturally line up left. Press **Tab** and your cursor will jump to the right margin where, as you type, your text will naturally right-align on that Tab you created. Voila, left-aligned and right-aligned text on the same line.

Want some centered text too? Just add a center-aligned Tab exactly in the middle of the line.

Reveal Codes

Want to start an excited conversation in a group of Word and WordPerfect enthusiasts? Utter the phrase "Reveal codes." WordPerfect users will hoist their swords and claim it's the killer feature that WordPerfect has and Word lacks. And . . . they're sort of right. But Word does have an analogue of sorts: **Reveal Formatting** (see Figure 4.24). Word doesn't really have codes so the best it can do is show you what formatting has been applied to the current paragraph section or selected text. The Reveal Formatting task pane can be launched by pressing **Shift+F1** and it will show you everything you need to know about the formatting applied to the selected text, current paragraph, or current section.

If you want to make a change to one of the formatting elements, just click the hyperlinked title of the element, and the appropriate dialog box will be opened so you can make the changes you want. Take some time to learn to use this tool—it's worth it.

FIGURE 4.24 The Reveal Formatting Pane

Wondering why one paragraph looks different from another? Click on the first paragraph, then check the box that says **Compare to Another Selection**, and then click on the paragraph you wish to compare it to. Word will show you the differences in formatting between the two, as you can see in Figure 4.25.

FIGURE 4.25 Comparing Two Paragraphs

Tables

One feature of Word 2013 that you'll probably use a lot is **Tables**. They have a lot of utility and can help you add some nice formatting to otherwise rough content. Tables can contain all kinds of custom formatting and can even perform some basic calculations for you.

Creating a Table

Creating a table is a pretty simple matter. Go to the **Insert** tab and find the **Tables** gallery (see Figure 4.26). The quick way is to just start at the top left corner with your mouse and drag down and over until you have the number of columns (up and down) and rows (left to right) you need. You can make a table of up to ten columns and up to eight rows that way. If you need something else, or you just can't get the hang of using the mouse for this task, you can click the **Insert Table** command to get the Insert Table dialog box you see in Figure 4.27. Then you can specify however many columns or rows that you need. If you guess wrong . . . don't worry about it. It's not that hard to insert additional rows and/or columns later if you subsequently discover that you forgot one.

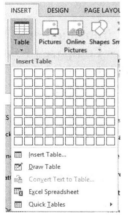

FIGURE 4.26 The Tables Gallery   **FIGURE 4.27** The Insert Table Dialog Box

There are two other useful features you'll find in the **Insert Table** window. The first is a way to control how **AutoFit** is going to work in this table. That means whether or not Word will automatically adjust the width of the column to fit the content. By default, Word 2013 will try to make some intelligent guesses about how the table should be laid out and will auto-size the columns accordingly. Those intelligent guesses will be based solely on the number of columns and the width of available space though—they won't have anything to do with the contents of the columns. If you'd like the columns to resize based upon the content of the column, here's your chance; just click the radio button next to **AutoFit to Contents**. The columns will automatically size to accommodate the widest bit of content in the column. Naturally there are limits; you can't have five columns that are each 3 inches wide on a letter-sized sheet of paper, for instance.

The second handy tool here is that you can tell it to remember these dimensions for new tables. If you think you're going to make several tables of the same size, checking that box will save you a tiny bit of time on your next few tables you create.

Quick Tables

Word 2013 provides you with some tools to help you create some tables that are a little more than basic. When you go to the **Insert** tab on the **Ribbon** and click the drop-down arrow on the **Table** button, you'll see **Quick Tables** listed at the bottom of the menu. Highlight it and the **Quick Tables** gallery, like in Figure 4.28, will appear. These are predefined tables you can insert—calendars, matrices, lists, and so forth. The colors schemes may vary a bit because they depend upon which Theme you have assigned to your document but the basic content will always be there. If you want to create a fancy table, check here first and see if there is a predefined Quick Table for that. If so you'll save yourself a lot of time trying to reinvent one.

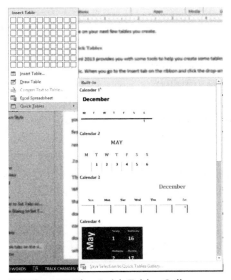

FIGURE 4.28 The Quick Tables Gallery

The Table Tools Tabs on the Ribbon

What's this? New tabs? Yes, one thing Word 2013 does to try to keep the Ribbon a manageable size is to utilize contextual tabs. There are a lot of tools for working with Tables in Microsoft Word, but you don't really need those tools if you don't actually have any Tables in your document. So Word conveniently stashes them away by hiding those tabs from you until you actually insert a Table. Place your cursor anywhere within a Table you've inserted, and you'll magically be presented with two new tabs on the Ribbon under the heading **Table Tools**.

The Design Tab

The Design tab (see Figure 4.29) gives you tools to control the basic look and feel of your table: colors, lines, shadings, and so forth.

FIGURE 4.29 The Design Tab

This is another example of Word 2013's live preview feature. Just by hovering your mouse over the sample tables in the gallery, Word will change your table to show you what it will look like *if* you select that option. No need to trial and error it, just move deliberately through the gallery until you find the look you like, then click on it.

The first group of commands in the **Design** tab includes some checkboxes that let you specify if your table has special rows or columns in it. If you have a header row or first column that contains data labels, check the appropriate boxes. If you have a total row or a last column that contains sums or summary data, check those boxes. Those will apply a bit of special formatting to set off those rows or columns a bit to make it clear that they're headings or summaries.

The checkboxes for banding just specify if you want the alternate rows or columns to be shaded for easier reading.

The next group on this tab gives you a gallery of Quick Table Styles (see Figure 4.30). By default, you've got a plain table (if you created your table with the **Insert** > **Table** tool), but you can pick from dozens of other choices in various styles, accents, and even colors just by selecting it from the gallery.

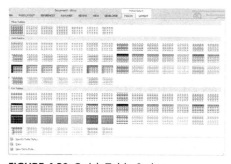

FIGURE 4.30 Quick Table Styles

You also have the ability to customize the shading and/or borders of your table from the Design tab. Click the drop-down arrow next to **Borders** and you'll see Figure 4.31. Here you can do all sorts of tricky things with custom borders like adjust the thickness of the lines or have borders only along the sides or top/bottom of the cell.

FIGURE 4.31 The Borders Gallery

Likewise with shading—clicking the drop-down arrow under **Shading** lets you choose what color to shade the currently selected cell or cells.

The Layout Tab

The **Layout** tab (see Figure 4.32) is all about configuring the actual functionality of your table. **Adding rows and columns**, **splitting cells**, **sorting**, or even i**nserting basic formulas**. Let's take a moment to look at the most important features of the Layout tab.

FIGURE 4.32 The Layout Tab

Table

The **Table Properties** dialog box seen in Figure 4.33 lets you set various settings about the table as well as the individual rows, columns, and cells. You can specify the **width**, **alignment**, and how you'd like the text to wrap around it. To give you some idea of **text wrapping**, Figure 4.33 is set for wrapping the text around . . . which is why you see this text alongside it. If text wrapping is set to **None** (which it is by default), then the table will stand alone, and no text will appear alongside it.

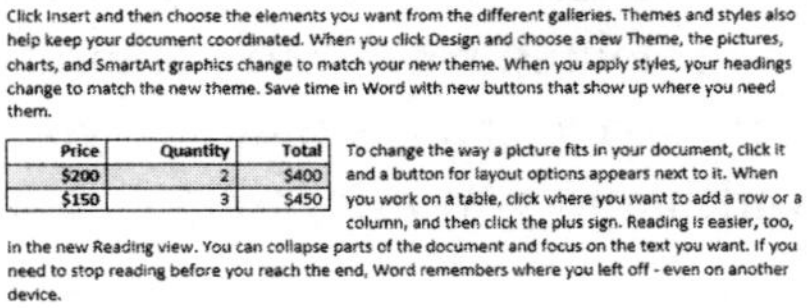

Click Insert and then choose the elements you want from the different galleries. Themes and styles also help keep your document coordinated. When you click Design and choose a new Theme, the pictures, charts, and SmartArt graphics change to match your new theme. When you apply styles, your headings change to match the new theme. Save time in Word with new buttons that show up where you need them.

Price	Quantity	Total
$200	2	$400
$150	3	$450

To change the way a picture fits in your document, click it and a button for layout options appears next to it. When you work on a table, click where you want to add a row or a column, and then click the plus sign. Reading is easier, too, in the new Reading view. You can collapse parts of the document and focus on the text you want. If you need to stop reading before you reach the end, Word remembers where you left off - even on another device.

FIGURE 4.33 Table Properties

Draw

The **Draw** group contains two sort of fascinating new tools. First the **Draw Table** tool lets you use your mouse or stylus and literally draw tables on the page. You don't have to be a great artist—Word will take your unsteady strokes and convert them to straight lines, columns, and rows.

The **Eraser** tool does just the opposite, letting you quickly scrub lines out of your table, effectively merging cells either vertically or horizontally.

Rows and Columns

If you don't want to draw your rows and columns, the **Rows and Columns** group contains commands for easily **adding rows or columns** to an existing table. If you underestimated how many you'd need, this is your solution. (You can also right-click your table and choose **Insert** to get at those commands.)

It also includes the **Delete** tool that lets you remove **rows**, **columns**, **cells**, or even the entire **table**.

Merge

The **Merge** group lets you merge or split cells or even the entire table. Sometimes you might want to merge cells, for example, if you wanted to create a heading above two columns of cells that spanned both columns. You'd merge those top two cells and type your heading into it. This is essentially the same as what the Eraser (which we talked about above) does.

Split Cells makes two (or more) cells out of one; also a handy way to undo an inadvertent or ill-advised Merge.

If you decide your table would be better as two tables, you can use **Split Table** to divide it in two.

Cell Size

The **Cell Size** group contains some tools that let you adjust your cells' width or height. You can use **AutoFit** to cause Word to automatically size your columns or rows or selected cells to accommodate the widest contents in them or you can manually size them.

Distribute Rows and **Distribute Columns** will automatically resize the selected rows and columns to evenly distribute them across the available space. That's handy if you've been playing around with the height or width and you want to get them back to equal heights and widths quickly.

Alignment

The **Alignment** group gives you some tools to adjust how your text will sit inside the cells—aligned to the top, bottom, left, right, middle—you get the idea. You can also control text direction here, in case you want your text inside the cell to rotate 90 degrees and appear landscaped, for example.

Data

The **Data** group contains some of the most interesting table features that Word has. First the **Sort** tool lets you sort any column based on the data. Sort alphabetically, numerically, or by date depending on the kind of data in the column. This is a great way to reorder data that you quickly input without having to worry about inputting it in a particular order to begin with.

▼▼▼▼▼
Tricks of the Pros

Lots of folks don't realize that you can actually sort lists of text that aren't in Tables in Word. Just select your list of terms and click **Sort** on the **Home** tab of the **Ribbon**. You'll get the **Sort Text** dialog box you see in Figure 4.34. You can do a three-level sort if your data is that complex, but most of the time you'll probably just do a simple ascending or descending (A–Z or Z–A) sort.

FIGURE 4.34 The Sort Text Dialog Box

Notice the **Header** row options toward the bottom? That lets you tell Word if your list has a header row at the top that you don't want sorted into the text.

Convert to Text lets you break down your table without deleting the data within it. Essentially this command will take a table and convert it directly to text.

The **Formula** command gives Word limited—very limited—calculation capabilities. You can create formulas to do a lot of things, but don't get too carried away. Creating and maintaining more than a few simple formulas is a chore in Word.

Tricks of the Pros

Most Microsoft Office pros wouldn't spend a lot of time creating a complex table, especially with a lot of formulas, in Microsoft Word. The Tables feature just isn't that robust. Instead we would create the table in Excel and just embed it into Word in the appropriate place. In Chapter 7 we'll dig into how to do that. Trust me, you'll like it.

Deleting a Table

Deleting a table is not quite as easy as you might think, but that's probably a good thing. If you took the time to create the table you probably really wanted it and you wouldn't want to just blow it away casually. The best way to delete the table is to click somewhere in the table, then go to the **Table Tools–Layout** tab of the **Ribbon** (which only appears if you actually have a Table in your document, and you are working with it), click the **Delete** button and select **Delete Table** as you can see in Figure 4.35.

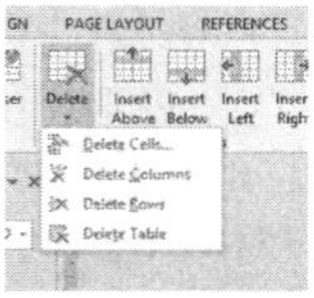

FIGURE 4.35 Deleting a Table

That's also where you can delete individual rows, columns, or cells.

Introduction to Templates

A Template is a starting point for a document. It generally includes formatting, layout (like margins and paper type), and it even often contains boilerplate text to get your document started. Consider a simple example: you print on a sheet of custom mailing labels frequently and you want to set up your page layout (margins, borders, etc.) to fit those labels. You can do that and then save it as a template for later reuse. Or consider a more advanced example: you have a standard retention letter that you send to clients to acknowledge the lawyer-client relationship. You could create the standard letter, minus the specifics like names, dates, and addresses, and save that as a template. Then in the future when you want to send that letter, you just start from the template, fill in the variables for that particular client, and you're ready to go.

Word has been based on Templates for years, and there are two kinds of Templates that you should be familiar with in Word:

- **Global** templates are always open, regardless of what kind of template you based the document on. *Normal.dotm*, the default Template in Word, is an example of a Global template.
- **Document** templates are templates that you base an individual document on. A few dozen of them come with Word (faxes, memos, letters, etc.) and hundreds more available (generally for free) from

Microsoft Office Online. Or you can build your own Document template, as we'll talk about in Chapter 8. Document templates are probably what you're thinking of when you think about templates.

Summary

It's not just what you say, it's how you say it. Your content is critical, of course, but we all know that legal documents have very precise formatting requirements and you have to make sure you have complete control of how that content is laid out. It does you no good to make a brilliant legal argument if the court rejects it because it's improperly formatted.

Word provides you with some great tools to control formatting—Styles, Tabs, Tables, Columns, and more. Mastering those tools will give you mastery over how your work is presented. If you only have time to master two of these concepts though . . . learn Styles twice.

Stuff Lawyers Use

5

Recognizing that I have no way of knowing what jurisdiction you're in (or even what country!), I can't get overly specific in this chapter. Each of you may have different requirements for documents in your specific jurisdiction. What I will try to do is show some of the features that tend to appear in legal-specific documents, and hopefully you'll be able to evaluate these tips in the context of your own court rules and make any adjustments you need to make.

Pleadings

Word has had, for quite some time actually, a Template for pleadings. Unfortunately it's not terribly easy to find, but once you have it, you can use it all you like. Your best bet for finding it is to go to **File** > **New** and at the very top of the **New Document** window is a search box for searching the Microsoft Online site for a particular kind of document. Type in *Pleading* and press enter as I have in Figure 5.1. What you'll get is a list of templates that match that keyword—as you can see in Figure 5.1, I've gotten five hits

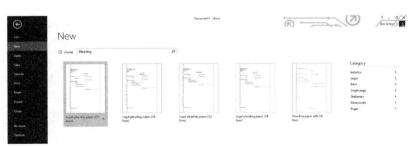

FIGURE 5.1 Finding Pleadings Templates

117

▼

Note: You'll need to do this, at least the first time, from a computer that is connected to the Internet. If you're disconnected at the time, you'll have to wait. Once you've downloaded the template the first time you can save it to your local hard drive and you'll always have it.

that are types of pleadings. Since this is a web search, by the time you do it you might see more (or fewer) pleading forms available. Select the pleading Template you want; I picked the one with twenty-eight lines for my test, but you can select whatever fits your jurisdiction best.

These Templates are provided free of charge, but it *will* check your Microsoft Office first using the Microsoft Genuine Advantage tool to verify that you have a legal and properly licensed copy of Microsoft Word 2013 in use. Assuming you do, the download should take mere seconds, and you'll be ready to roll with your new pleading template.

Using Line Numbers to Roll Your Own

As a general rule, using the pre-built Templates we looked at above is easier, but if you really just want to use a document with your own line numbering, you can. Click the **Page Layout** tab of the **Ribbon** and then the **Line Numbers** button to get the dialog box you see in Figure 5.2. Most lawyers just want to start from 1, increase the numbering in increments of 1, and then restart on each page. Select **Restart Each Page**, and you'll get the effect you're looking for.

FIGURE 5.2 Line Numbering Dialog Box

Unfortunately Word only puts Line Numbers on lines where there is content (even if it's "blank" content), so when you turn on Line Numbers you'll just get a *1* until you actually start adding content. If you want the numbers to continue all the way to the bottom of a page, even though you ended your text halfway down, you'll have to hit **Enter** ("blank" content) a bunch of times to create those lines.

Also the line numbering respects the Paragraph and Line Spacing rules. Line Spacing isn't a problem—typically it's double-space, and that's fine. If your Paragraph Spacing is anything other than the same spacing, however, you may end up with unevenly spaced Line Numbers—so make sure you've got your spacing set correctly.

If you're trying to do something different or create custom numbering, you can go into **Line Numbering Options** > **Line Numbers** and specify that you want the numbering to start at a different number or increment by 3 or whatever you like.

Citations and Bibliography

Word 2013 includes pretty powerful tools for marking Citations and creating a Bibliography. To get started, you'll want to go to the **References** tab of the **Ribbon** and look for the **Citations and Bibliography** group as you see in Figure 5.3.

FIGURE 5.3 Citations and Bibliography

The first step is to select the Bibliography Style you want to use. MLA is a pretty common choice so that's what I'll use for my examples here, but there are eleven other options you can select from including Chicago and APA. Don't worry if you're not completely sure which style you'll want to use—you can change it later if you need to.

Next create your list of sources. To do that, click **Manage Sources** to get to the **Source Manager** you see in Figure 5.4.

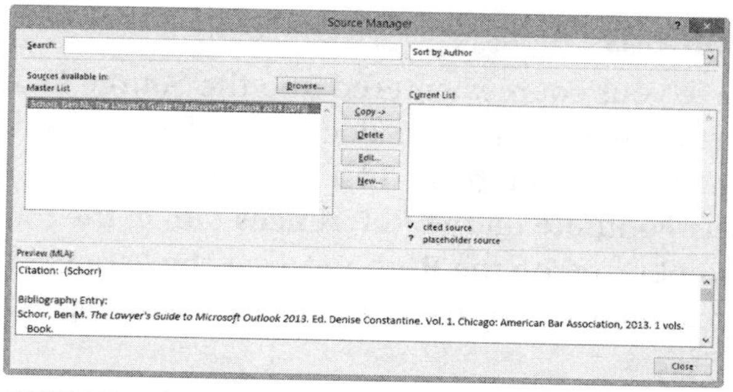

FIGURE 5.4 The Source Manager

Clicking **New** will give you the dialog to create a new source item that you see in Figure 5.5. You'll want to specify what kind of item it is (**Book**, **Journal Article**, **Article in a Periodical**, etc.) and then fill in the relevant details on the rest of the form. When you get the form finished, click **OK**.

FIGURE 5.5 Adding a New Source Item

Sources to Go

Want to take that list with you or share it with a friend? The master source list is stored as an XML file in the C:\Users*[username]*\AppData\Roaming\Microsoft\Bibliography folder, and you can easily copy that file to any other machine or share it with other users. Word to the wise, if the other person has their own master source list, they may want to rename the one you give them from sources.XML to something else before putting it in their folder, otherwise it will overwrite their list.

Repeat the process for each source you want to use. Don't worry if you don't have all of them, or if you have incomplete information. You can always add additional items or update your existing items, later by returning to the Source Manager.

Adding sources to the Source Manager is a bit of a chore, but it's a chore you won't have to repeat. As you add each entry, Word will add it to a master list of sources that will be available to you in all of your future documents. If you want to use some of those sources in a future document, simply open the **Source Manager**, find those sources on the **Master List** on the left, and click **Copy** to copy each one to the **Current List** on the right. Once they're in the Current List they'll be available from the **Insert Citation** button in that document.

Adding Citations

Once you have your sources entered into the Source Manager, you're ready to start using them in your document. To add a Citation, type the text you want to cite, and then add a footnote at the end of that cite by clicking **Insert Footnote** on the **References** tab. In the footnote click the **Insert Citation** button on the **Ribbon** to get the list of sources you entered (see Figure 5.6), and select the one you're referencing.

FIGURE 5.6 Inserting a Citation

Inserting Your Bibliography

Once you've gone through and added all of your Citations, inserting the Bibliography is a pretty simple process. Typically you'll create a blank page at or near the end of your document, click on that page, and click **Bibliography** on the **Ribbon** to get the **Bibliography Gallery**. Select the format you want, and Word will insert it and populate it with the Citations you've used in this document.

Table of Authorities

Lawyers love to create Tables of Authorities. A Table of Authorities is a list of references in the document, along with the page number indicating where the reference can be found. Creating a Table of Authorities is pretty easy actually. You simply insert your Citation into the document where you want it, then highlight it, go to the **References** tab on the **Ribbon**, and click **Mark Citation** under the **Table of Authorities** group. Doing so will launch the dialog box you see in Figure 5.7. The Selected Text box shows how the Citation will be listed in the Table of Authorities. You can also edit the Short Citation (it should match how you're going to reference the citation elsewhere in the document; i.e., *Carter v. Bruha*), and change the category if you like.

FIGURE 5.7 Mark Citation

If none of the categories built into Word suits you, you can edit the list of categories by clicking the **Category** button on the right side of the dialog box. Add or change the categories to whatever you like.

Tricks of the Pros

You can also press *Alt+Shift+I* (capital *i*) to mark the citation.

Once you've got the Category and Short Citation the way you want them, click **Mark**. If you have (or may have) multiple instances of this citation, click Mark All to flag every citation that matches either the selected text or the Short Citation. That will insert the field code that flags that item as a Citation and will turn on Show/Hide so you can see that it's tagged as a Citation. If you want to turn off that display, because if we're honest, it's distracting, just click the **Show/Hide** button (¶) on the **Ribbon** (or press **Control+Shift+8**) to hide the display again. You'll want to hide those marks before you insert your Table of Authorities (that's next; be patient) so that your document paginates correctly.

Once you've marked all your Citations, you're ready to insert your Table of Authorities into the document. Just go to where you want it and click **Insert Table of Authorities** from the like-named group on the **References** tab of the **Ribbon**. That will open the Table of Authorities dialog box you see in Figure 5.8. You can select a specific category of citations you want to include or, more likely, just select "All" for the categories.

FIGURE 5.8 The Table of Authorities Dialog Box

If you subsequently add authorities that you want included in the table, just go back to the **References** tab and click the **Update Table** button in the **Table of Authorities** group.

Make sure that you come back to the **References** tab and click **Update Table** to refresh your Table of Authorities before you finalize your document. That will ensure that the page numbers are correct and reflect any repagination that might have occurred since you originally inserted (or last updated) the table.

Numbered and Bulleted Lists

One feature that lawyers use quite often are lists—both numbered and bulleted. The difference is fairly straightforward—a Bulleted List is used when the order of the items isn't as important. A Numbered List is a way to create a list when you want to specify an order of events (like a set of step-by-step instructions), or when you want to create a list of items that are set off with unique identifiers so they can be more readily referred to later. For this last reason, Numbered Lists are more common in legal documents.

Word is pretty intelligent about recognizing when you want to create a bulleted or numbered list. If you just start a new paragraph with *1* followed by a period, Word will assume that you intend to create a Numbered List and will apply the default style for that. This is also true if you start an outline with the classic Roman numerals (*I.*, *II.*, etc.) or an alpha list with *A*.

If you want to start a Bulleted List instead, you can just preface your line with an asterisk (*) followed by a space, and Word will convert that automatically to the default bullet.

You can change the numbering format just by clicking the drop-down arrow to the right of the numbering button on the Ribbon like in Figure 5.9. Here you can select an alternate format for your numbered list or define a new number format.

FIGURE 5.9 Change Numbered List Formats

That's fine if you just want to do a very simple numbered list. The problem is lawyers often want to do far more complicated Numbered Lists by numbering paragraphs and sub-paragraphs and sub-sub-paragraphs and . . . well, you get the idea. When you do those kinds of more complicated Numbered Lists, you've probably discovered that things in Word can go very wrong, very fast. That's why in a few pages I'm going to show you a better way to do those deep Numbered Paragraphs and Numbered Lists.

Understanding Numbering in Word

It's probably a good idea for me to give you a rudimentary understanding of how numbering works in Microsoft Word. We could do an extensive study of the subject, but if you're a lawyer, you've already had a lot of years of school, and you probably don't want to spend two more just trying to figure out Word's little complexities in the area of numbered lists. So let's try for the short-course version.

There are two basic kinds of lists in Word: Simple Lists and Multilevel Lists (yes, I'm oversimplifying just a bit, but just come with me on this). The defining characteristic of a **Simple List** is that it has only one level: 1., 2., 3., 4., . . . and so on, or A., B., C., or even bullets. Whatever the delineating character, the point is there's just the one level of list. **Multilevel Lists** are outlines and similar lists that contain multiple levels with different symbols or numbers (typically) to delineate the levels. Like this:

I. This is the first level.
    a. This is a second level.
    b. This is another second level item.
       i. You can have a third level.
       ii. Or more levels, but you get the idea . . .
II. And another first level item to finish my example.

WARNING: GEEK CONTENT AHEAD!

In reality all lists are Multilevel Lists. Word always sees a list as having nine levels, no matter how many levels you actually use.

All of these lists are really a series of Paragraphs (each line is a new paragraph), which have been formatted as List Paragraphs. You can sometimes run into problems with lists if you use the List Galleries instead of Multilevel Lists to apply your list formatting.

There isn't any real difference between a Bulleted List and a Numbered List as far as Word is concerned. The only difference between them is the kind of character prefacing each paragraph.

You can create a numbered list from scratch, or you can convert existing text to a numbered list.

Tip

If you want extra space after an item or if you want to type another paragraph within your list without preceding that paragraph with a number, press **Shift+Enter** instead of **Enter**. When you press **Enter** again, Word will resume your list.

To create a new list, just type the number you want to start with (such as *1* followed by a period) and start typing your list. At the end of each item, press Enter to get the next number.

If you want to convert an existing set of text to a list, just select that text first, then use the Numbering or Bullets Gallery to apply your list format. Each paragraph in your selected text will be formatted as a separate list item. Note . . . you may have to clean it up a bit by separating or recombining items, depending upon how diligent you were in using paragraphs to create the set of text to begin with. If you want to separate something as a new list item, just move your cursor to the beginning of that word or phrase and press **Enter** to make it a new paragraph (and thus a new list item). If Word has made two list items (1 and 2 perhaps) out of something that should be a single list item, just go to the beginning of the second item and hit **Backspace** to delete the paragraph definition and move the second item up to the previous line.

Automatic Lists

Word will often create lists for you automatically—sometimes whether you want it to or not. To start a numbered list automatically, just start a paragraph by typing *1* followed by a period and pressing the space bar, as we did above to start our new list. Word will start a numbered list. *A.* or *a.* or *I.* will have the same effect alhtough the format of the items in the list will correspond to the format you used to start the list. To start a bulleted list, type an asterisk (*) and then press the space bar.

If that behavior annoys you and you would like to have more control over your lists (and non-lists), you can turn it off. Like a lot of the things Word does automatically; that capability is provided by AutoCorrect. To turn it off, just click **File**, go to **Options** > **Proofing**, and click the **AutoCorrect Options** button. Then go to the **AutoFormat As You Type** tab and under the **Apply As You Type** group, you'll find entries for **Automatic Bulleted Lists** and **Automatic Numbered Lists**. Clear one or both of the checkboxes as you desire, and Word will stop making automatic lists for you.

Continuing a List

Maybe you've ended a numbered list and somewhere later in the document you want to resume that list, or maybe you got tired of pressing **Shift+Enter** to insert unnumbered paragraphs and decided it would be easier to just end the list, type your additional paragraphs, and resume the list later. Either way, there is a fairly simple way to continue a previous list. Just type the next number in your sequence and Word will pick up where you left off and automatically join these new items to the previous list.

For example, if you had something like this:

1. An item
2. A second item
3. A third item

Then you added some unnumbered text like this, before adding . . .

4. A fourth item
5. A fifth item

I simply had to type the *4.* to have Word continue my previous list. And yes, if I were to go back up and add another item between *2.* and *3.*, Word will automatically renumber the items below (including 4 and 5) to account for that. Don't be disheartened if you were to add an item between 2 and 3 and the fourth item doesn't instantly update to 5. When you press **Enter** to complete your new item, the numbers below the break will automatically update. Be patient.

Restarting Numbering

If you want to restart your numbering back at 1, just type *1.* in front of your first item, and Word will create a new list for you starting at 1.

You can also have numbering start at any number you want. Start a new list with *1.* (or any number) and then right-click that number and choose **Set Numbering Value** to get the Set Numbering Value dialog box you see in Figure 5.10. You can pick any number you like to start your new list, and Word will pick up from there.

FIGURE 5.10 Set Numbering Value

When you're ready to end your list, just press **Enter** twice.

Now that's all well and good for relatively simple lists. But what about more complicated lists and paragraph numbering where you have multiple levels and sublevels? For that we need to roll up our sleeves and do some work. What we're going to do is create a set of Custom Paragraph Styles and a new Paragraph List Style to tie it all together.

Creating the Styles

First we need to create nine new custom styles. Why nine? Because, as we learned above, all multilevel lists (including numbered paragraphs) are actually nine levels deep. Even if you're only using three of them in a given list.

Now I'm going to make some assumptions here because I don't really want to write 200 pages on customizing numbered paragraph styles. The assumptions I'm going to make are as follows:

1. You want to number your paragraph levels as *1, 1.1, 1.1.1, 1.2, 1.2.1,* etc.
2. You want to use the same formatting on all of it. You don't want *1.1* to be bigger than *1.1.1* or different colors or any of that.

3. The formatting you want to use is basically the same as the Normal style in Word.

If any of these assumptions are wrong, you'll be able to make adjustments to the styles to compensate. I just don't have the time (or paper) to explain every possible divergent scenario.

▼▼▼▼▼

Normally when setting up Paragraph Styles for List Numbering we'd want to use the built-in Header 1, Header 2, and so on, styles. That comes with the associated formatting and the inclusion of those headers in the Table of Contents (if you have a Table of Contents). There are actually a whole bunch of good reasons to use the built-in header styles for regular Numbered Lists. But for Numbered Paragraphs, I think we're better off with the custom styles because we usually *don't* want them in the Table of Contents and we *don't* want each level to have different formatting, and so on.

To create your styles, type a bit of sample text in Normal style and then select that text, go to the **Styles** group of the **Ribbon**, and click the drop-down arrow to expand the gallery (see Figure 5.11). Click **Save Selection as a New Quick Style**. Give your new style a name as I have in Figure 5.12. I've chosen to name my style *ParaNum1* to indicate that it's a paragraph numbering style for level 1. Repeat those steps for levels 2–9. When you're done, you should have identical styles named *ParaNum1, ParaNum2, ParaNum3*, and so on. Once you get the hang of it, you should be able to create the whole set in about thirty seconds.

FIGURE 5.11 The Styles Gallery

FIGURE 5.12 Creating a New Paragraph Numbering Style

Next we create a new List Style for our Paragraph Numbering.

Create the List Style

Click the drop-down arrow next to the **Multilevel List** button on the **Paragraph** tab of the **Ribbon** (see Figure 5.13). Select **Define New List Style** and you'll get the dialog box you see in Figure 5.14. Give your new list style a name: I'll call mine *ParaNums*. Click the **Format** button at the lower left and select **Numbering**. Now you'll see the **Modify Multilevel List** dialog you see in Figure 5.15. This is where the work gets done. (Don't worry, we only have to do it once.)

▼

If your Modify Multilevel list dialog box looks a little different than mine, click the **More** button at the bottom left. You'll need the options it reveals for this.

FIGURE 5.13 Multilevel Lists

FIGURE 5.14 Creating a List Style

FIGURE 5.15 Modify Multilevel lists

To start with, click **Level 1** in the left-hand column. Then follow these steps:

1. Click Link Level to Style and set it to ParaNum1.
2. Under Enter Formatting for Number delete the text that appears there and then click Select 1, 2, 3 from the Number Style for This Level field. Click after the number that appears and type a period.
3. Under Click Level to Modify, select Level 2.
4. Repeat step 1 and assign ParaNum2.

5. Click in the Enter Formatting for Number field and where it says Include Level Number From, click the drop-down arrow and select Level 1.

6. Type a period after the number that appears, and then in the Number Style for This Level select 1, 2, 3.

7. Type a period after the number that appears in the Enter Formatting for Number field. It should look like Figure 5.16.

8. Under Click Level to Modify, select Level 3.

9. Repeat step 1 and assign ParaNum3 (notice a pattern developing?).

10. Click in the Enter Formatting for Number field and where it says Include Level Number From, click the drop-down arrow and select Level 1. (Yes, *Level 1.*)

11. Type a period after the number that appears in the Enter Formatting for Number field.

12. Click in the Enter Formatting for Number field and where it says Include Level Number From, click the drop-down arrow and select Level 2.

13. Repeat step 6.

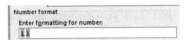

FIGURE 5.16 Correctly Formatting the Paragraph Numbering

Rinse, repeat for all levels through Level 9. Yes, it's a bit tedious and will take you some time to do it. Once you have it set up though, you won't have to do it again. One key point . . . at each level you need to do steps 10 through 12 once for *each* preceding level. So for Level 9 you're going to start by selecting **Level 1**, type a period, and then select **Level 2**, type a period, and then select **Level 3**, type a period, and then select **Level 4** . . . you get the idea.

Once you have that all set, you can click **OK** repeatedly to back out and save your new list style. At this point, exhale and perhaps get a refreshing beverage. You've just accomplished something.

Note: if you want to automatically indent any (or all) of the paragraph levels, you can set that up in the Modify Multilevel list while you're assigning number formats. The bottom section of that dialog box is all about text indents. Naturally you can also turn off all indentation here too.

Tricks of the Pros

If you'd like to precede your paragraph number with some text, such as **Section** or **Article** or **Paragraph**, just type that text in the **Enter Formatting for Number** field, followed by a space, and then insert your numbers as described above.

Using the Paragraph Numbering

Using your new paragraph numbering is simplicity itself. Just apply the appropriate style to your paragraphs! Apply *ParaNum1* and watch your paragraph number magically appear. Apply *ParaNum2* to the next style and voila, your *1.1* paragraph number appears. *ParaNum3*? You guessed it . . . *1.1.1* will appear. The numbers will increment and should be stable. Want to skip a paragraph? Just apply *Normal* style and it won't be numbered.

Ready to number another paragraph? Apply the proper ParaNum level and it will automatically continue the numbering from where it left off. All that setup work was worthwhile.

Table of Contents

Building a Table of Contents is somewhat like creating a Table of Authorities. You mark text and then insert the Table of Contents, and Word will build the table for you and update it whenever you ask. Marking the text is actually a little more automatic with the Table of Contents than it is with the Table of Authorities because the Table of Contents builds with the predefined Heading styles in Word that you're probably already using (or at least you *should* be using).

Whenever I create a long document, I use the Heading 1, Heading 2, Heading 3, and so on, styles to format section and subsection headings. If I want to add a Table of Contents, it's thus quite easy to do; just go to where I want the Table of Contents, switch to the **References** tab, and click the **Table of Contents** button to display the **Table of Contents Gallery** of predefined styles. I can also create my own if I don't like any of the built-in tables. When you select a Table of Contents from the gallery, it will be inserted in the document at the current insertion point.

Maybe you want to add some body text to your Table of Contents though—not text that's actually in a heading but rather text that's . . . well, just text. You can do that, but it's not quite as easy as you might think. You might think it's really easy because the Table of Contents group on the References tab of the Ribbon (see Figure 5.17) contains a button called **Add Text**, which, if you highlight it, claims that it will just add your plain old body text to the Table of Contents. Except it doesn't. Well, that's not true, it *does* . . . but it does it by reformatting your text like a heading.

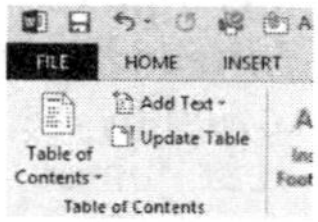

FIGURE 5.17 The Table of Contents Group

No, if we want to have proper body text in our Table of Contents, we need to make a Custom New Style . . . that doesn't look like a Custom New Style. Here's how:

1. Select the text you want to add to the Table of Contents.
2. Click the drop-down arrow on the **Styles** gallery to expand the Styles gallery.
3. Click **Save Selection as a New Quick Style**.
4. Give your new style a name like . . . *TOCText*.

OK, job done. Now whenever you want to flag some body text for the Table of Contents, just select that text and assign it the TOCText Style.

Once you have all of your text thusly flagged, there is one other thing you have to do. Go to the **References** tab of the **Ribbon**, click **Table of Contents** > **Insert Table of Contents**, and then click the **Options** button. You'll get something like what you see in Figure 5.18. Scroll down until you find your *TOCText* (or whatever you named it) style and assign it to a **TOC Level**. You can give it *Level 3*, so it's on the same level with *Heading 3 text*, or you can give it *Level 4*, so it's indented below. Click **OK** repeatedly until you've backed out.

FIGURE 5.18 Customizing the Table of Contents

Next time you update your Table of Contents, your marked body text will be right there where you want it.

Electronic Filing

Electronic filing is rapidly becoming the rule rather than the exception and Word is even more compatible than any version before with those e-filing rules. Though the specific requirements will vary slightly from jurisdiction to jurisdiction, virtually all of them will accept your e-filing in PDF/A format, which means that Word 2013's native PDF capability gets you to where you need to go in order to file electronically. There is just one thing you have to make sure to check before you create those PDF/A files. When you go **Backstage** by clicking **File**, then **Export**, and **Create**

PDF/XPS Document, make sure to click the **Options** button before you publish the PDF file. On the Options dialog (see Figure 5.19), you'll notice an **ISO 19005-1 Compliant (PDF/A)** checkbox. I circled it in red on the figure. Make sure that's checked, so your PDF is created in the proper format.

▼▼▼▼▼
CAUTION: Geek Content Ahead!
PDF/A is the PDF Archive format that includes all of the information needed, including font information, to completely rebuild the original text. PDF/A files tend to be a bit bigger than standard PDF documents due to the added information.

FIGURE 5.19 Configuring PDF Options

If you're in a jurisdiction that accepts Word documents, it probably still requires the *.DOC* (Word 97-2003) format files, which you can also easily produce with Word 2013 by simply doing a **Save As** and changing the **Save As Type** to **Word 97-2003 Document** (see Figure 5.20).

FIGURE 5.20 Saving Documents in .DOC Format

Process Diagrams and Flow Charts

Sometimes you'll want to illustrate a flow or a relationship in Word using graphics. This can be an effective way of communicating a concept, an organizational chart, or a process to a client or even an opposing counsel. Word does have the ability to create those kinds of diagrams.

On the **Insert** tab click **SmartArt**, and you'll get a dialog box similar to what you see in Figure 5.21. Here you can choose from a variety of different charts and diagrams to insert. Insert a diagram and you'll be able to type the appropriate text inside the shapes. Additionally, when you have the diagram selected, you'll now have two new tabs on the Ribbon.

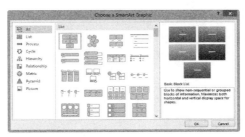

FIGURE 5.21 Creating Diagrams with SmartArt

Design

The **SmartArt Design** tab (see Figure 5.22) has the tools you need to control the layout of the chart itself. You can add shapes above, below, left, or right of existing shapes; promote or demote the shapes; and even change your mind about which layout to use. You can also adjust the colors or shading of the diagram. Finally, if you feel you've goofed up your diagram beyond easy repair . . . a simple click of **Reset Graphic** will put it back the way it was before you started messing with it.

FIGURE 5.22 The SmartArt Design Tab

Format

The **SmartArt Format** tab deals more with the text and the formatting of the individual shapes. You can change colors, fill (which means "background"), and other effects here (see Figure 5.23).

FIGURE 5.23 The SmartArt Format Tab

Summary

Lawyers make heavy use of a number of pretty specific features of Microsoft Word in the creation of the documents we use in our practices. Among those features, the Table of Authorities, Electronic Filing, and List Formats have improved in Word 2013. Master those capabilities and you'll be more effective than ever before.

Collaboration

6

Microsoft approached Office 2013 with a very heavy emphasis on collaboration and the Cloud. This plays nicely into how lawyers tend to use their tools. Partners, Associates, Co-Counsel, Clients, Witnesses, Paralegals . . . on any given document there may be anywhere from one to many authors and editors. Effectively working together to produce a professional finished document is key to running a great law practice.

SharePoint

SharePoint is Microsoft's browser-based collaboration portal. If you have **Windows Server 2003** (or later), then you already have a license for **Microsoft SharePoint Foundation**, which is all you need to create shared document libraries and a fair set of other collaboration tools. Creating and configuring SharePoint sites is a little beyond the scope of this book, but I'll try to offer you a few tips for working with SharePoint from a user's standpoint.

> Want to know more about how to collaborate to produce documents in your practice? Visit the ABA Online Bookstore and pick up a copy of Dennis Kennedy and Tom Mighell's excellent book: *The Lawyer's Guide to Collaboration Tools and Technologies*.

Microsoft SharePoint Foundation

Microsoft SharePoint Foundation is the basic set of services that provide collaboration and a web-based interface. Microsoft SharePoint Standard (we'll talk about that next) is built on top of SharePoint Foundation. However, SharePoint Foundation is all you need for most collaboration. SharePoint Foundation installs right on top of any Windows 2003 or later server and runs there as a service. Check with your IT consultant or systems administrator—you may discover that you already have SharePoint Foundation installed and running in your firm. Did I mention that if you have a Windows 2003 (or later) server, then you already own the SharePoint Foundation license? Effectively, it's free.

Microsoft SharePoint Standard

Microsoft Office SharePoint Server adds a lot of bells and whistles on top of WSS. Most of those bells and whistles involve search, communities, and personalized portals. For most firms, especially small firms, SharePoint Standard is overkill—especially because it's definitely not free. You'll have to buy it separately to install on your servers.

Microsoft SharePoint Online

If you are a **Microsoft Office 365** subscriber, you may have one of the Office 365 plans that includes SharePoint Online. If so you should find that SharePoint site already integrated into your Office apps, as you can see in Figure 6.1.

FIGURE 6.1 SharePoint Online as Part of Office 2013

Using SharePoint

OK, so you've got SharePoint installed on your server. Now what? Word 2013 integrates natively with SharePoint, so you should see your SharePoint site listed as a native location to open or save files. If you're not seeing SharePoint listed under File Open or File Save As, check with your IT guy—he should be able to get it working for you.

Uploading Existing Documents to SharePoint

If you want to upload documents you've already created, just go to your SharePoint site in your web browser and click the **Upload** button on the document library's toolbar.

It will ask you where the document is and walk you through the upload. Easy enough for one document. If you want to copy a *bunch* of documents, however, you may want to use a slightly different technique. For that you'll want to use Explorer View.

Click **All Documents** and select **Explorer View**. That will open your document library in a view that looks just like Windows Explorer. Now alongside this view open the real **Windows Explorer** (**Windows Key+E** will do it) and navigate to the folder that contains the documents you want to upload. Select those documents and just drag and drop them to your SharePoint Explorer view.

Co-Authoring

One of the interesting features in Word 2013 is the co-authoring capability. Basically that allows multiple users to work in the same document, at the same time.

As the other author makes changes to the document or adds content, that content is automatically highlighted on the screen in almost real time. The highlighting is color-coded and shows the initials of the author or editor who created it. Word's version support makes it easy to see when (and by whom) changes were made and gives you the ability to see quickly changes relative to an earlier version of the document.

Office 2013 offers co-authoring functionality for **Word 2013, PowerPoint 2013, OneNote 2013,** and **Visio 2013** documents as long as they're hosted on Microsoft SharePoint Server 2010 or later. Additionally you can co-author **Word, Excel, PowerPoint,** or **OneNote** documents using the Office Web Apps that are included with SharePoint, including SharePoint Online.

Important to note: this functionality *only* works on documents stored on a SharePoint 2010 (or later) server.

OneDrive

Microsoft's Office Live service, aka OneDrive (see Figure 6.2), offers you 25GB of free online storage for your documents and files (as of this writing). Recently Microsoft sweetened the deal with the release of **Microsoft Office Web Apps**—browser-based versions of Word, Excel, PowerPoint, and OneNote—that let you view *and* edit

Don't have a OneDrive account and want one? Just go to http://live.com. If that link doesn't work (the Internet changes a lot faster than this book does) just Google or Bing for *OneDrive* and you'll find it. OneDrive accounts are free.

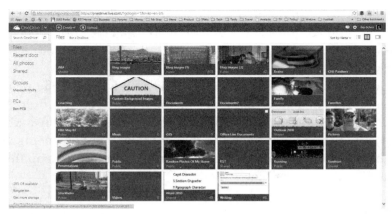

FIGURE 6.2 OneDrive

your documents and files in the browser. Are the web apps full-featured? No. But they're pretty good, and it's hard to beat the price.

OneDrive folders can be easily shared with one or more other users; in fact, I've used a OneDrive folder to share the chapters of my books with my editors as I get them done. You can control the permissions to a limited extent—designating some users as "Read-only" while giving others permission to create, edit, or even delete files.

Collaboration via E-mail

Over the last decade or so lawyers have gotten very comfortable collaborating via e-mail—by sending documents back and forth. This method is tried but not really true . . . and that's because this method tends to generate an unwieldy number of document versions, and especially if you're working with more than one other party, it can become a nightmare of tracked changes and trying to merge different versions of the content into a single master document.

Tracking Changes

One of Word's most controversial features—if a word processor can have controversial features—has got to be Track Changes. Why? If you're not careful, you can inadvertently transmit those tracked changes to other, potentially adverse, parties in your case. And that can be bad. Really, really bad. See Chapter 11's section on metadata for more on that. But here we're going to focus on using Tracked Changes' power for good and not evil.

Track Changes features can be found on the **Review** tab of the **Ribbon** (see Figure 6.3).

FIGURE 6.3 Track Changes

If you're going to use Track Changes, the first thing you'll need to do is turn it on. Just click the **Track Changes** button to do that. On the Status Bar (see Figure 6.4) it should change from **Track Changes: Off** to **Track Changes: On**, and the Track Changes button itself should light up blue.

If you don't see the Track Changes status on your Status Bar at the bottom of Word, then you really **do** want to turn that option on. Right-click the **Status Bar** and click where it says **Track Changes** to turn that on and add it to the Status Bar. Believe me . . . if Track Changes is on, you **want** to know it.

FIGURE 6.4 The Status Bar Shows If Track Changes Is On or Off

You can also set and change a number of options for Track Changes. To get to those, click the **Dialog Launcher** on the **Tracking** tab. That will display the Track Changes Options dialog box that you see in Figure 6.5. Click the **Advanced Options** button to get the **Advanced Track Changes Options** dialog box you see in Figure 6.6.

FIGURE 6.5 Track Changes Options

FIGURE 6.6 Advanced Track Changes Options

Most of these options just have to do with how the changes will be displayed—which colors or font effects you want to apply—but a couple of them are especially useful. For instance, I find it hard to read a document that has *too* many highlighted changes, and I want any substantive changes that get made to stand out really. So I tend to turn off the ability to track formatting changes. Not many formatting changes are going to get made to a legal document anyhow (since the formats are fairly proscribed), and for the stuff that I write, I don't care much about the formatting. To turn tracking of formatting changes off, just uncheck the box next to **Track Formatting**.

The next field I want to point out in Track Changes is the **Display for Review** field (Figure 6.7), and it really is important. You want to make sure that if Track Changes is on, either you have the **All Markup** option selected *or* you are *very* aware of the fact that you don't. Again, Track Changes can be great, but it can also be seriously bad if you accidentally allow a document with tracked changes into the hands of another party who shouldn't see those changes. If you change your Display for Review to **No Markup** or **Original**, Word will hide the tracked changes from you, even though they will still be embedded in your document. **Simple Markup** shows you that changes exist, but it's very subtle so you could easily miss it. If you find editing a document with the markup displayed to be too distracting, it's OK to turn the markup display off . . . but be darned sure you turn it back on and give the document a look-over—plus run it through a metadata checker—before you send it along to anybody who isn't collaborating on its creation. That may include the client or court as well as adverse parties.

FIGURE 6.7 The Display for Review Field

Under the **Show Markup** button (see Figure 6.8) you can control which markup is going to display. Again with the possible exception of formatting, I think that you really should have *all* of it showing.

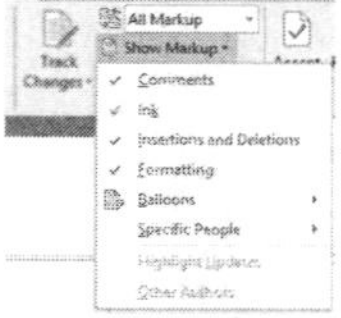

FIGURE 6.8 The Show Markup Button

The **Specific People** list (see Figure 6.9) lets you control which reviewers you want to display markup from. In my document, John Simek's comments are going to appear along with comments I've made

FIGURE 6.9 The Specific People List

from either of the machines I've edited this document on. If you want to hide markup from a particular reviewer, you can turn those changes and comments off (or back on) here. Usually you should leave this alone, though, so you can see all markup from all reviewers.

The other tool you're going to find handy, I predict, is the **Reviewing Pane** (see Figure 6.10). When the Reviewing Pane is turned on, it shows a summary of changes (either vertically along the left side of the document or horizontally at the bottom) and lets you quickly navigate them. I use this tool all the time when I'm dealing with the many comments and edits my editors come back with. When you have 91 edits in a 300-page document, it can be nice to have that tool there to help you address them quickly.

FIGURE 6.10 The Reviewing Pane

Once you have changes in your document and you want to start merging (or rejecting) those changes, the next Ribbon group, appropriately titled **Changes**, provides just the tools you need.

When you select a particular change in your document, you can click **Accept** to make that change part of the final document or **Reject** to delete that change and leave the document as it was before the change was made.

Clicking the drop-down arrow on **Accept** (or **Reject**) will give you a couple of tools that may speed up the process somewhat (see Figure 6.11)—most notably the ability to **Accept** (or **Reject**) **All Changes** in the document in a single stroke (well . . . a couple of clicks anyhow). If you have supreme confidence in your editor, or if you've already reviewed and agree with (or hate) all of the edits they've suggested, you can accept (or reject) them all at once. A huge time saver!

FIGURE 6.11 Efficiently Accepting or Rejecting Changes

▼▼▼▼▼
Tips of the Pros

If you want to accept or reject all changes made by one particular reviewer, there *is* a way to do that in Word 2013. On the **Review** pane of the **Ribbon**, click **Show Markup**, highlight **Specific People**, and uncheck **All Reviewers**, which is the default. Annoyingly, Word will now make you again click **Show Markup** and highlight **Specific People**. Now you want to select only the reviewer (or reviewers) whose changes you want to work with. With that done, you can go back to the **Accept** button, hit the drop-down arrow (as we did above) and select **Accept All Changes Shown**, and only the changes from that reviewer will be accepted en masse. Yes, you can also use this trick to reject all changes from that reviewer.

The Previous and Next buttons in the Changes group just take you to the Previous (or Next) change in the document without doing anything to the current change. Handy if you're just reviewing changes without wanting to take any action on them. As a general rule, however, I recommend acting upon the changes while you're there—it's poor time management to touch the same change twice if you don't have.

Version Tracking

If you have **Save AutoRecover Information** *and* **Keep the Last Autosaved Version if I Close without Saving** turned on in Word (see Chapter 9),

Word will periodically save a version of your document, which you can revert to if you need to. With the current version of the document open go to **File** > **Manage Versions** (on the **Info Tab**) and you'll see that Word offers you the last five Autosaved versions of the document.

If you open one of those files, you'll be given the option to compare that version to the current version, highlighting the differences (see Figure 6.12). You'll then have the option to Restore the older version as the current version or you can File > Save As to permanently save the older version with a new name.

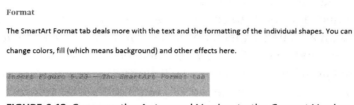

Format

The SmartArt Format tab deals more with the text and the formatting of the individual shapes. You can

change colors, fill (which means background) and other effects here.

FIGURE 6.12 Compare the Autosaved Version to the Current Version

If you need something a little more extensive, you're probably looking at document versioning in your document management or file system, if you have one, or fashioning something a little more manual.

When you're creating and/or collaborating on documents, it is often handy to have some way to track what version you're currently working with. Word provides a rudimentary way to do that automatically, in the Advanced Properties. Click **File**, then **Properties** (see Figure 6.13), and then **Advanced Properties**. What you'll get is a dialog box similar to Figure 6.14, and on the **Statistics** tab you'll find the **Revision Number**. All that really is, unfortunately, a count of how many times the document has been modified and saved. If you press **Control+S** after every word, the Revision Number will increase awfully quickly.

FIGURE 6.13 The Properties Link Is Deceptively Hard to Find

If you're using a fancy third-party document management system, it will handle the version tracking for you.

FIGURE 6.14 The Advanced Properties

There is also a simple, manual way to track versions and also keep old versions around, and that's to simply always use **Save As** on your document and save it with a name that includes a version number. Like *Smith Memo v1*, *Smith Memo v2*, and so on. The new version won't overwrite the old version, and if you're faithful to this system, you'll always be able to tell easily which version you're on. The downside is that your folders may quickly fill up with a bunch of outdated versions of your documents, and you may find yourself frequently needing to do some cleanup to get rid of them.

The key is to find a balance—using Save As for major revisions, but a simple Save to reflect minor changes to the current version.

Reviewing

An important element to collaborating is reviewing the results of that collaboration. Microsoft Word provides you with some tools to use in reviewing those documents. The **Review** tab of the Ribbon (see Figure 6.15) provides quick access to those tools.

FIGURE 6.15 The Review Tab

Comments

When you're reviewing a document, you can use Word's Comment feature to add your own comments to the document for review. Select the text you want to comment on and click **New Comment**. Type your comment in the balloon that appears, and it's just that easy. Your Comments will appear in one color, and Comments by other reviewers will appear in different colors.

You can quickly navigate to the Next (or Previous) Comment in the document with the buttons on the Ribbon.

Word 2013 adds threaded comments so that you can actually reply to a Comment by clicking the reply icon on the right side of the Comment or right-clicking the Comment you want to reply to and selecting **Reply to Comment** (see Figure 6.16). Using threaded comments you can actually have a conversation back and forth among multiple reviewers.

Tip

Comments can be one of the more dangerous bits of metadata in a document if you're not careful. There have been a number of instances where a document with inappropriate comments ended up in the hands of a client. Be circumspect about what you say and be sure to use a metadata checker to remove the comments (see Chapter 11) before you send it on to somebody who shouldn't read those comments.

FIGURE 6.16 Replying to a Comment

Additionally if a Comment was an action item such as "Rewrite this sentence to reflect the new offer," you can mark that Comment done. Right-click the **Comment** and select **Mark Comment Done**. The Comment will be grayed out to indicate that it's been marked as done.

Compare Versions

One of the features that gets a good workout by law firms is the blacklining feature (what we often call redlining), which is where you have the system compare two versions of a document, and Word will highlight the changes for you.

To use it, click the **Compare** button on the **Ribbon** and select **Compare...**. You'll get the **Compare Documents** dialog box (see Figure 6.17), which lets you specify the documents to compare and set some of the

FIGURE 6.17 The Compare Documents Dialog Box

options for the pending comparison. I usually just accept the defaults but there are one or two settings here I want to spend a moment on.

First of all, under **Show Changes** you should leave the **Show Changes At** to **Word Level** instead of character level. Character level is OK, but it tends to be rather distracting since most character changes that don't also change the word aren't worth looking at. Any character change of significance also changes the word and would be flagged anyway.

▼

If you're not seeing those options, click the **More** button at the bottom left of the **Compare Documents** dialog box.

The second setting you should be aware of is the **Show Changes In** setting. You can have the changes reflected in the **Original** or **Revised** documents but I prefer to have a new document created showing the changes. The reason for that is that I like to leave the original document unchanged, just in case I need to go back to it at some point.

Once you're satisfied with your options click **OK**, and you'll get something that looks like Figure 6.18. The original document is at the top on the right side, the revised document is on the bottom on the right side, and the compared document (showing the changes) is right in the middle. On the left side of the screen you'll see a list of the changes, and you can quickly navigate to a change by clicking it on that list.

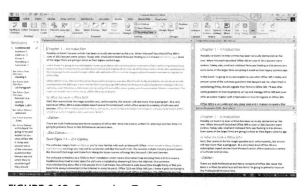

FIGURE 6.18 Comparing Two Documents

If you don't want to see the source documents, you can close any of the four default windows by clicking the **X** in the top right corner of that window.

At the top of the revisions list you'll see a summary of the revisions in the compared documents (see Figure 6.19). Here you can see the total number of revisions along with a breakdown of how many insertions, how many deletions, how many comments, etc.

When you're satisfied with the combined document (and yes, you can edit the combined document right there in that window) just click **Save**

FIGURE 6.19 The Revisions List

(or press **Control+S**), and you'll be prompted to give the new document a new name and save it.

Third-Party Document Management Systems

I have to admit that I sort of resent third-party document management systems. They're an expensive crutch whose sole reason for existence is simple human weakness. With any modern computer if you use an intelligent file naming convention in a disciplined fashion and a good file searching system—**Windows Desktop Search** (WDS) is perfectly capable—then you really don't need a third-party document management system. Document management exists to help you and your colleagues intelligently save, store, and find documents. You can accomplish the same thing by setting up a policy that says "All memos will be saved to the client's folder, under the matter subfolder, with a file name in the format of 'Memo to [X] regarding [Y]'," and then adhering religiously to that policy. Everybody would be able to find a document they were looking for and the search tool (like WDS) would help cover those scenarios where simple good file names and directory structures don't fit the bill.

Unfortunately in the real world people get rushed and corners get cut. Pretty soon the root folder of the structure starts to fill up with files named *Memo1, Memo2, Jonesmemo*, and so forth as people cut the handful of steps required to save the file properly and just save it as quickly as they can with whatever name they can bang in fast and move on. Soon you have the filing equivalent of kindergarten, and nobody can remember which cubby they put their shoes in.

Document management systems solve this problem by automating some of the process (extracting keywords from the document itself, and inserting the author and editor IDs) and by forcing other parts of it, for example, requiring the user to type in a client and matter number, for example. They also generally include a search engine that can be used to search the document profiles as well as the document itself. In addition to the purpose-built document management tools I'm going to mention momentarily, many case management suites like **ProLaw**, **PC Law**, or **Clio** have the capability to do some document management. If you already have a full-featured case management suite deployed, you might want to check to see if it can suit your document management needs before you invest in a separate document management tool.

DocsOpen by Open Text (Formerly "Hummingbird")

The venerable **DocsOpen** system is one that just about any lawyer who has been around a decade or two has probably run across in at least one firm. It was, for a time, the most popular system among the AmLaw 100, and if it has fallen from that perch, it has only been due to cost, competition, and perhaps some firms' disillusionment with the product—which, to be honest, is probably inevitable with a product as complicated and ubiquitous as a document management system.

More information about DocsOpen is available at http://www.open-text.com/2/global/sol-products/sol-pro-edocs-products2/pro-llecm-docsopen.htm. If the URL is any indication you can already sense, this is going to be complicated.

Interwoven WorkSite (Formerly Known as iManage) . . . Now HP Autonomy

Probably the other leading vendor in the AmLaw 100 for document and content management is **Interwoven**. Their **WorkSite** is extremely modular and can be customized for a particular firm. Interwoven has been acquired by HP as part of the Autonomy product line.

More information is available at http://www.autonomy.com.

Worldox

Worldox has been around since the late 1980s and is widely deployed in small to mid-sized firms. Unlike its competitors, Worldox has always been Worldox and hasn't evolved through acquisition and change of ownership. It started out as a small, reasonably priced solution for smaller firms and has grown a bit from there. It's still pretty reasonably priced for what you get.

More information is available at http://www.worldox.com.

Collaborating with Other Word Processors

As much as Microsoft would like to make it so, the reality is that not everybody is using Microsoft Word 2013. You may have to work collaboratively with people who are using older versions of Microsoft Word or even—Bill, forgive me for saying so—products from other vendors like WordPerfect from Corel.

Older Versions of Word

Operating with older versions of Word is actually fairly easy. The **Office OpenXML** file formats were all new to Office 2007, and the older versions of Word don't understand them natively. Microsoft has found a great way to accommodate users of the older versions however. They've created **File Converters** that you can install on older versions of Microsoft Office (Office 2000 or later), which enable those versions of Office to read *and* write the newer file formats natively! How cool is that? Better still, these file converters are free. I won't try to post the cryptic URL for them here, just Google for *Office 2010 File Converters*, and you will quickly find the site to obtain and download them along with simple instructions. Most, but not quite all, of the document features will be available to the older versions after the File Converters are installed.

OK, you dragged it out of me. Examples of what might not be available to a Word 2003 user running the File Converters include things like equations created using the new Word equation editor. When the Word 2003 user opens an OpenXML document with equations, they will be converted to images. The equations will be converted—not the Word 2003 user.

Even if they're *not* interacting with Office 2013 users, the File Converters convey the benefits of the new file formats to the older software—such as the smaller file sizes.

If the other party isn't interested in installing the File Converters, all is not lost. You can still click **File**, do a **Save As**, and choose **Office 97-2003 Document** (see Figure 6.20) to save the document in the old, binary, .DOC format. It shouldn't surprise you that if you do that you lose all of the benefits of saving in the new OpenXML formats. You've simply created a classic .DOC file, which can be opened and edited by any application capable of working with those documents (such as Word 2002, aka Word XP).

When you save a document in the older file formats, you're saving in what Word calls Compatibility Mode. Word will caution you that certain elements of your document might not quite translate properly into Compatibility Mode. Luckily, most of those things are not elements that

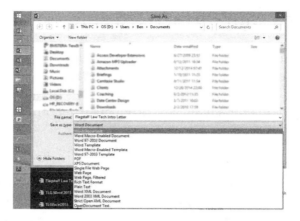

FIGURE 6.20 Use Save As to Convert Document Format

most lawyers will care about. Mostly it's about Themes and SmartArt for example.

Microsoft Word for Mac

If you happen to be collaborating with one of that small, but vocal, contingent of users who believe that putting an *i* in front of anything and painting it white makes it cool, then you're in luck— Microsoft Office 2008 and 2011 for Mac supports the Office OpenXML format (.DOCX) natively. There are File Converters for older versions of Office for Mac; just like the PC versions.

WordPerfect

Amazing how times change. When I first started in legal technology, about two and a half decades ago, **WordPerfect** (for DOS back then) was easily the dominant word processor in law firms. Today you still find it here and there, but for the most part, it's a distant second to Microsoft's Word. You obviously know what I mean since you bought this book. Unless you're my mother and just bought a copy to give my Aunt Susan, I suppose.

That said, if your colleagues are using **Corel WordPerfect Office X4** or later, then they can already read and write the Word Open XML format files. No special hoops to jump through for you. Corel users, however, should save their documents in **Office OpenXML** format (.DOCX) before they send the documents to you so that you can read them.

Corel's WordPerfect X3 support for Office OpenXML is a little more uncertain. There are a number of vague statements inferring that X3 would support Office OpenXML, but X3 didn't support it when the product was new, and there are a lot of documented instances where working between X3 and Office 2010 (and even older versions of Word for that matter) resulted in some fairly frustrating issues—particularly around the way fonts were translated between the two products. Your best bet, if you have to work between those two products, would be to use a format that is more common to both products. You could try saving the documents as **Word 97-2003** format, but again, be prepared for possible formatting inconsistencies.

LibreOffice

LibreOffice (formerly known as "OpenOffice") is the open source productivity suite that has a certain amount of popularity among the technorati. At the time of this writing it's at version 4.2 but, as for all things open source, that could change at any time. Working with LibreOffice users is relatively easy since OpenOffice supports OpenXML natively and Word 2013 supports the OpenOffice formats natively too.

In It for the Short Term

If you have to collaborate with somebody who has an obscure, or rather old, word processor and it's only going to be a short-term collaboration (a few weeks perhaps), then maybe you can persuade them to download and install the trial version of Microsoft Office 2013. It's fully functional and free; it just stops allowing you to edit documents after about sixty days. Great solution? No. But may be better than beating your head against the wall trying to share documents with somebody who uses StarOffice 5.2.

Working on the Road

We're an increasingly mobile bunch, and the technology has evolved to the point where we don't have to be sitting at our desks in order to access and edit our documents. A number of technologies have emerged (and continue to emerge and impress) that allow you to work from anywhere at any time.

Mobile Devices

Just about everybody is carrying a mobile device these days—most of you are carrying phones that function as personal information devices. **Windows Phone 8**, for example, includes a very good version of Microsoft Word. It's a mobile-enhanced version that you can use to read, edit, or even compose documents on . . . if you're really desperate. Let's be honest, working on a document of any size on a four-inch screen with an on-screen keyboard is not exactly an optimal experience. You can create bulleted lists, use primitive fonts, add and edit text, and even send your completed document via e-mail when you're done.

Word Mobile has the ability to access documents stored in your **OneDrive** or **SharePoint** accounts—assuming your SharePoint can be accessed from the Internet.

I think I can safely say that this is not something you'll choose to do if you have other options, but it's nice to know that in a pinch, if you really have to review and edit a document while you're stuck somewhere and can't get access to a real computer to do it, this option can get the job done if you're patient enough.

That applies to DataViz's **Documents to Go** (for Android devices) too.

The increasing popularity of tablet devices like the **iPad** and **Kindle Fire** means that mobile users are getting larger screens (but often still no physical keyboard) to work with. The iPad can read Word documents natively (assuming you can get them on your iPad to begin with), but if you want to edit them, you have to get an additional application. As of this writing the best solution is probably **Pages for the iPad** ($10) though a rumored version of **Word for the iPad** seems imminent.

For **Android** the story is substantially the same as the iPad. There are third-party applications like **Documents to Go**, and expectations are that Microsoft will be releasing an official Word application for the Android platform soon too.

Microsoft's **Surface** tablets come with a full version of Microsoft Office, which means you can work with Word documents as long as you can get to those documents—either via Internet or via a USB drive typically.

Regardless of the tablet you opt for, if you think you're going to do any kind of serious document editing on it, then it's a no-brainer that you will want to invest in an add-on keyboard for it.

Another option would be to use **Google Docs** to read documents (as long as they're under 10MB). Be careful with the free version of Google Apps, though, their terms of service give Google generous access and rights to your content—including the right to republish or "perform" (whatever that means) your documents.

By the time this book is in print and in your hands, there's a good chance that some newer and better solutions for working with Word documents on your tablet device will be available.

Telecommuting

One of the things technology is increasingly enabling is the ability to work from anywhere at any time. This can be a blessing and a curse. There are three main technologies for telecommuting—which you use is up to you and your IT department or consultant.

Remote Node

Remote Node computing is the **Virtual Private Network** (VPN) solution where you connect to your office via the Internet and establish a secure "tunnel" across the Internet that lets you join your local computer (home computer or laptop typically) to your office network. Then you work on your local computer just as if you were sitting in your office. You have access to all of the files and resources of the office network just as you do from your desk—albeit probably a little slower since you're limited to an Internet connection.

If you have Microsoft Word installed on your local computer, then you can use it just as you would Word on your desk at the office. Easy as that. All of the processing occurs on your local computer. One nice advantage of Remote Node is that it's not too hard to work off-line (which means disconnected from the office) because your local computer is a stand-alone machine with Word installed. You can simply copy or check out documents to your local hard drive, disconnect from the office, and work on those documents locally. Later when you connect back up, you just copy or check in those documents back to the office.

This is pretty handy if you're taking a laptop on an airplane and want to work rather than watch the movie.

Remote Control

Remote Control is the old **pcAnywhere** or **GoToMyPC** solution. With this solution, you connect to the office, again typically across the Internet, and with an application on your local computer, you take control of a remote PC sitting idly at the office—usually your office computer. As the name sort of implies, you are remotely controlling your office computer and that means you quite literally have everything you have at the office. The office computer is transmitting to you images of the screen and you are transmitting to it keystrokes and mouse movements. All of the processing occurs on the office computer.

Remote Control is fairly easy to set up but does have one big drawback . . . if you don't have an Internet connection, you're out of luck. You *have* to be able to connect to the office to use it, which means that you sometimes can't do it from airplanes (aerial WiFi is here but not ubiquitous quite yet) or other disconnected areas. It also means you probably have to remember to leave the machine you're remotely controlling turned on when you leave the office, which may introduce other security issues. Also if the office machine is shared with other users, it won't be accessible to you while another user is logged into it, either remotely or locally (sitting at the keyboard).

With Remote Control you're literally using the same machine you use when you're sitting at the office, so you are using the same copy of Microsoft Word (complete with any customization) that you are used to.

Remote Host

The third basic technology you'll find is Remote Host. This is the **Citrix** or **Terminal Server** solution where a server at your office hosts some number of simultaneous users who connect in remotely with virtual Windows desktops. The advantage to this is that you don't need to leave your office computer turned on—you're connecting to a server that is always on. Also if you have a number of remote users, you don't need to provide office machines for each of them; they can remote into the Terminal Server from their home machines or laptops and work from there. It may be a little pricier to set up and configure than GoToMyPC, but the results are a tad more professional, especially in an office where you may have a lot of simultaneous remote users.

With Remote Host you can install and run Microsoft Word on the Terminal Server or Citrix Server, and all of the functionality we've described in this book would still apply.

NOTE: If you have a Remote Host server and you want to install Word on it, you have to make sure you get the **Volume License** version of Word. You can't install the Word that came with your PC (known as the OEM or Original Equipment Manufacturer version) or a retail version of Word that you bought at the computer store or from Amazon.com. Volume license versions are actually less expensive than the retail version, and contrary to popular belief, you don't have to have fifty machines to qualify. You need only buy five (or more) licenses to get Volume Licensing.

As **Bring Your Own Device** (BYOD) becomes increasingly common, firms are increasingly moving toward Remote Host—aka **Virtual Desktop Infrastructure** or VDI—technologies to standardize the resources available to mobile and remote users and improve security and manageability.

In "The Cloud"

The newest player in the telecommuting market is actually an old concept [Application Service Providers (ASPs)] brought back to life. **Software as a Service** (SaaS) is what you've got when an outside provider is hosting your software on their servers, across the Internet, usually for a monthly subscription fee. Google Apps (free and paid) are examples of SaaS products. Microsoft's new Office 365, which provides stripped-down web versions of Word, PowerPoint, Excel, and OneNote across the web is another. Every week it seems like new SaaS products are popping up. SaaS can be a great solution for the mobile legal professional—you can access it from anywhere, don't need to maintain your own servers and it's constantly updated and monitored. But there are some downsides too:

- **Cost.** It seems like SaaS would be cheaper than having your own software, and often it is, but sometimes it's not. If you're paying

$30 a month to use that suite of apps that cost you $499 to buy . . . in 18 months you'll have spent more on the SaaS than the purchase price of the product. It pays to do the math.

- **Security.** Google's free apps have a very liberal terms-of-service agreement that gives them the right to reproduce and republish any content you submit to their service (i.e., documents you're storing there). Will they ever do that? I don't know, but are you comfortable agreeing to a contract that gives them the right to? (**Note:** Their *paid* version of apps does not suffer from this same shortcoming.)

- **Shared Tenant Environment.** Additionally almost SaaS services are in what's called a Shared Tenant Environment. That's how they keep the price down: economy of scale. You're on a server with dozens or hundreds of other users and customers. The chances of that server getting compromised (or seized by authorities) have to be weighed.

- **Access.** If your Internet connection goes down or is otherwise unavailable, so is your data. If you're going to be dependent upon SaaS applications, it's wise to have redundant Internet connections and a plan for what to do in case of a total outage.

- **Local Copy of Data.** Also, make sure your SaaS provider lets you have a local copy of your data. You don't want them to have all of the control over your critical data—heaven-forbid you ever have a billing dispute or mistake and they cut off your access to the data while you're under deadline.

- **Geolocation.** When your data is hosted somewhere else, you don't always know where that somewhere else is. Make sure to ask. If your data is being hosted in Iowa or Seattle, that's probably OK. If your data is being hosted in Canada or Scotland . . . that might be OK. If your data is being hosted in China or North Korea . . . that's probably not OK. Don't forget to ask where their backups are too.

Summary

Collaborating and working remotely help to maximize your productivity, and Microsoft Word has been designed with these benefits in mind. The Office OpenXML format is the most open and portable format yet for Microsoft Office, and increasingly other word processing products, such as Corel's X5 and LibreOffice 4.2, will be able to comfortably support it natively. Additionally Word now supports the LibreOffice formats natively.

Working with Other Programs

7

One of the advantages of purchasing the Microsoft Office Suite is that the applications in the suite tend to work well together. Office 2013 continues this trend.

Outlook

Outlook is the application that is open the longest during the day for most users of Microsoft Office and it's the place where a lot of information that is useful to Word documents (like names and addresses for instance) is stored. Naturally there is an interest in wanting to be able to use that information in Word as seamlessly as possible.

Mail Merge

Commonly, lawyers and firms keep a list of clients in Outlook in the form of a **Contacts** folder. You can leverage that list of information to create mailing labels or form letters in Word. The way you do that is called a Mail Merge, and basically involves creating a document template with fields where your variable data goes; things like Name, Address, City, and so on.

You can start your Mail Merge from either Word or Outlook, but I generally recommend you start from the Outlook side because Outlook offers better filtering capabilities than Word does.

1. To begin, you'll want to switch to your **Contacts** folder in Outlook and select the contact items you

Tricks of the Pros

Mail Merge is a great reason to use **Categories** in your Contacts. Categorize your contacts as *Clients* or *Holiday Card* or whatever, and then filter your view either with the **Search Contacts** tool at the top right or by setting an actual **Filter** on the view with **View** > **View Settings** > **Filter** > **More Choices**. Once your Contacts folder is only displaying the contacts from the category you wish to merge from then you can proceed with step 2 of the merge.

want to use for your merge. If there are only a handful of them, just hold down the **Control** key and click on each one to select them, or if they are contiguous, hold down **Shift** and click the first and then last one in the group. If you want to select All of the contacts in the current view, then you can skip right to the next step.

2. Click the **Mail Merge** button on the **Home** tab in Outlook. You'll get the **Mail Merge Contacts** dialog box like you see in Figure 7.1. If you're sending to *all* of the displayed contacts, then check the **All Contacts in Current View** radio button. If you've selected specific contacts and only want to merge those, then select the **Only Selected Contacts** radio button. Leave **Fields to Merge** set to **All Contact Fields** if you have the option.

FIGURE 7.1 Mail Merge Contacts Dialog Box

3. Select the Document you want to merge to. Usually it will be a new document, but there may be times when you have a preexisting Main Document (that's what Word calls the document that contains the text and information you're merging into) that you want to use.

4. If you plan to do this merge repeatedly with the same, unchanging, group of contacts you can save this contact data to a permanent file. I discourage this except in *one* scenario: you want to keep a snapshot of the merge data for reference—to show to whom you sent the newsletter or what address you had on file for them at the time. The rest of the time your merge data will likely change from month to month and year to year as new contacts are added and old contacts removed (not to mention as addresses change).

5. Under **Merge Options** select the **Document Type**. Normally it will be either **Form Letters**, **Mailing Labels**, or **Envelopes**. A **Catalog** is essentially a directory. I've yet to find a practical use for that option in a law firm setting.

6. Under **Merge Options** you can change the **Merge To** setting from **New Document** to either **Printer** or **Email**. I discourage using Printer because that's going to perform your merge to the printer and if something isn't right with the merge, the first indication you might have is blowing through fifty pages of paper before you realize it. I always merge to a New Document so I can preview my results *before* I send them to the printer or out via e-mail.

7. Click **OK**. Word will open with what looks like a blank document (assuming you chose New Document in Step 3) but there is a key difference . . . the **Ribbon** will open to the **Mailings** tab, and a number of the buttons will be active.

8. Create your document as you would like it to appear. Type the text that isn't going to change, and in those places where you want to insert data from the merge (like **Full Name** or **Mailing Address**) click the **Insert Merge Field** button to get the gallery of possible fields from your data set to merge (see Figure 7.2). Select the field or fields you want to insert there, for example: *Dear «Title»«Last_Name»*.

FIGURE 7.2 Insert Merge Fields

9. When you have the document completed—with fields in place that will be replaced with Outlook contact data—you can preview your results by using the **Preview Results** button. Click that button and Word will perform the sample merge.

10. Use the forward and back arrows on the **Go To Record** command to move forward and backward through your previewed results and make sure everything looks the way it should.

11. When you're happy with the results, click the **Finish & Merge** button and then you can print (or e-mail) the results.

One-Off Envelopes

One of the features I've liked since the days of **WordPerfect 5.1 for DOS** (Remember that one?) is the ability to print envelopes. It just looks a lot more professional to have a printed envelope, and it's a pain to have to load your envelope into a typewriter and type the address—especially since I don't even own a typewriter anymore. If you don't want to have to do a whole mail merge just to print a single envelope, then Word's **Envelopes** feature is for you.

▼

I've always liked being able to print a barcode on the envelope for the destination address. Word 2007 did away with that feature. The reason it was pulled was that the POSTNET codes that the **Barcode** field in Word produced were no longer compliant with US Postal Service (USPS) regulations. It could be argued that Microsoft could have fixed the POSTNET codes but to be honest the USPS is using high-speed scanners on all mail now and they are perfectly capable of reading a printed address on an envelope. So there really isn't any advantage to printing the barcodes on the envelopes anymore.

To print an envelope with Word, just go to the **Mailings** tab and click the **Envelopes** button. That will give you the **Envelopes and Labels** dialog box you see in Figure 7.3. You can type your delivery (destination) address in the provided field or click the address book icon just above it to the right to access your Outlook Address Book and have Word pull the address from there. If you click the drop-down arrow *next* to the Address Book (as I have in the figure), you'll see the last few addresses you've selected so you can reinsert a common address if you need to.

You can add your return address or check the **Omit** button if you have preprinted envelopes or if you're going to use a sticker for it. When you're ready to print the envelope, just load the envelope into your printer and click the **Print** button. Voila, a lovely envelope.

FIGURE 7.3 Printing Envelopes and Labels

If you'd like to change the default return address that Word uses, just go to **File** > **Options** > **Advanced** and scroll down to the **General** section where you'll find the **Mailing Address** section.

Labels

You can create labels with addresses from your Outlook Address Book the same way you created envelopes just above. You can print a whole sheet of the same label or you can print just a single label—and even use a partial sheet of labels! Word will let you specify which column and row you want to print the single label on.

Tricks of the Pros

If you have your destination address in the document, such as in an address block at the top of a letter, just select that address first, then click the **Envelopes** command in the **Mailings** tab. When the **Envelopes and Labels** dialog box opens, that selected text will already appear in the Delivery Address field.

In reality you don't always *have* to select the address. Word will try to guess intelligently what address you want to address the envelope to, but it doesn't always guess correctly. Selecting the address first makes sure you get the address you want.

Excel

Word and Excel make it easy to embed Excel data into a Word document—either as a static table or even as a live link that updates as the data in Excel updates. There are a few different ways to do it, but let's start with the easiest way. Create your spreadsheet in Excel, select the cell or cells that you want to embed in your Word document, and click **Copy**. Switch to your Word document, place the insertion point where you want the data, and click **Paste**. There's your data (see Figure 7.4). Easy as that!

Of course that's a static representation of the data. If it changes on the Excel spreadsheet, it won't change in the Word document. If that's what you want, great. If, on the other hand, you were hoping for something more dynamic, then there is one more step you need to take.

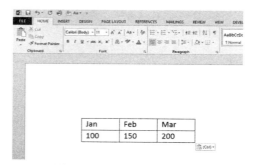

FIGURE 7.4 Inserting Excel Data in a Word Document

See the little clipboard at the bottom right corner of Figure 7.4? That's a tool that gives you Paste options, and in this case it's pretty useful. If you click it, you'll get the options you find in Figure 7.5. The six basic options relate to how the table of data will appear. **Keep Source Formatting** means that any Formats in Excel (including colors and lines) will come over. **Match Destination Table Style** will bring the data but replace those Formats with a Table Style from your document.

FIGURE 7.5 The Paste Options Dialog Box

The default is to paste the data in as a table, but **Paste as Picture** won't paste it as a table at all, but rather as a static image. That's a good one to use if you want to maintain the source formatting and also make sure the data can't be easily edited.

Keep Text Only doesn't paste the data as a table, but rather as plain text. This is good for simple content, but not very good if you have a lot of data to paste.

All of those options differ in how the data is presented, but they're the same in one very important way: they're all going to paste the data statically. In other words, the data is the data and that's it—there's no link back to the source Excel workbook. If the data changes in the source workbook, it won't be updated in the Word document.

I guess I should point out that this only works as long as the Excel workbook is available. If you e-mail this Word document to a colleague at another firm, the link will be broken since your colleague doesn't have the source workbook. The colleague will see the Excel data as of the last time you updated it, but any subsequent updates won't be reflected. If you move the Excel file to another location in your organization, Word will cleverly update the link to reflect the new location . . . so future changes will still be reflected, as long as you can still access the Excel file from that computer.

The two middle options in Figure 7.5 address that shortcoming. Basically you're just going to choose if you want to keep the **Source Formatting** (i.e., have the data look like it does in Excel) or if you're going to match the **Destination Formatting** (i.e., have the data look like a default Word table), but either way the data *will* be linked back to the Excel workbook. If the data in the workbook changes, then the data in the Word document will change as well.

The converse is not true, by the way. If you change the data in Word, it will *not* update the data in the Excel spreadsheet. In fact, the next time you make a change in Excel any changes you made to the Word version of the data will be lost—overwritten with the current version of the Excel data.

This is a pretty useful feature for documents that are a work in progress—for example, if you have a complicated purchase offer and you're still running all the "what-ifs" and scenarios in Excel. You can link the relevant Excel data to your Word document and Word will always reflect the latest numbers for you until you're ready to send or print. When you've got what you want, just print it or PDF it and send it off. When you PDF the document, you essentially affix the numbers as they are—they won't change in the PDF no matter what happens to the Excel workbook.

The other place this feature is really handy is in recurring reports. You can set up your report in the Word document and link in relevant data from Excel workbooks. For each period, your Word document will already have the relevant numbers from your Excel workbooks—making much shorter work of preparing the report. Print your report to PDF each month and the PDF will reflect that snapshot of numbers.

If you'd like to break the link so that Word no longer automatically updates the data, just right-click the table in Word and choose **Linked Worksheet Object** and then **Links**, as I have in Figure 7.6.

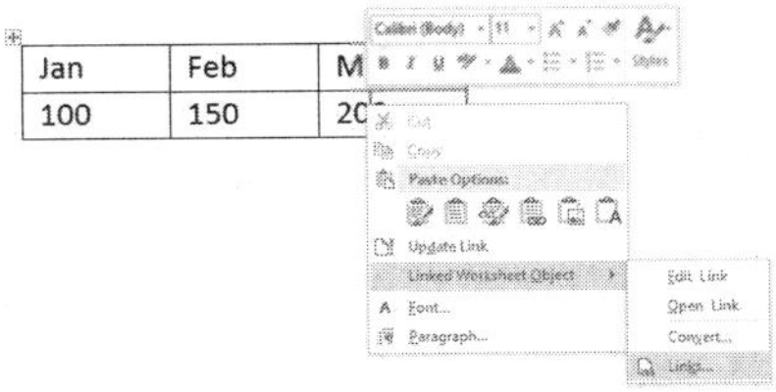

FIGURE 7.6 Breaking the Links

The Links dialog box (see Figure 7.7) includes a number of clever tools for working with the linked data, including a **Break Link** dialog box that will effectively convert your linked table to a static table. If you only want to prevent the link from updating temporarily, click the **Locked** checkbox under **Update Method** on the **Links** dialog box instead of the

FIGURE 7.7 The Links Dialog Box

Break Link button. Later, when you want to resume updating, just go back in and uncheck **Locked**.

OneNote

OneNote is Microsoft's free-form note-taking software. It's an application that should be extremely popular with lawyers because it is essentially an electronic version of the yellow legal pad but with a *lot* more power. One of the things that OneNote is exceptionally good at is serving as a starting point for Word documents. When I start to write a long memo (or a book for that matter) I'll often start it as an outline in OneNote. I can do my Internet research, collaborate with colleagues, and reorganize things until I'm ready to write the actual detailed content. In OneNote (see Figure 7.8) you can create your outlines and other content, and when you're ready to send it over to Word for finishing and formatting, you just click **File > Send > Send to Word** as you see in Figure 7.9. When you do that, you'll get a fresh new Word document with your outline ready for content.

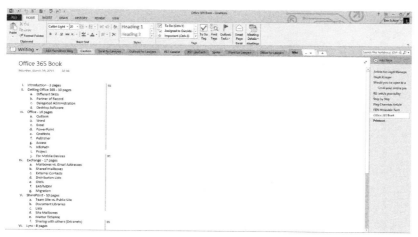

FIGURE 7.8 Microsoft OneNote

FIGURE 7.9 Send to Microsoft Word

You can also readily Copy and Paste **content**, **images**, **diagrams**, and other items from OneNote to Word.

Linked Notes

OneNote and Word have another interesting integration trick. You can click the **Linked Notes** icon in the **OneNote** group of the **Review** tab in Word (see Figure 7.10). That will open OneNote and dock it to the right side of your screen. OneNote will ask you in what section you want to put the linked notes, similar to what you see in Figure 7.11. Pick a section to locate the linked notes in and OneNote will give you a blank page to start taking notes in. At the top right corner of the OneNote page you'll see a little chain link icon as you can see in Figure 7.12. That's your cue that these notes are linked to a document.

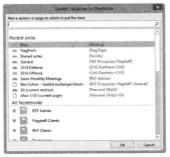

FIGURE 7.10 The Review Tab

FIGURE 7.11 Select a Section

FIGURE 7.12 The Linked Notes Button

Now here's where the fun begins. You keep working in your document. As you go, you can take notes on the document in the OneNote window docked to the side. You can see that I'm doing that with some sample content in Figure 7.13. "So what?" you might be thinking. Well, this is OneNote's party piece . . . if you look to the left side of the notes I've typed there, you'll see a little Word icon. If you click that icon . . . you'll be taken to the place in the Word document that you were working on when you took those notes.

FIGURE 7.13 Taking Linked Notes

> OneNote linked notes also work for **PowerPoint** and web pages too!

OneNote becomes a powerful repository for you to take notes and do document review. None of the OneNote notes appear in the Word document, so you don't have to worry about any metadata from them.

PowerPoint

Microsoft PowerPoint is a way to take information and present it to a live audience. Word integrates with PowerPoint in two ways that are interesting to us.

Send to PowerPoint

If you have a document that you want to present to an audience, you can use it as the basis for a presentation. The first trick to doing that successfully is to format the document you're sending to PowerPoint properly.

PowerPoint uses the styles you're using in the document to decide what text goes where (as if you needed another reason to use styles). **Heading 1** text becomes slide titles. **Heading 2** is the first level bullet point. **Heading 3** is the second level bullet point. And so on. Perfect! If you've properly formatted your document, every major heading becomes a new slide and the subheadings within that are the bullet points.

Body text that doesn't have a heading applied won't appear on your slides.

Now that you've got a properly formatted document, you're ready to send it to PowerPoint. Great! Now how do we send it? There's no button on the Ribbon. Nothing Backstage under the File menu.

No, we have to add the button. You could add it to the Ribbon, but that would require adding a Custom Tab, and it seems silly to add a whole tab just for this one command. If you already have a custom tab, go ahead and add this to that if you want to. If you've created a custom tab before, you already know how to add this button. For the rest of you . . .

Click the drop-down arrow on the end of the **Quick Access Toolbar** (QAT) and choose **More Commands** from the menu that appears. On the left-hand column set the **Choose Commands From** to **All Commands** and then scroll down to **Send to Microsoft PowerPoint** (see Figure 7.14). **Add** that to the QAT and then click **OK** to go back out to your document.

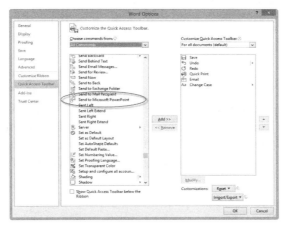

FIGURE 7.14 Adding the Send to PowerPoint Button to the QAT

Now, ready to send to PowerPoint? Just click the new button for that on the QAT and Word will start the process. If you don't think you'll ever use it again, you can always remove the button from the QAT when you're done.

Word for Handouts

The other handy integration between Word and PowerPoint comes when you already have a PowerPoint slide deck and you want to make a set of handouts to give to the audience. In **PowerPoint** just go to **File** > **Save & Send** > **Create Handouts** and click the **Create Handouts** button. PowerPoint will ask you how you want to lay out your handouts (**notes next to slides**, **blank lines below slides**, **outline only**, etc.). Select the style you like, then click **OK**, and a Word document will be created for you with your PowerPoint content. Ready to print and present!

> **Tricks of the Pros**
>
> That's not a bad way to create speaker notes to have at the podium during your presentation too—in case you're not using PowerPoint's Presenter View for some reason.

Pictures and Diagrams

They say a picture is worth a thousand words, and there may well be times in your documents when you'll want to include a picture, diagram, or graphic. Word 2013 makes even easier to do than previous versions did. For images that you have on your system or network, go to the **Insert** tab, click **Pictures**, and use the **Insert Picture** dialog box to navigate to the picture you want to insert. When you've found it, click once to select it and then click **Insert**.

> **Tricks of the Pros**
>
> If you're working with an image that you might change in the future, consider inserting the picture as a link to the file by clicking the drop-down arrow on the Insert button and choosing **Insert and Link**. Later if you want to change or update the image, simply replace the image file on your hard drive with the new file, using the same name.

Word 2013 makes it easier to insert clip art and images from the web than previous versions did too. To do that, go to the **Insert** tab of the **Ribbon** and click the **Online Pictures** button. Word will pop up a different **Insert Pictures** dialog box (seen in Figure 7.15) and you can have it search for clip art or online images based on search criteria you offer. Want pictures of a dog? Conference table? Airplane? Belgium? Just type in the search and Word will do its best to find matches.

FIGURE 7.15 Insert Online Pictures

Once you have the image inserted in your document, you can resize it by pointing at one of the tiny squares around the edge (called handles) with your mouse cursor and drag the handle to resize it. If you need to be more precise in your image sizing, just right-click the image to get the context menu you see in Figure 7.16 and choose **Size and Position . . . .** In the size dialog box, not only you can specify the size of the image but you can also rotate the image or change the way that text wraps around it.

As long as I'm on the subject . . . there are a couple of other items on the context menu in Figure 7.16 that you should be interested in. The

FIGURE 7.16 The Image Context Menu   **FIGURE 7.17** Insert Caption

Change Picture . . . command lets you select a different image—handy if you realize that you inserted the picture of what was supposed to be a photo of a disputed property line, but is actually a shot of your family at the Grand Canyon.

Hyperlink is handy in electronic documents if you want to be able to click on the picture and open a file or website. It doesn't do anything for paper documents of course.

Insert Caption brings up Word's Captioning Tool (see Figure 7.17), which I happen to find a bit inflexible and primitive, but can be handy if your needs align with what it does.

Scanned Documents

Just like inserting pictures there may be times when you'll want to insert a scanned document. There are two basic ways you might want to do that:

1. **As an Image.** You want the other person to see and probably be able to read the document, but not edit it. Perhaps it's just an exhibit that you're including in your document.
2. **As Editable Text.** You've received the document in paper form and now you want to be able to edit the text like any other Word document. To do that you'll have to scan the document and run it through an **Optical Character Recognition** (OCR) program.

When you first scan in a file, or receive an image of a document via e-mail or other electronic transfer, the computer just sees a picture. It doesn't know a document from a building or an elephant; it's all just pixels to the computer. When you run the OCR program, it will look at the image and try to recognize the text so that it can be converted into A's and B's and 4's and so forth. The results are saved as a document file that you can then edit.

The best OCR programs include spell checkers and some context-sensitive capabilities that make good guesses at what a word should be, but even so, they're not perfect. Even the very best tend to achieve only about 99 percent accuracy.

When it comes to OCR, the cleaner your original, the better your results. If your original is clearly printed, in a nice clean font, black text on white paper, then you'll probably get very good results. If your original is a little wrinkled, on colored text, with highlighted text or handwritten notes scrawled in the margins, and so forth, then your results may be somewhat unpredictable. Either way, be sure to carefully proofread the results before you trust them. Especially in legal documents, a single word or number that's wrong could have serious consequences.

Adobe Acrobat

Acrobat has become the de facto standard for portable documents, especially in law. Word has some pretty good integration with Acrobat both in creating documents and, now, in reading them.

Creating Acrobat Documents

There are a few different ways you can create Adobe Acrobat documents from your Word documents, and we've already looked at most of them.

- You can do a **File** > **Save As** and change the **Save As Type** to **PDF**.
- You can do **File** > **Export** > **Create PDF/XPS** to create one.
- You can do **File** > **Share** > **Email** > **Send as PDF** to start a new e-mail message with your Word document in PDF format.

There are a number of third-party tools like **CutePDF** or **NitroPDF** that you can install, which will create PDF files for you. Now that Word creates competent PDF files natively, I only really ever bother with those tools if I have *other* programs that don't have native PDF support already and I wish to create PDF files.

Or, of course, you could use actual Adobe Acrobat to create PDF files from Word documents. Don't want to buy and install Acrobat? Adobe offers an online PDF creator that you can subscribe to for a monthly fee.

Reading Acrobat Documents

Word 2013 has a pretty impressive new party piece and that's the ability to do **PDF reflow** natively. What does that mean? Well . . . it means that you can open a PDF file in Microsoft Word and Word will convert it to an editable document. Word does the OCR we talked about above and tries to preserve as much of the original look and layout as possible.

Some of you are thinking "Wow, that's really cool!" Others are realizing that it means that any PDF file you send somebody—that you put in PDF format because you didn't want them to edit it—has just become easily editable.

To use **PDF reflow** all you need to do is go to **File** > **Open in Word**, find the PDF file you want to open, and open it. Word will give you a little notification (see Figure 7.18) indicating that it's going to convert the PDF to an editable document, and moments later you're in business.

The other way you can use it is to find that PDF file using Windows Explorer. Right-click the file and choose **Open With** > **Word**.

FIGURE 7.18 PDF Reflow

Summary

Word is part of a suite of applications that are designed to work together. Over the years, that statement has garnered chuckles or snarls from users who have tried to make them work together without much success, but Word 2013 and the Office 2013 suite go further than ever before to try to help the applications work together more smoothly. Whether you're doing mail merges from Outlook or embedding data from Excel, Microsoft Word 2013 can help you be more productive, more effective, and generally happier. Adding PDF reflow to Word 2013 adds even more utility and will save lawyers time (along with finally dispensing with the myth that PDFs can't be edited).

Automating Word

8

Microsoft Word 2013 offers some very powerful tools for automating your document creation and editing—reducing repetitive tasks and giving you better quality control while reducing errors.

Document Assembly

Document assembly is the usage of tools like **macros**, **scripts**, or **applications** to automate the building of standardized documents. Mail Merge is a form of document assembly too. There are a lot of third-party tools that can do document assembly, as well as some tools built right into Word. The key to document assembly is to create a library of reusable parts (phrases, images, even entire pages of boilerplate text) so that you don't have to re-create them from scratch every time.

HotDocs (and Others)

HotDocs (owned by LexisNexis) is an example of a third-party document assembly application. The premise is pretty straightforward: you create a model document that is going to be the basis for all of the future documents of this type. In the document, you identify those bits that are going to vary from document to document—the **client's name**, **dates**, **amounts**, **locations**, and so forth. Once you have your model document completely built, you run the document assembly software, and it performs an "interview" asking you for the variable information you previously specified for the document. The assembly software will take your answers and plug them into the places you specified in the model document, and the result is a fully built document!

Kiiac

Kiiac takes a slightly different approach from HotDocs. You show Kiiac a library of documents, and it analyzes those documents, finds the documents that are similar, and identifies the most common clauses. Later when you need to build a new document, Kiiac presents you with the most common or successful clauses for you to choose from and helps you build a document that most closely resembles the model documents you've identified. Kiiac helps you build and maintain clause libraries and document templates. It's not cheap, but especially if you're creating a lot of documents on a value-based billing system, it could be worth it.

Building Blocks

A popular feature among lawyers in earlier versions of Word was the **Auto-Text** feature. Commonly lawyers and staff would create custom AutoText entries with oft-used phrases or paragraphs and then use AutoText to quickly and easily insert those bits where they were needed. In Word 2010, **Building Blocks** (sometimes known as **Quick Parts**) replaced the **AutoText** feature, making it simultaneously more powerful and more difficult to use. Building Blocks let you create and save snippets of a document that you expect to reuse often. One way Building Blocks improve on AutoText is that it's not just limited to text. You can make a Building Block out of just about any element of a document. For lawyers, that will still usually mean text, but it could just as easily mean an image like a logo or scanned signature file.

To create a Building Block you just select the element—highlight the text for example—you want to add to the **Building Blocks** gallery and then go to the **Insert** tab, **Quick Parts**, and **Save Selection to Quick Parts Gallery**. What you'll get is what you see in Figure 8.1.

FIGURE 8.1 Creating a New Building Block

Give the Building Block a name. In Figure 8.1, I've created a Building Block consisting of directions to my office and named my Building Block {OffDir, because the name you have needs to be descriptive, and the left bracket makes the text unique and thus unlikely to be typed in normal writing, but should be fairly easy to type quickly. (I'll explain why in a moment.)

Pick a gallery to add your new part to—you'll see several of the known galleries like **Cover Pages** listed. Generally speaking, you'll want to choose either **AutoText** or **Quick Parts** if you're just adding text or maybe a scanned signature image as most lawyers will. Choosing Quick Parts has the added benefit that your new block will appear on the Quick Parts gallery under the button on the Ribbon.

The next field is for **Category**, and this one is purely up to you. You don't have to use Categories if you don't want to—put everything in **General**. But if you're going to use a lot of custom Building Blocks, you might want to organize them a bit by creating custom categories. Click the drop-down arrow for **Category** and you'll see that **Create New Category** is a choice.

Give your new Building Block an optional description and then choose which template to save it in. For the most part, you'll want to just save in the Building Blocks template. The one exception I can think of is a Building Block you want to share with others. In that case, you might create a Custom Template and save to that—then you can send that template to other people, and they can open it.

▼▼▼▼▼

To share Building Blocks with others, create a new template by saving a new document (create a Word document with a brief description of your intended Building Blocks for example) as a template. Click **File > Save As > Change the File Type to Template** and give it a name. Save your Building Blocks to that template and send the template to the people you want to share with. They can save the template to Word's Startup folder (C:\Users\[*USERNAME*]\AppData\Roaming\Microsoft\Word\STARTUP is the default), and the next time they start Word the custom Building Blocks will be available to them.

Finally you have an **Options** field that lets you configure how your Building Block should be inserted into the document you're working on.

- **Insert Content Only** just inserts the contents of the Building Block at the current cursor point. This is what I usually use as most of my Building Blocks are just bits of boilerplate text that I save as Building Blocks to save myself the time of having to retype it or having to search it out and copy and paste it from another document.
- **Insert Content in Its Own Paragraph** sets off your Building Block as a paragraph of its own. Useful for signatures or if your block is . . . well . . . a paragraph.

- **Insert Content on Its Own Page** creates page breaks before and after your Building Block. This is a nice option if you have an entire page of boilerplate that you want to be able to add quickly to your documents. For example: a biography page, or one or more pages of standard contract language that you don't change often.

Tricks of the Pros

If you have pages of text that change only a bit, use them to create Building Blocks that are their own pages. Then when you need to build that document, insert the pages and then go back make the subtle changes to each of those pages. Building Blocks, once inserted, are edited as easily as any other bit of text. This way you can quickly build a several-page document with the benefits of, but not the hazards of, document reuse.

With the old **AutoText** feature you'd type the name of your AutoText entry, and it would offer to replace your AutoText name with the actual text. With Building Blocks, you have to type the name of your Building Block (which is why we want it to be something easy to type) and then press **F3** to activate it (i.e., replace the name with the actual Building Block).

To organize your Building Blocks, go to the **Insert** tab and click on the **Quick Parts** button. You'll find the **Building Blocks Organizer** pictured in Figure 8.2.

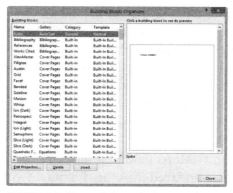

FIGURE 8.2 The Building Blocks Organizer

The Building Blocks Organizer is how you can edit the properties of a Building Block after the fact—for example, if you decide to change the category you assigned the Builidng Block to or what Gallery it appears in. You can also preview and insert your Building Blocks from the Building Blocks Organizer.

If you want to edit the text of an existing Building Block, however, that's a bit of a different matter. There isn't any really easy way to do it—the best I can offer you is this: insert the Building Block you want to edit into a blank document and make the changes you want. Then highlight and save the edited text as a new Building Block with the same name as the old one. Word will prompt you by asking if you want to "redefine" the existing Building Block. Click **Yes** to replace the old one with the new version. If Word doesn't prompt you to redefine, then double-check to make sure you used the same name and saved the new version of the Building Block to the same Gallery and Template as the old one.

Macros

Word's macro language is amazingly powerful. So powerful, in fact, that it became the basis for a number of Word macro viruses a few years ago. The macro language that Word uses is **Visual Basic for Applications** (VBA). Entire books far thicker than this one are devoted to the subject, so I won't attempt to cover it in detail here; besides the reality is that most of you will never do any VBA coding. What I'll do instead is show you how to use the **Macro Recorder** to create simple macros yourself, and then later in this chapter give you a taste of what VBA is capable of and point you toward some resources if you want to know more.

Insert Text from File

One way to build a document is to assemble it from a collection of other documents. If you'd like to insert the entire text of another file into a Word document, you have a couple of ways you can do that.

1. Open the file you want to paste into in Word—the destination (recipient) document.
2. Open the file you want to paste from—the donor document.
3. Select all of the text in the donor document.
4. Copy that text.
5. Switch to the destination (recipient) document.
6. Find the spot you want to put that text and paste it.

Or you could just go to the document you're trying to create, place the cursor where you want to insert the other document's contents, go to the **Insert** tab of the **Ribbon**, and click the drop-down arrow next to **Object** and select **Text from File**. Word will let you browse for the file you want to insert. Select it and click **Insert**. Done.

Quick Parts—Fields

Some content in your document may be dynamic—either metadata or calculated content. You don't have to type (and update) that data manually. Word has a long list of fields you can insert that will dynamically update as you need.

To access the list go to the **Insert** tab on the **Ribbon** and click **Quick Parts** and then **Field**. You'll get the Field dialog box like you see in Figure 8.3. From here you can insert any number of things from a **formula** that will automatically calculate and present the result to various **dates**, **author names**, **numbers**, **page count** . . . a vast array of things. By placing the appropriate field code, you can save yourself some time and effort and let Word insert the appropriate data for you.

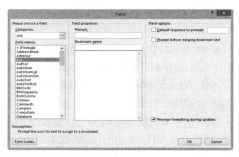

FIGURE 8.3 Fields Dialog Box

One thing to know about Fields is that most of them don't update automatically. For example, if you insert the **NumPages** field to display a count of the pages in the document and you subsequently add or subtract pages, you'll need to update the field manually to get the number to change and reflect the correct count. You can go to that field, click on it, and press **F9** to force it to update. If you have multiple fields in the document, you can select them all and press **F9** or just press **Control+A** to select the entire document and press **F9** to update all fields in the document.

Recording Macros

The easiest way to create a new macro is simply to record it, and Word provides a capable feature to do just that. To access the Macro Recorder you can go to the **View** tab of the **Ribbon** and to the **Macros** group on the far right-end of the Ribbon and click the drop-down arrow on the button (see Figure 8.4) to find **Record Macro**.

FIGURE 8.4 Record Macros

So, let's say for our example that you'd like to create a macro that prints only the current page of your document. All we need to do is start recording, name our macro, step through the actions we want to record, stop the recording, and save it as a macro. So let's give it a go . . .

1. Go to **View Tab** > **Macros** and choose **Record Macro**. The Record Macro dialog box (see Figure 8.5) will appear. Give your macro a name—I called mine *CurPrint* for *Current Page Print*.

FIGURE 8.5 Recording a Macro

2. You can assign the macro to a button that you might put on the QAT (Quick Access Toolbar), which we covered in Chapter 2, or you can give it a keyboard shortcut. If it's not a macro you'll run often or if you want to invoke it using something like **AutoHot-Key**, then you can do neither and just save it by name. I chose to assign it to **Control+Alt+P**, replacing InsertPageField, which I rarely do.

3. If you only want this macro to be part of a custom template, you can change the **Store In** field, but realistically you'll almost always leave that alone. If you're sophisticated enough to want precise control of which template the macro gets saved in, then you've probably skipped these simple step-by-step instructions anyhow.

4. You may want to give a description of what your macro does, especially if you have a lot of them and may not remember later, or if you're going to share it with other users and want to make sure they know what the macro does.

5. Click **OK**, and you'll be returned to your document and your mouse pointer will have a small "cassette tape" (remember those?) icon attached to it, which indicates that recording is currently on.

6. Perform the actions you wish to record. In our example we're going to click **File**, then **Print** and click **Print All Pages**, and change that to **Print Current Page**. Then we'll click the **Print** button.

When recording macro actions the speed with which you perform the tasks is irrelevant. The macro will be replayed much faster than it was recorded. But you don't want to record mistakes, so I tend to move very deliberately when I'm recording. Plan ahead, click on things deliberately, pause to make sure you know what your next action is, and then take that action. You'd rather not record mistakes or have to stop and start over.

Your document should print, and you should find yourself returned to the editing screen. Since clicking Print was the last step of your macro, you can go back to the **View Tab** > **Macros** button and click **Stop Recording**. Recording will stop, and your macro will be saved for future use. The next time you invoke that macro—via **View** > **Macros**, or the button or keyboard shortcut you selected—the *exact* same set of steps will be repeated. Those steps can do anything in Word that you can do—including type entire documents of text, perform a series of actions, order a pizza . . . well, OK, ordering pizza requires somewhat more advanced programming skills.

What Can VBA Do?

Just about anything you want it to do and even a few things you don't. You can manipulate data or files, automate repetitive tasks, or even roll your own more advanced application extension. In the previous section, we used the Macro Recorder to record a macro, but what that really did was create some VBA code for us. We could have written that code manually, but in that example we used the recorder to automate the process of creating the code.

Creating a Form Template

There may be times when you want to create a form using Word and have some custom controls on the form to enable more professional data entry. I can't account for every possible form scenario you might have, but let me introduce you to the controls at your disposal and let your creative juices flow.

The first step is to create your sample form. In Figure 8.6 I've created an oversimplified New Client Intake form. Now that you have the form, you need to add controls to the form, which is how the user will fill out the form.

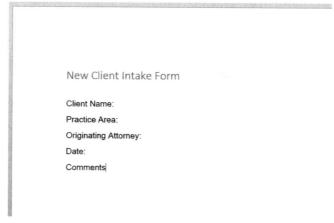

New Client Intake Form

Client Name:

Practice Area:

Originating Attorney:

Date:

Comments

FIGURE 8.6 The New Client Intake Form

Controls

On the **Developer** tab there is a group called **Controls**, which contains a number of tools for creating professional-looking forms.

Don't see the Developer tab? Right-click the Ribbon, choose **Customize the Ribbon,** and check the box in front of **Developer** in the right-hand column.

To start with we need a field to enter the client's name. The first Control in the group is the **Rich Text Content** Control. Click to insert one of those. If your cursor isn't at the place in the document where you want the control, just drag and drop it with your mouse where you want to put it. In our sample, I'll put it next to the *Client Name:* label.

The next field is *Practice Area* and I'll use a Drop-Down List control for that. Click **Drop-Down List Content Control** in the **Controls** group and insert it where you want it—in this

Note in Figure 8.7 that I've also checked the box to prevent the user from deleting the content control. Just a little extra precaution to keep somebody from messing up your form.`

case next to *Practice Area*. It may have occurred to you that you now have a lovely field that lets you choose a Practice Area . . . but you haven't told it what practice areas you have.

To do that just click once on the **Practice Area** Control on your form, then click **Properties** in the **Controls** group on the **Ribbon**. You'll get the dialog box you see in Figure 8.7—and I've taken the liberty of naming our control and entering some sample options.

Unfortunately there isn't an easy way to default the Date Picker to today's date; but the user can just click the **Today** button at the bottom of the Date Picker to easily insert it.

FIGURE 8.7 Control Properties Example

The next field we want to fill in is the *Retainer Received* field. And we're going to use a checkbox for that field. This control is pretty simple—just add it where you want it, and it inserts a clickable box.

Next we have a *Date* field to enter. Click the **Date Picker Content Control** from the **Controls** group and place that next to *Date*. The user can enter a date or click the drop-down arrow on the right end to get a **Date Picker** as you see in Figure 8.8.

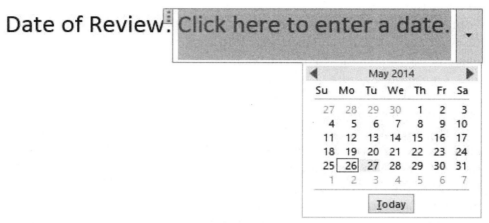

FIGURE 8.8 The Date Picker Control

Finally for the *Comments* field we're going to do it a little differently; we're just going to draw a text box to provide a place for the user to write optional comments. To do that, go to the **Insert** tab of the **Ribbon**, click the drop-down arrow under **Text Box**, and choose **Draw Text Box**. Using your mouse draw a nice big rectangle next to *Comments*.

The end result of our sample form looks like Figure 8.9.

New Client Intake

Prospective Client Name: Click here to enter text.

Practice Area: Choose an item.

Retainer Received: ☐

Date of Review: Click here to enter a date.

Comments:

FIGURE 8.9 The Completed Form

Obviously, this is just a very simple sample form. You can make far more complex and detailed forms if you like. Once your form is done, save it, mark it **Read-Only**, and then you can make it available to your users. When they fill it out and click **Save**, it will force them to give it a new name (since the original is Read-Only).

Other Tools

VBA isn't the only way to do macros and scripting in Microsoft Office. There are tools both built-in and from third parties that can help you with that as well.

AutoCorrect

Word's built-in AutoCorrect can be found **Backstage** by clicking **File** > **Options** > **Proofing** > **AutoCorrect Options**, which launches the dialog box you see in Figure 8.10.

FIGURE 8.10 AutoCorrect Options

AutoCorrect is a handy tool to fix typos as you go. If you accidentally type "teh," Word's AutoCorrect will fix it to *the* on the fly. In fact, I had to undo an AutoCorrect in order to type that example! That's the typical usage of AutoCorrect, but it can also be customized to replace any text with any other text. Leaving aside the potential for clever practical jokes, this gives you a tool for replacing short strings of text with much longer ones. For instance, perhaps you work for Jones, Smith, Jones, Smith, Jones and Rumpelstiltskin. Naturally you don't want to have to type that out very often. It would be easy to add an AutoCorrect entry so that if you type

If you're typing away and Word has autocorrected something for you that you didn't want it to autocorrect, you can press **Control+Z** to Undo that autocorrection, and it will restore your originally typed text in this one location.

JSJSJR (or even just *JSJ*), Word would replace it with the full firm name (which I don't feel like retyping here).

Hopefully you're seeing a lot of possibilities here. Have clients you work with a lot? You can put their name in and have it replace their initials with their full name. Use it for **addresses**, **location names**, **court names**, or other words and phrases you use a lot. It'll save you a lot of typing time *and* reduce the chances that you inadvertently send out a document in which you refer to your firm as Jones, Smith, Jones, Smith, Jones and Rumpledsuitman.

That's great for working in Word but what if you want those same replacements to work in other apps? Keep reading . . . our next tool gives you a universal AutoCorrect capability.

AutoHotKey

One of my all-time favorite free tools, **AutoHotKey** (http://www.autohotkey.com), is an all-around scripting language that, with a little bit of effort, you can use to automate tasks not only in Word but in the entire Office suite and, in fact, any application in Windows. You can launch programs with it, you can script installations in it, you can create blocks of text that will be inserted with a short string of characters, you can create mouse gestures, and you can do a lot of really cool things.

> ▼▼▼▼▼
> ### What's a Mouse Gesture?
> A mouse gesture is an action with the mouse that triggers an action. For example, if you hold down the right mouse button and move the mouse to the left, you could have that action tell your web browser to go Back. Or hold down the right mouse button and draw a clockwise circle to make your browser refresh. With a little effort you can create just about any gesture you like and have AutoHotKey do whatever you'd like it to do in response.

For example . . . I have a little bit of script in AutoHotKey that whenever I type "bwa" and press the spacebar, it will replace that with *Best wishes and aloha*, which is my typical e-mail sign-off. Easy way to insert a signature block.

Coding something like that in AutoHotKey is quite easy. You just open the AutoHotKey script in any text editor (like Notepad) and add lines that say this:

```
::bwa::Best wishes and aloha,
return
```

The first bit defines what keystrokes you're going to type; "bwa" in my case. The second bit tells you what it's going to replace that with when you do so; "Best wishes and aloha," in my case. (In fact, I just used my bwa tool to put that in!) And "return" just tells AutoHotKey that you're done with what that action does.

While AutoHotKey is a good way to insert text quickly and consistently, it can also be used to automate any repetitive series of keystrokes or mouse clicks, and since it's not tied to any one application, scripts you create in AutoHotKey are available everywhere. I use it to launch applications too.

Did I mention it's free?

Customize Word's Hotkeys

One feature most people don't realize Word 2013 has is the ability to customize the Hotkeys that Word uses. Don't want to use **Control+B** for boldface? You can change it. To get to the Customize Keyboard dialog box like the one you see in Figure 8.11, just go to **File** > **Options** > **Customize Ribbon** (yes, I know) and at the bottom left, next to the label Keyboard Shortcuts you'll find a button for **Customize**.

Let's try a useful exercise. One of the symbols that lawyers commonly use is the section symbol: §. So let's assign it to a keyboard shortcut to make it easier to access. Go to the **Customize Keyboard** dialog box (instructions are still above if you need a refresher), and on the left side

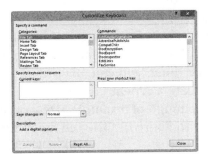

FIGURE 8.11 Customize Keyboard

where it says **Categories** scroll all the way down to where it says **Common Symbols**. It's the very last thing on that list. Then in the box on the right that now says Common Symbols scroll down until you find the **Section Symbol**. Select that one and you'll notice that under **Current Keys** the box is empty. There aren't any Hotkeys assigned to it yet. On the right where it says Press **New Shortcut Key**, click there and press **Alt+S**. You'll notice that when you enter that in the box, you'll get a little message below the Current Keys box that tells you what that Hotkey is currently assigned to (as far as Word knows). By default, it's available. Well, it's sort of available. By default, **Alt+S** will open the References tab on the Ribbon. But you can still get to the **References** tab by pressing and releasing **Alt**, then pressing **S**. So you can assign Alt+S to the section symbol, and just use Alt and then S to get to the References tab.

To finish assigning Alt+S to your Section symbol click the **Assign** button. Then you can exit back out to your Word document and give it a try. Sure enough, Alt+S should immediately put a § at your insertion point. Nice, eh?

Word can only tell you about Hotkeys that it knows about. If some other program, like **AutoHotKey**, has **Alt+S** for something there's no way Word can know that and warn you about it. The other limitation here is that any Hotkey you set up in here is only going to work in Word.

The Roland Schorr 10-Most Method

If you're a fairly quick typist, I want to encourage you to use keyboard shortcuts and automation to make your Word experience substantially more efficient. Here's the way you do it . . .

1. Put some kind of notepad next to your keyboard. You can use an online thing like OneNote's docked page if you want to but I really think it'll be easier to just have a piece of paper and a pencil.
2. Use Word in the course of your normal workday.
3. Each time you grab the mouse to click an icon or launch a command (like **Print**, **Save**, **Boldface**, etc.) quickly note down what it was. The first time you do it make a note; each additional time you do the same thing, you can just put a tick mark next to the first one to indicate a repeat.
4. After you have enough of a sample size—perhaps a day or two—go back and try to figure out the ten most common tasks you use the mouse for.
5. Learn, or create if necessary, the keyboard shortcuts for those tasks. If the shortcut takes more than two or three keystrokes to do it, then use **AutoHotKey** or Word's **Macro Recorder** to automate the task down to a single keystroke. It may be too much to try to master all ten in a single day, so it's OK to break the list down into chunks. Start with the most common tasks and learn two or three every day.

Tip

This is also a great use of Building Blocks. If you can identify bits of text that you type often and can convert to Building Blocks, you can save time. Bonus . . . use AutoHotKey to insert a Building Block and then perform some common action upon it like applying a style.

If you can get to the point where your five, ten, or fifteen most common non-editing tasks (e.g., formatting, printing, launching applications, etc.) can be done with a just one or a few keystrokes or Hotkey combinations, you can save yourself a lot of time in the course of your normal day.

Resources

Like all URLs (Uniform Resource Locators, aka web addresses) you see in print, the following URLs could change between the time that I type them here and you read them there. In those instances . . . .Google is your friend.

- http://msdn.microsoft.com/en-us/office/ff688774.aspx—This is Microsoft's **MSDN site for Visual Basic for Applications**. It has a lot of useful resources and tools here for people doing development with VBA.
- http://en.wikipedia.org/wiki/Visual_Basic_for_Applications— **Wikipedia's article** on Visual Basic for Applications. It's a nice starting point with some general background, and it also includes a nice collection of references and links to more information.

Summary

Microsoft Word is an application that requires a high degree of user interaction—by that I mean that unlike some applications where you start a process and just let it run, Word is an application where virtually everything that happens occurs because the user pressed a button or clicked a mouse. A lot of those interactions the user has with Word are repetitive, so there are a lot of efficiencies to be gained by learning to automate Word and make those interactions easier and faster. Lawyers, and legal staff in particular, tend to create a lot of repetitive documents—documents that don't vary greatly from one to the other. Using tools for document assembly and automation can help make the law office operate more efficiently and with fewer mistakes.

There are a number of tools available to help in that process.

Document assembly lets you automate the process of building standardized documents. By asking only for the variables (e.g., the stuff that changes; names, dates, places) and placing it in the document where you need it, document assembly software can significantly reduce the time it takes to build standard documents and ensure consistent quality.

Visual Basic for Applications is a very powerful macro language. In fact, I daresay it's the most powerful macro language ever implemented in an office productivity suite like Microsoft Office. It can manipulate data, run various functions of the application, and even interact with the operating system in powerful and potentially dangerous ways.

AutoHotKey is a free utility that can help you create powerful scripts that automate tasks not only in Word but in any other Windows application as well.

AutoCorrect and Hotkeys are built-in Word tools that can be extended by the user to help automate tasks or simplify how things are initiated.

With just a bit of thought and practice you can easily find a lot of new efficiencies! Especially as law firms and in-house legal departments move increasingly toward value-based billing, it's important to find new and powerful ways to streamline the process of practicing law and creating documents while improving accuracy and quality.

Managing and Maintaining Word 2013

9

In this chapter we'll take a look at some of the configuration options of Microsoft Word. To get to these options click **File** and toward the bottom of the **Backstage** menu you'll find a button labeled **Options**. I'm not going to cover every single option; I'll skip over some of the things I don't think you're likely to care about.

General

The General group (see Figure 9.1) contains a few of the most commonly used Options in the program. If you find the **Mini Toolbar** more annoying than useful, you can turn it off right here. Likewise the **Live Preview** (Galleries) and updating

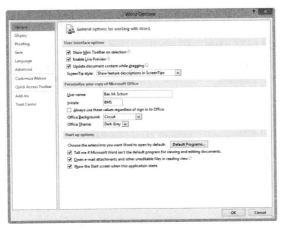

FIGURE 9.1 The General Group of Options

document content while dragging may be a burden to a slower system, though if they're not causing you problems, I would leave them on. They'll save you more time than they could cost.

The next settings on this page that interest us allow you to customize how Word identifies you. It lets you tell Word what your **Initials** and **Full Name** are. These are used in instances like inserting **comments**, **metadata** about last editor and author, **signature blocks**, and such where this information can be automatically inserted for you. If you inherited this copy of Word and user profile from a previous user and that person's name and initials are still appearing in the product, this is one place you should go to change it.

Note that changes you make to your identity in any Office program will be reflected in the rest of the suite as well. So you don't need to change your name and initials in every program—just once. The checkbox for **Always Use These Values Regardless of Sign In to Office** is for users who have multiple Windows Live identities connected to Office (we'll get to that later in this chapter). Personally, I leave it unchecked.

After you've told Word how you'd like to be identified, you have some, rather limited, control over how Word looks.

▼▼▼▼▼
The Feature's So Bright, I Gotta Wear Shades

One of the first things we hear from people who first fire up Microsoft Office 2013 is how white and bright it is. There's much less contrast in the interface than there was in earlier versions. That was a deliberate design decision at Microsoft to try and make it look crisper and cleaner and more modern. Unfortunately it's generated a lot of complaints from users who find it difficult to look at for long periods. Suggestions to remedy it include dialing down the brightness on your monitors—though that then penalizes your other applications that are not as bright. I've settled for just using the darkest color scheme Office currently offers, **Dark Gray**, and I've managed to get used to it.

Office Background lets you enable a pattern that appears in the upper right corner of Word, spanning the Title Bar and Ribbon. Figure 9.2 shows you the **Circuit** background. As you can see, it doesn't make a dramatic difference, but it does help to introduce a little bit of texture, I suppose.

Office Theme has been disappointing users of previous versions of Office. Previously you could select **Black**, **Blue**, or **Silver**, which let you add a splash of color or some dramatic dark headings. In Office 2013 you're currently limited to **White**, **Light Gray**, or **Dark Gray**. White is too

FIGURE 9.2 The Circuit Background

bright for my tastes, and Light Gray isn't much better. Dark Gray gives you the most contrast on the screen, so that's my preference.

The other settings that you should be concerned on this tab are whether you want e-mail attachments to open in Full Screen Reading view. This is a feature I get a lot of questions about—lawyers receive e-mailed document attachments, and when they double-click them to open them (after acknowledging all of the **Are You Sure You Want to Open this?** prompts), they expect an attachment to just open in Word the way they're used to seeing it. Instead it opens in **Reading View** that looks a bit odd and can be unsettling. That view *is* useful in many ways, but if you'd rather that Word just do what you expect it to, uncheck the **Open Email Attachments in Full Screen Reading View** box and Word will just skip that screen and open normally for you.

Finally I do like to leave the box checked for **Tell Me If Microsoft Word Isn't the Default Program for Viewing and Editing Documents**. On the odd chance that some other program gets installed that tries to take over viewing and editing documents, you'd probably want Word to warn you and give you the chance to restore Word as the default program for that task.

Display

The Display group (see Figure 9.3) lets you control how Word will display documents.

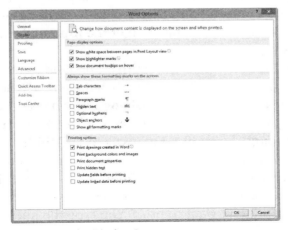

FIGURE 9.3 The Display Group

The first option is **Show White Space between Pages in Print Layout View**. That option basically just shows the top and bottom margins, just like you'd see on the printed page. If you want to save a bit of screen real estate, you could turn that option off, or just edit your documents in Draft Mode.

> The problem with **Draft Mode** is that you lose a lot of the layout features, especially any embedded images. Most people work in Print Layout mode because that's the default. I work in it because, as you may have noticed, I have a lot of screenshots and figures in the book, and the figures don't display in Draft Mode.

The **Show White Space . . .** option will also show the Headers and Footers on a page. If you want to quickly turn it off (or back on) just point to the top or bottom edge of the page and double-click.

If you've used any highlighter marks in your document, which is a pretty common action when reviewing and collaborating on documents (you did read Chapter 6, right?), you may want to turn off the display of high-lighter marks. Worth noting that turning them off here not only suppresses the display of them on the screen but also keeps them from printing too.

Show Document Tooltips on Hover turns off (or on) the display of balloons detailing the changes made to the text. Essentially, if you make a change to the text and then later hover over that text with your mouse, the change will be displayed in a tooltip that will "magically" appear above your cursor. If those balloons annoy you, here's where you turn them off. Note that you have to have Track Changes enabled for this to work.

The next section of the dialog box is where you control the **display of formatting marks**. I tend to leave all of these off myself. I may occasionally have it display paragraph marks because those can be significant in document formatting, but unless I'm troubleshooting document formatting issues (we'll talk about that in Chapter 10), I tend to just leave them all off. It's just a much cleaner look to the document.

If you want to turn all of the formatting marks on (or off) at once, you can just press **Control+Shift+8** from within the document or click the **Show/Hid**e button on the **Home** tab of the **Ribbon**, which looks like a paragraph mark (¶).

There is *one* option in this section that I do tend to turn on, and that's the option to Display Hidden Text. "What's hidden text?" Glad you asked. If you open the **Font Panel** (click the **Dialog Launcher** at the bottom right of the **Font** group on the **Ribbon**) you may notice that among the font effects (**Strikethrough, Subscript, Emboss**, etc.) is **Hidden**. Apply that effect to text on your page and . . . it disappears unless you have **Display Hidden Text** turned on in the **Display Options**. So why would you use that? It's handy if you want to create a document with annotations, notes, or answers that you don't want to print. You type the questions and you type your notes. You mark your notes as Hidden, however, and when you go to print the document, the hidden text doesn't print (unless you've changed another setting I'm going to explain in the next page or two). But you can still see the hidden text on your screen—and you can choose to print the document *with* the hidden text for your own copy. Keep reading.

The last section of the Display group controls **printing options**. The first option lets you speed up your printing. The description is a little misleading—implies that only drawings created in Word (how many drawings do you actually create in Word?) are affected. Actually unchecking that box will suppress printing any graphics or text boxes—just a blank box will be printed in their place. Fine for printing quick drafts I guess, but in reality I don't know anybody who changes that setting. You probably *do* want to see your graphics, even on the drafts.

The next option enables the printing of background colors and images. I've never seen a legal document that had a background color or an image; but maybe you're creating a marketing material and want to print those things. Here's where you'd turn it on.

If you want to print a copy of your document with the document properties (author, created date, etc.) you can enable that here as well.

If you used the hidden text trick we talked about a few paragraphs back, you can change the setting here to have that hidden text print.

The last two options on this screen are actually pretty handy. **Update Fields before Printing** and **Update Linked Fields before Printing** will ensure that your Tables of Contents, linked Excel data, and other dynamic content is up-to-date before you click Print. It's a bad feeling to realize, as pages 35, 36, and 37 are rolling off the printer, that you forgot to update your Table of Contents and it's a few pages off.

Proofing

The Proofing group (see Figure 9.4) contains tools that are essential to your document assembly (see Chapter 8). It handles how Word will take care of **Spell Checking**, **Grammar Checking**, and **AutoCorrect**.

We already talked in Chapter 8 about configuring the AutoCorrect options, so here we'll talk about some of the other settings on the Auto-Correct Options dialog box.

Math AutoCorrect

The **Math AutoCorrect** tools let you type the names of mathematical operators and symbols and have them replaced by the actual symbol. For example: type \approx, and Word will replace it with ≈. Note that if you want

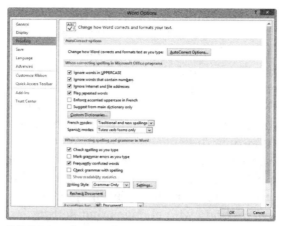

FIGURE 9.4 The Proofing Group

these changes to happen outside of the "math regions" (which means outside of where you have inserted an equation using the **Equation** tool on the **Insert** tab of the **Ribbon**), you'll need to check the box next to **Use Math AutoCorrect Rules Outside of Math Regions**.

AutoFormat As You Type

These settings are, as you might have guessed, primarily concerned with automatically applying some stylish tweaks to your documents. For example—changing **straight quotes** to "**smart quotes**," which are the curly quotes and changing **fractions** to the **fraction characters** (see Figure 9.5).

FIGURE 9.5 AutoFormat As You Type

One of the options on this dialog box that we do get asked about are the options that automatically start a numbered list if you start an item with *1* follwed by a period (.) or a bulleted list if you start a line with an *asterisk* (*) followed by a period. Those are handy features, but they do annoy some people . . . so here's how you can turn them off.

▼▼▼▼▼

The fractions character option is a lot more limited than it may seem. There are "hidden" ASCII characters for three of the common fractions: **1/4, 1/2, 3/4**. If you type one of those three fractions, Word will automatically replace it with the ASCII character for that: ¼, ½, ¾ (assuming you have the setting enabled in **AutoFormat As You Type**, which it is by default). Type any other fraction and you'll just get what you typed since Word has nothing to change it to.

The sharp-eyed among you may have noticed that there are both **AutoFormat** and **AutoFormat As You Type** tabs in the AutoCorrect options. And that they have many of the same options! So what's the difference? Word has a carefully hidden feature called AutoFormat that allows you to apply these settings to a document that has already been typed. Don't remember that feature from our extensive Chapter 2 review of the Ribbon? That's because it's not on the Ribbon. In fact, to use it you'll have to add it to either the Ribbon or the QAT. If you go to customize the Ribbon (or QAT), change the left-hand column to show **All Commands**, and locate **AutoFormat Now** . . . that's what you need to add to use the feature.

Never used that feature before? Neither have I. Moving on . . .

Actions

The **Actions** tab of **AutoCorrect** gives you a few custom behaviors that Word can take if it recognizes particular kinds of text in your document. They're like tags. Really intelligent tags. You might even call them **Smart Tags**. Well, that's what Word 2007 called them.

Smart Tags are a feature that debuted with Microsoft **Office XP** (aka Office 2002) in which Office applications can recognize certain bits of text, like a date or a phone number or an address, and then give you some options of what you can do with that. For example, if you have a street address typed in your document, you can select that text, right-click it, and choose **Additional Actions** (see Figure 9.6) to get a list of other things you can do with that data.

Note that this functionality was deleted in Word 2010. In earlier versions of Office, a Smart Tag might recognize that you've typed in a street address and underline that address with a purple dotted underline. Word no longer automatically recognizes and underlines your tags—you have to select the text and right-click to access that functionality.

FIGURE 9.6 Using Actions, Aka Smart Tags, in Word 2013

Additional Actions can be useful however . . .

They do take up a tiny bit of additional resources, so many people have them disabled by default.

1. They're only useful on the electronic copies of the document. Obviously a printed document has no use for the actions.
2. Powerful though they may be, you might not really have much use for them yourself. They're often a solution in search of a problem. I've never asked Word to give me driving directions to an address I had in a Word document.

A few of the default settings back on the **Proofing** page are worth noticing. For example, **Ignore Words That Are in UPPERCASE** or **Ignore Words That Contain Numbers**. In those cases, Word is going to assume that you're typing an acronym or a custom word or formula for which traditional Spell Checking is likely to be of limited value. If you're in the habit of typing regular words in ALL UPPERCASE, then that's a habit I strongly suggest you break. Words in ALL CAPS are really rather hard to read, and it looks like you're shouting. However, if you really insist upon shouting, then you might want to have Word not ignore those words. You can make that happen by unchecking the box here.

Another interesting option that appears on the main Proofing page is the option to have Custom Dictionaries in Word. Click the **Custom Dictionaries** button to launch the dialog box you see in Figure 9.4 (the Proofing group). Here you can see the Custom Dictionaries that Word is going to use—the CUSTOM.DIC file is there by default and contains all of the words that you've added to the dictionary yourself. You can add **new custom dictionaries**, **remove dictionaries**, **enable** or **disable** them, **edit** the word lists, and do all sorts of other tricky things.

▼▼▼▼▼

You may be tempted to add or buy—or even create—a "legal" custom dictionary, but in my experience it's rarely needed. Most legal words (*abatement, jurisprudence,* and even *venire*) are already in the Word dictionary, and for the ones that remain (*voir dire* may trip your red squiggly lines), you can easily right-click the misrecognized word and select **Add to Dictionary** to just add it to your main dictionary.

Medical dictionaries are a little more useful as the words are somewhat more complex and esoteric.

The next section on the Proofing tab offers a few useful choices.

- **Check Spelling As You Type** lets you turn off the live spell checking. I recommend you leave this on, but if the red, squiggly, lines distract you too much, you can turn it off.
- **Frequently Confused Words** will make intelligent guesses about how words are supposed to be spelled based on their context. This was a new feature in Word 2010—it's supposed to help you figure out when to use words like *than* versus *then*, and so forth.

One option that may have caught your eye is the **Readability Statistics**. Enabling that will let you check to see how complex your writing style is—at least according to a few computer algorithms. To use it, enable it in the proofing options, and then go to your document and run a **Spell Check** from the **Review** tab of the Ribbon. Unfortunately you'll have to go

 Tip

There is also an occasionally handy button in this section. **Check Document** will run the spell check against your document (just as pressing **F7** will) except Check Document will reset the "ignore" options you may have previously selected. You can use this if you suspect you may have ignored actual spelling errors and would like to reset those.

through the entire document before it will give you the readability results, a minor pain when you're doing a 287-page book and just wanted to do a quick Readability Check so you could grab a screenshot. But if you were to lose patience with that process perhaps and choose instead to check a much shorter document, you might get a result that looks like Figure 9.7. Note, you *do* have to let Word check your grammar too in order for the readability statistics to appear.

FIGURE 9.7 Readability Statistics

Tired of the Spell Checker or Grammar Checker getting on your back in that particular document, but you don't want to turn them off completely? The last settings on the proofing dialog let you tell Word to just **Ignore Spelling and Grammatical Errors in This Document Only**.

Save

The **Save** section of the **Word Options** helps you control options with how (and when) Word will save things (see Figure 9.8).

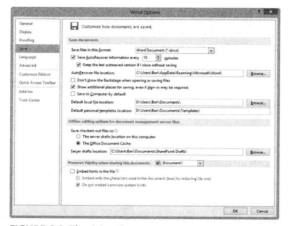

FIGURE 9.8 The Save Group

First up, you can control the **default document format**. You'll probably want to leave that set to **Word Document (*.docx)**, which lets you take advantage of the new document formats. But if you have to share a lot of documents with users of older versions of Word and they refuse to install the File Converters, you can change the default here. Even if you change the default to .DOC, you can still manually save a new document as a .DOCX file; you'll just have to manually set that each time you save.

Some of you may remember the days when computers crashed fairly often (no **Vista** or **Windows ME** jokes, please!), and losing the document you'd been working on was a real possibility. A lot of old-timers (like me) are in the habit of saving quite often, specifically so if the machine reboots suddenly, you aren't going to lose your work. Word is, and has been for quite some time, smarter than that however. It saves **AutoRecover** information on a regular schedule. What's AutoRecover information? It's what enables Word to offer to recover your work for you when you restart Word after a crash. By default, Word will save this information, quietly in the background, every ten minutes. If you're paranoid or have a machine that crashes a lot, you can set that to be a little more often—every five minutes perhaps. If you're supremely confident, you can set it to a longer interval, though there really isn't much reason to do so unless your machine is so underpowered that saving AutoRecover information actually slows it down or unless you're really trying to milk every ounce of battery life out of that laptop and want to reduce disk activity.

Don't Show the Backstage When Opening or Saving Files only comes into play if you use **Control+S** to Save and **Control+O** to Open files. With that setting checked, if you press either of those key combinations, Word will take you right to the **File Navigator** you may be traditionally used to without taking you Backstage first. Figure 9.9 shows you what that looks like.

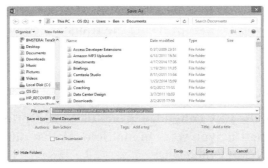

FIGURE 9.9 The File Navigator

Show Additional Places for Saving, Even If Sign-in May Be Required is a fancy way of saying "Don't Tease Me Bro." Word really really wants you to use OneDrive. So much so that if you don't have a OneDrive account, or if you have one but aren't signed into it, Word is going to show it to you as an option as a place to save your files there. If you'd rather it not do that, uncheck this box. Note that unchecking has no effect on services you *are* signed into.

The **Save to Computer by Default** option just underscores how tightly coupled to the Cloud Word 2013 is. It assumes you're going to want to save to a Cloud storage location (OneDrive or SharePoint most likely) unless you specify otherwise.

The **Default File Location** is where Word is going to save documents by default. Usually that's set to your own **My Documents** folder. You can change it to be anything you like—including a server location if you have one.

Word also gives you the option to specify your default **Personal Templates** location, in case you plan to use a lot of templates and want an easily accessible location (like \My Documents\Templates). This is also handy if you're in a firm with a lot of shared templates on a network location. You can set your default Personal Templates location to S:\Office Files\Templates or somesuch.

The only other setting in this section I want to point out is under the **Preserve Fidelity When Sharing This Document** section, and it lets you embed fonts in the file. Usually that's a waste of space, but it can be handy if you're using a nonstandard font in your document and you're sharing the document with a user who doesn't have that font installed or for whom the document just doesn't look quite right. Embedding the fonts in the file does just that—saves a copy of the fonts you used within the document file so that when the other party opens the document, they get the fonts too. The upside to this is that it helps the person you're sharing the document with see the document as you intended it. The downside is that it inflates your document size somewhat so that it uses more storage space. If you're e-mailing this file to your collaborator, the extra file size may also slow down (or even prevent) the transfer.

Language

Figure 9.10 shows the new **Language** group in Word Options. Office 2013 is a LOT better at letting you work in multiple (or just different) languages than earlier versions of Office were.

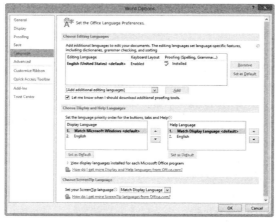

FIGURE 9.10 The Language Group

You can configure your editing languages, including Keyboard Layout and Spell Checker. Note that even though you can pick from an enormous list of additional languages (including Hawaiian), that doesn't mean that those languages support spell checking and other proofing tools right out of the box. Some languages are listed but not included. Selecting them will simply tell you that the Keyboard Layout and proofing options are **Not Installed**. In some cases, you can download a language pack for that particular language; in other cases . . . *a'e*. (No.)

If you want to try to change the languages for the buttons and Help system, you can also configure that here.

Advanced

The Advanced page has a lot of sections and options in it. We'll take it section by section but I'm only going to spend time on those options that I think you're going to care about.

Figure 9.11 shows the **Editing Options** section where you can control how Word is going to behave while you're editing. The first option is **Typing Replaces Selected Text**. I'll explain it, so you know what it does, but I don't recommend you change it. Basically what it does is that if you select some text and then start typing, Word will delete the selection and replace it with whatever you type. That's the default behavior and what most people expect to happen. If you clear that checkbox, Word will instead *insert* what you're typing before the selected text. In which case, forgive me for suggesting it, there's no point in selecting the text to begin with. Just place your insertion point where you want to insert the text and type away.

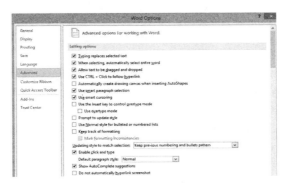

FIGURE 9.11 The Advanced Editing Options Section

The second option is a little more helpful if you often find yourself wanting to select parts of a word and being frustrated that Word tries to be overly helpful and select the entire word. Clear the **Select Entire Word** checkbox, and your word selections can be a little more precise, but a little less efficient. I more often want to select entire words, rather than parts of words, so I leave it checked.

Word is increasingly smart in little ways. **Smart Paragraph Selection** makes sure that when you select a paragraph, the hidden paragraph mark (which is what holds the paragraph's formatting) is selected with it. That's good because if you select the paragraph to cut or copy it to somewhere else, you'll probably want to cut or copy its formatting too.

Smart Cursoring means that when you scroll through a document, for example, by dragging the vertical scroll bar up and down, the insertion point (i.e., the vertical bar that marks where you're typing) will jump to the page you're viewing if you touch an arrow key. To illustrate: if you drag the scroll bar several pages up or down, you will no longer see the insertion point. That's because it's still back at the last place you were editing. But if you press the left or right arrow key, the insertion point will suddenly jump to the page you're looking at. This saves you the extremely difficult task of using the mouse and actually clicking on the page you're looking at.

Wondering why the Insert key on your keyboard seems dead in Word? Probably because you have the Use the Insert Key to Control Overtype Mode option unchecked. That option was added because some users would inadvertently toggle on Overtype Mode by accidentally hitting the Insert key on their keyboard.

If you change the formatting of text that has been formatted with a particular Style, Word can ask you if you want to update the style to match that new bit of formatting. The assumption being that maybe you want *all* of the text in that style to have this new formatting. The checkbox Prompt to Update Style is what you check if you want Word to ask you about that. It can be a quick way to update your styles with custom formatting; but I find it fairly annoying to be asked every time I apply a little Direct Formatting (remember Chapter 4?), so I leave it turned off.

Speaking of formatting and styles, the next options of interest are the **Keep Track of Formatting** and **Mark Formatting Inconsistencies** options. These options alert you to text that looks the same but is styled in two different ways. For example, let's say you use a Style, such as Heading 2, to format some text. Later you use Direct Formatting (font size, font attributes like bold, etc.) to format other text in the document in a very similar way. Word will underscore that text with a blue wavy line to indicate that you appear to be formatting two pieces of text in a similar way but with inconsistent methods. That's to suggest that you should use the same Style for both. The idea is to help you create documents where you're using Styles consistently throughout rather than formatting different paragraphs with different methods—which can lead to some interesting issues later.

The final option of the Editing Options section is the rather handy **Enable Click and Type**. The default is Enable, and that's the right way to go. This is what lets you basically click anywhere on the page with your mouse and just start typing. Gone are the days of having to manually insert a bunch of tabs or spaces if you want to start typing one-third of the way across a page.

The next set of options is for Cut, Copy, and Paste as you can see in Figure 9.12. They let you configure how Word will behave when you make use of the Clipboard.

FIGURE 9.12 The Cut, Copy, and Paste Options

The first four settings let you configure the default behavior for various kinds of copy-and-paste operations, and for those you have four basic choices:

- **Keep Source Formatting**. This will paste the text and whatever formatting came with the text. If the original text in the other document was 24 point and green, then it will be 24 point and green when you paste it regardless of what the document you're pasting it into looks like.
- **Merge Formatting**. This is going to change the formatting of the text so that it matches the text immediately around it in its new location.
- **Use Destination Styles**. This will bring over the text and any style definition associated with it, but it will apply the characteristics of the matching style (if there is one) in the destination document. For example, let's say you copy some text formatted for Heading 3 in a source document, and in that document Heading 3 text is Bold, Italics, and Red. You paste it into your destination document where Heading 3 is Bold, Underline, and Blue. The text will come over but the formatting will be changed to Bold, Underline, and Blue. If the original text had no style definition applied, then the text will be assigned the style of the paragraph you're pasting it to (which will usually just be Normal).
- **Keep Text Only**. This is sort of similar to the last option except that *no* formatting information will be brought over. Just the pure text. If you're having problems with formatting after pasting in some text, try using this option to eliminate any odd formatting elements that might have been brought over in the paste operation.

One exception to this is found in the first of the four checkboxes at the bottom of this group: **Keep Bullets and Numbers When Pasting Text with Keep Text Only Option**. The description is fairly self-explanatory. Word won't bring over formatting, *however*, if the source text was in a bulleted or numbered list, Word will preserve that formatting element.

The next setting lets you control how you want pictures inserted or pasted into your documents by default. This lets you choose which of the **Text Wrap** options (**In line with text** or **Square** or . . .) you wish to make the default.

Keep Bullets and Numbers When Pasting Text with Keep Text Only Option simply means that if you copy and paste something that was in a bulleted or numbered list, and you choose to **Keep Text Only** for that paste . . . Word will still keep the bullets or numbers it had before.

If you do a *lot* of pasting and don't often change the insert (overwrite) option, the next checkbox is actually pretty nifty: **Use the Insert Key for Paste**. With that option selected, anytime you want to paste, instead of pressing **Control+V** you can just press the *Insert* key on your keyboard. You can still use **Control+V** if you want to, but Insert would do the same thing.

The next checkbox I want to mention is the **Show Paste Options** checkbox. Have you ever pasted something into an Office application, like Word, and seen the little clipboard icon that appears immediately alongside your freshly pasted content? That's the Paste Options icon. It has a drop-down menu, which gives you a few options for how you want that pasted text handled (mostly what I've described above about keeping source formatting, etc.). It lets you override the defaults you specified just above on a case-by-case basis.

Finally you have a checkbox that asks if you want to **Use Smart Cut and Paste** followed by a Settings button that lets you specify a myriad of granular configuration options for how Cut and Paste will work. Honestly . . . stick with the defaults here. These settings mostly concern merging lists, spacing, and alignment of pasted items, and the defaults generally work just fine. If you're really having problems with how pasted items space or align, then you might want to tweak these settings. I have yet to meet a lawyer who did.

The next section is **Image Size and Quality** (see Figure 9.13). Not a lot here that excites us, though if you find that pictures you insert into your Word documents don't look very good, then you can either come in here and check **Do Not Compress Images in File** or set the default target output to a higher resolution than 220 ppi or get a better photographer.

▼

If you're running Word on an old workhorse of a computer that is really gasping and wheezing to get the job done . . . well, then you probably need to buy a better machine. Until your new machine arrives, however, you might disable the Smart Cut and Paste and Show Paste Options features. That might get you a barely perceptible performance improvement.

FIGURE 9.13 Image Size and Quality Options

The next section I want to talk about is **Show Document Content** (see Figure 9.14), which lets you control how Word displays certain bits of custom document content. There isn't really much here that is of interest to us, but do be aware of the **Font Substitution** settings because if you receive a document that was created with a font you don't have, then Font Substitution is how Word tries to imitate the original font using a font that you *do* have. This is usually not an issue but when it *is* an issue . . . it really is an issue. Font Substitution can be one of the bigger headaches in troubleshooting why documents don't look right when transferred between different machines.

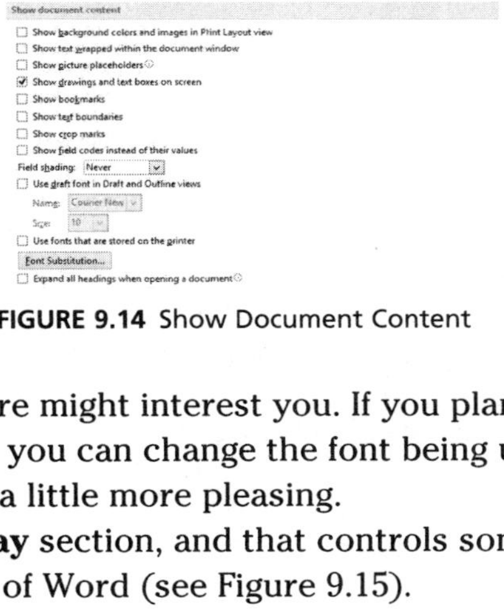

FIGURE 9.14 Show Document Content

One setting in here might interest you. If you plan to use the Draft View or Outline View, you can change the font being used in those views to make it something a little more pleasing.

Next is the **Display** section, and that controls some of the more general display elements of Word (see Figure 9.15).

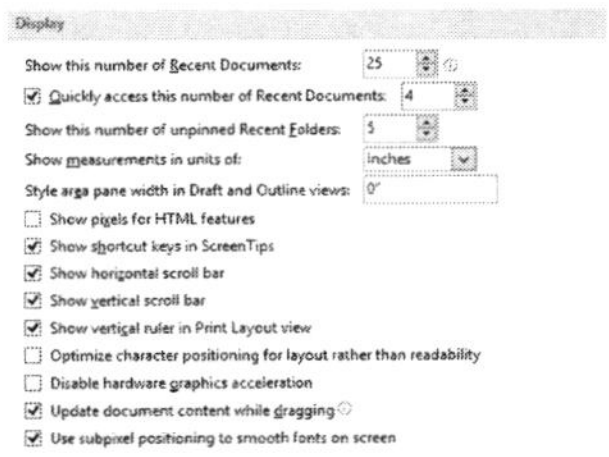

FIGURE 9.15 The Display Section

The first option lets you control how many **Recent Documents** will appear when you click **File**. Twenty-five is the default, but you can set it as high as fifty. Of course, your screen size/resolution might not support *displaying* fifty files in that area, but you can give it a try if you really want to.

While you're displaying files for quick access, you can check the box for **Quickly Access This Number of Recent Documents**. When you check that box, Word adds the specified number of documents to the bottom of the **Backstage Navigation Pane**, as you see in Figure 9.16.

FIGURE 9.16 Showing Four Recent Documents for Quick Access

If you prefer to work metrically rather than imperially, you can change from Display Measurements in Inches to Display Measurements in Centimeters (or Millimeters). You could also choose Points or Picas if you are so graphically inclined.

The only other setting in this group that I think is worth mentioning is the ability to turn on or off the Scroll Bars.

The **Print** group (Figure 9.17) offers a couple of useful options too.

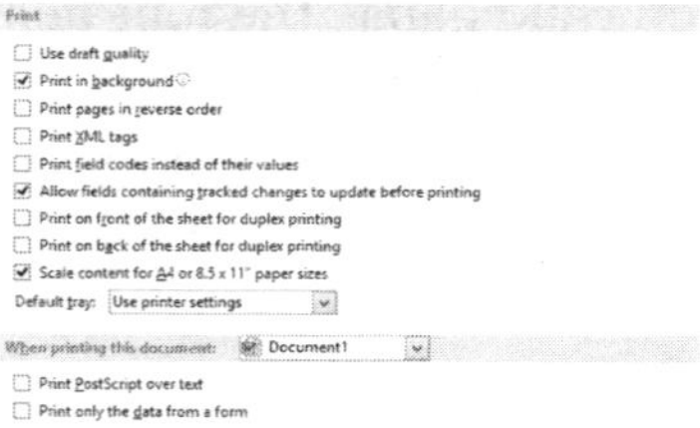

FIGURE 9.17 The Print Group

Use Draft Quality is handy on slower printers or if you're printing large documents and want to reduce the amount of ink or toner you're using. It's great for documents you're printing for internal use and don't intend to show a client.

Print in Background speeds your RTA (Return to Application) time by letting Word return to editing while the printing occurs in the background. If your machine is low on resources, this might not work that well, but most modern systems can handle printing in the background while you get back to editing.

The last settings I'll mention here, but won't go into detail on, are **Control Printing Pages in Reverse Order** (in other words printing the last page first), and **Printing on the Front and Back** (duplex printing). Those are little-used but occasionally handy options for dealing with certain kinds of printers. If your pages come out of your printer face up instead of face down, you might want to have Word print in reverse order, so that the pages are already in order when you take them off the printer.

In the **Save** section (see Figure 9.18), there are some options we should look at.

FIGURE 9.18 The Save Section

Never been clear to me why these are under the Advanced group instead of under the Save group we talked about earlier but anyhow . . .

Prompt before Saving Normal Template is a safety feature. A lot of Word malware attempts to infect the Normal template. This feature causes Word to warn you that changes have been made to Normal.dotm, which might alert you to something unfortunate before it can cause any problems. If you get prompted to Save Changes to the Normal Template but didn't intend to make any, you should click **No** just as a precaution. I advise you to leave this setting checked unless you're in the habit of making a lot of changes to Normal.dotm and just don't want to be troubled.

Always Create Backup Copy will give you primitive document versioning. With this feature, when you go to save your document, the prior saved version is renamed to *Backup Copy of filename.wbk* and saved in the same folder as the document you're saving. That way if you realize you made a bad change, it's easy to restore the backup copy. Each time you save the document the backup is replaced with the most recent prior save so you only have one prior version.

To restore a backup just click **File** > **Open**, set the **File of Type** field to **All Files**, and then locate and open the appropriate .wbk file. Once it's open you can **File** > **Save As** to save it as a regular Word document again—including re-saving it over the bad copy of the document (which will then itself get saved as a backup).

The **Copy Remotely Stored Files onto Your Computer, and Update the Remote File When Saving** option is not just long-winded; it's also sort of useful. With this option enabled, if you open a document from a network location, Word will create a temporary copy of the document on your local hard drive and work from that temporary copy. That gives you better performance than trying to work off the original remote copy of the document and also protects you in case you lose network connectivity in the middle of editing the document. When you do a Save of the document, Word will save your changes to the remote location.

Allow Background Saves is another performance-enhancing feature—when you do a Save, Word will do the Save operation in the background, so that you can continue editing. If you're saving a 5-page document, it probably doesn't matter. When you're saving a 205-page document, it can matter a lot in terms of your RTA (Return to Application) time. With this option turned off, Word will stop to save the document and not let you do anything else (in Word) until the Save is complete.

The **General** group has a few options that cover things that don't fit anywhere else.

I always uncheck **Provide Feedback with Sound** because as I work, I get tired of Word chirping at me to notify me of things.

I do like to let Word **Update Automatic Links at Open**—that way if I've embedded some Excel data for example (remember Chapter 7?), and that data has changed, Word will get the latest data automatically. Handy because I don't always remember to update manually.

The only other option in here that I think you might care about is the one that lets you enter your **Mailing Address**. That's the address Word is going to use, by default, in places like the envelopes where it asks for your mailing address.

Near the bottom of the General tab are two buttons. Web Options you probably don't care about. **Web Options** are used if you're creating web documents with Word, which I generally discourage.

The **File Locations** button, on the other hand, is occasionally useful. Click that button to get the **File Locations** dialog you see in Figure 9.19. Here you can specify the locations of key Word directories—from where User Templates are located to where AutoRecover files will be stored to

FIGURE 9.19 File Locations

where the Startup folder is. Most of this you don't need to change, but if you want to find (or change) them, here's where you can do that.

Customize Ribbon

Next in **Word Options** you'll find the **Customize Ribbon** page. This page is primarily about customizing the Ribbon, which you may want to do. It's fairly self-explanatory—you select commands from the left side, and then click **Add** to add them to the Ribbon. Note that you can't add commands to the predefined groups on the Ribbon. You have to create a Custom Group—which you can do on any of the Ribbon tabs—and add commands to that. You can see it in Figure 9.20.

FIGURE 9.20 Customize the Ribbon

Quietly hidden on this page is the button to **Customize the Keyboard Shortcuts**. Click it, and you'll get the dialog box you see in Figure 9.21. We talked about it a bit in Chapter 8. You can choose a Category from the

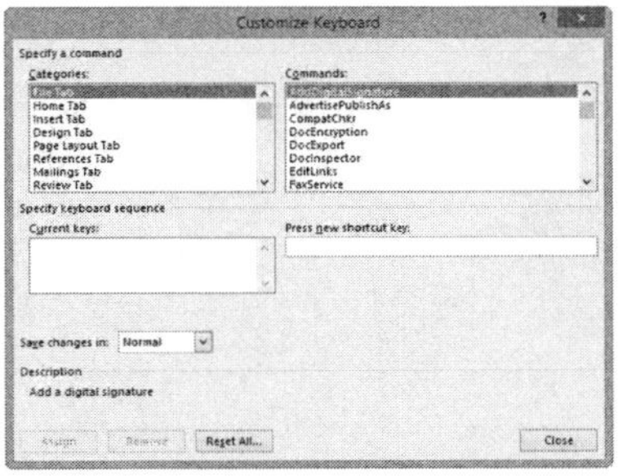

FIGURE 9.21 Customize the Keyboard Shortcuts

field on the left and then a command from that category from the field on the right. If there is already a keyboard shortcut for that command, it will appear in the Current Keys window once you have the command selected. Otherwise (or even so), you can click in the **Press New Shortcut Key** field, and press a Hotkey combination that you would like to assign to that command.

If the combination you select is already assigned to something, it will show up under the Current Keys field on the left. Otherwise it will say [unassigned], which means it's available for use. If you select something that is already assigned and click the **Assign** button, it will reassign it to your new command. That means you can remap the current Word Hotkeys if you want to.

When you have the shortcut key you want, just click **Assign** to make it so. If you later decide you'd like to undo those custom assignments (and restore the default assignments) you can do that in one move with the **Reset All** button at the bottom.

Quick Access Toolbar

The next group (see Figure 9.22) is very much like the previous group. This one lets you customize the Quick Access Toolbar (QAT) though. Again, something you probably do want to do. It works about the same as the previous group too—except it's simpler. Select commands from the

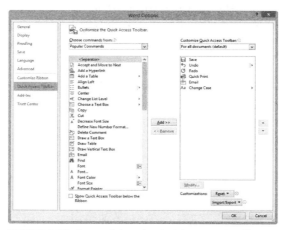

FIGURE 9.22 Customizing the Quick Access Toolbar

left side and click **Add** to add them to the QAT. Click them on the right side and select **Remove** to remove them from the QAT. Simple.

If you build a QAT that you're especially proud of, you can export those customizations to a file that you can use to preserve them or take them to another machine. Click the **Import/Export** button at the bottom right to access that functionality.

Add-Ins

The **Add-Ins** group (see Figure 9.23) lets you control the helper programs that are running with Word. Honestly not only will you rarely need to use this, but you really *shouldn't* mess around in here too much if you don't know what you're doing. The most common things you would do here would be to disable certain add-ins for the purpose of troubleshooting issues.

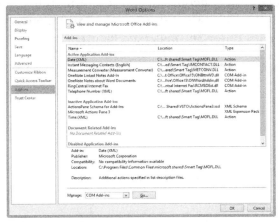

FIGURE 9.23 Controlling Word Add-Ins

The initial screen you see in Figure 9.23 only displays the Add-Ins. To actually manage them you need to click the **Go** button at the bottom of the page.

Trust Center

The **Trust Center** (see Figure 9.24) is where you control the security set-tings of the application, and in Microsoft Word, it's pretty basic—primarily concerned with privacy and how Macros are handled. I wouldn't change any of the settings in here unless you know exactly what you're doing or you have the guidance of a good technical support person. The welcome

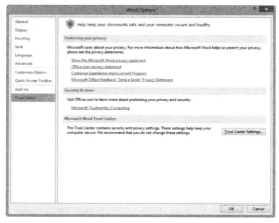

FIGURE 9.24 The Trust Center

screen has a lot of administrivia on it—privacy policies and such. There is a link here to let you opt in (or opt out) to the **Customer Experience Improvement Program**. I encourage you to opt in, but it's up to you. To explore further in the Trust Center, click the **Trust Center Settings** button to display the Trust Center Settings (see Figure 9.25).

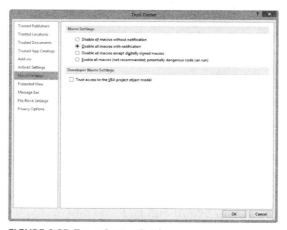

FIGURE 9.25 Trust Center Settings

Again, most of what you see in Figure 9.25 you should leave alone. There are a few features of the Trust Center that I do want to highlight for you though . . .

Trusted Locations

One common complaint with Office has been the security features added to the more recent versions. You open a document and have to click thru a variety of warnings just to open your own documents! Well, Office 2013 gives you a way around that; you can specify folders on your computer (or on your network) that are automatically trusted (see Figure 9.26).

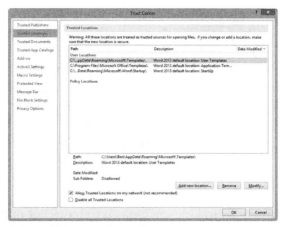

FIGURE 9.26 Trusted Locations

Documents you open from those locations won't prompt you. If you add a trusted location on your network, you'll need to check the box that says **Allow Trusted Locations on My Network** for it to work. If you're particularly paranoid, you can disable all trusted locations. Unless you're particularly fond of dialog boxes, I wouldn't do that, as you'll be prompted nearly every time you open any kind of document.

Trusted Documents

Sometimes you'll open a document and Word will warn you that it contains Macros or other content and will ask you if you want to trust this document. If you click **Trust Document**, then Word will shut up and let you use the document in all its glory—Macros and all. You can decide if you want to let documents on a network to be trusted (as opposed to only documents on your own computer) and you can even disable the feature entirely, so that *no* documents are trusted. Word remembers when you trust a document, so you don't have to re-trust it every time. You can clear that cache of trusted documents with the **Clear** button.

Trusted App Catalogs

As we saw earlier Office 2013 added the capability to have Office apps—specialized apps that run within Office programs. Trusted Catalogs lets you specify stores of apps that you trust, so you can add those apps to your Office installation. Mostly this would be used if your firm develops custom Office apps and you want to be able to install them.

Protected View

Protected View is a feature that was introduced in Word 2010. It opens documents from e-mails or the Internet in a restricted mode that doesn't allow Macros or other active content (also doesn't allow you to edit).

Word will prompt you to trust those documents and enable those features, but if you really want, you can actually turn off Protected View here. I strongly discourage that—Protected View is a very nice safety feature, but on rare occasions, we've seen problems with opening e-mailed documents, and **Disabling Protected View for Outlook Attachments** has fixed the problem. Again, I'd leave it alone unless you're having a problem.

If documents from a particular location, like a network drive, are continually opening in Protected View, add that location to the Trusted Locations list.

File Block Settings

Another safety feature: Word lets you choose to block (or open in Protected View) certain types of files. In Figure 9.27, you can see the settings for controlling the kinds of files Word will treat that way. Can you guess what I'm going to say now? Yep, it's best to leave these alone unless you have a special need.

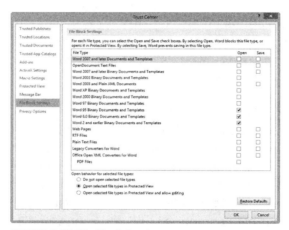

FIGURE 9.27 File Block Settings

Privacy Options

In the Privacy Options window (see Figure 9.28) you can tell Word how paranoid you want to be. If you don't want Word to search Office Online for help content when you're connected, you can turn that off here (though honestly you really should use it; it's good).

If you've decided that you don't want to participate in the Customer Experience Improvement Program, which you had to opt in to begin with, you can opt back out here. Again, this is a really useful program, so I encourage you to participate and assure you that there's no good privacy reason not to . . . but if you'd really rather not, then here's one place that you can say so.

There are a couple of settings here that let Office check for and download updates and new features and services. I've never seen any problems as a result of these settings.

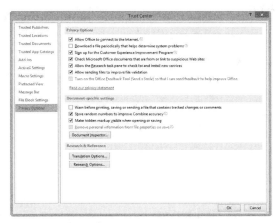

FIGURE 9.28 Configure Privacy Options

Under **Document-Specific Settings**, one sort of cryptic setting is **Store Random Numbers to Improve Combine Accuracy**. That setting is about letting Word quietly stamp the documents in the background, so that when multiple authors are editing the document at the same time, Word can do a better job of keeping track of which is which. If you don't think you'll ever do coauthoring of the document, you can clear that checkbox, but since the numbers are random anyhow, there's no harm in leaving it checked.

The final setting in here that I want to point out is the **Warn before Printing, Saving, or Sending a File That Contains Tracked Changes or Comments**. It's probably a good idea to turn this option **ON**, just to minimize the chances that you might inadvertently distribute a document with embarrassing metadata in it. See Chapter 11 for more on that subject.

The **Document Inspector** button just launches the same Word Document Inspector you can get from **File** > **Check for Issues**. We'll talk more about it in Chapter 11.

At the bottom of the screen there are two buttons: Translation Options and Research Options.

Translation Options

The **Translation Options** dialog (see Figure 9.29) lets you control how Word's multilingual translation features are going to work. There are two kinds of translation available:

- **Bilingual Dictionary.** This is what you use to translate individual words or phrases within Word. Unless you tell it otherwise, Word will try to use its installed dictionary first, and then fall back to an online dictionary to perform the translation if it has to.
- **Machine Translation.** This is what you use when you translate an entire document. Word will send the document to the online service listed, and the translation will appear in a web page.

Be careful with machine translation—sometimes "consequences unpredictable can be resulted."

FIGURE 9.29 Setting Translation Options

Research Options

The Research Options dialog (see Figure 9.30) lets you configure what reference books you want to have available on the Research pane in Word. You can **add or remove** services, **enable or disable** services, **update** them, or even turn on **Parental Controls** to block certain reference sources from your kids. I like to have resources, so I tend to enable all of the English services that look useful. Most of the services listed here are in languages I don't speak, so I don't bother enabling them.

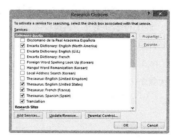

FIGURE 9.30 Research Options

Summary

For such a seemingly simple product, Microsoft Word can be configured and personalized in a lot of different ways. Some of these features are really useful to tweak; most of them you're better off leaving alone.

Among the features that you'll probably want to pay some attention to are the Proofing tools and the way Word is going to display the documents you enter. It can make a big difference if the Proofing tools are working for you, rather than against you, and if you're comfortable with how the document editor actually *looks*.

Troubleshooting

10

Word 2013 is probably the most robust and resilient version of Word Microsoft has ever created. That doesn't mean that nothing ever goes wrong with it though, so in this chapter we'll take a look at a few of the common problems and talk about how to resolve them.

Getting Help

Microsoft Word 2013 is a remarkably well-understood and well-documented application. There are a plethora of forums, websites, books, classes, and other resources out there to help you get the most out of it.

In the old days, you used to get a big thick manual with your software—it explained all of the features and capabilities in language that was rather dry but made up for its poor organization. Software publishers quickly found out, mostly via calls to their support lines, that most users didn't bother to read the voluminous printed documentation. So these days they save a lot of money on printing, paper, and shipping, and just include that content—occasionally better written—as either online or digital content in the Help system. Office 2013 is no different. On the right end of the Title Bar, right next to the Window Controls, you'll find a small question mark like what you see in Figure 10.1.

FIGURE 10.1 The Help Button

Clicking that will launch Word Help and if you're connected to the Internet, it can be a powerful and rich tool. Without Internet connectivity you *still* get the off-line Help, but that system is not quite as robust.

At the bottom of each Help topic in Word 2013 (when you're connected), you'll find something surprising . . . comments, left by other users! These are tips and tricks that other users have chosen to add to the Help system, and sometimes you find some real gems in there! Just pick a Help topic and scroll to the bottom to read the comments. *And* . . . you'll get the chance to leave your own comment if you want to.

The other thing I encourage you to do is to use the **Was This Information Helpful** feedback too. The Microsoft Office documentation teams *do* look at that feedback, and it really does help them to craft better articles for you. So please, take a moment to click **Yes**, **No**, or **I Don't Know** to express your opinion on the article.

Activating

If you find that certain features of the product don't seem to be available or if you get an error message telling you that a certain selection is **Blocked**, it may be either that you haven't activated the product yet or that you're using a trial version of the product that has expired. A lot of computers come from the manufacturer with only trial versions of Office installed, and those will expire in approximately sixty days. If you then go out and buy the full version, you can install over your trial and all of your data and documents will be just fine. It's easy.

If you're sure you have a full version, just go to **File** > **Account**. If the product is already activated, you'll see what you see in Figure 10.2. If the product isn't activated, you'll see a link to activate it.

If for some reason it refuses to activate over the Internet, try again and select **Telephone Activation**. When you call the number provided, you'll

FIGURE 10.2 Activating Office 2013

get an automated attendant that will walk you through activating. I've used the Telephone Activation method several times, always successfully.

Safe Mode

Word 2013, like (almost) all Office 2013 applications, has a Safe Mode it can start in. Safe Mode basically means that the program opens without any Add-Ins, Customizations, or Advanced Features running—it's a quick way to find out if the problem is the result of a faulty Add-In or something else. To start any Office product in Safe Mode, just hold down the **Control** key when you start the application. When Word starts up, it will prompt you to confirm that you want to start in Safe Mode (see Figure 10.3). Click **Yes** and Word will start.

If the problem you're troubleshooting doesn't occur when Word is in Safe Mode, then try disabling Add-Ins by going to the **File** > **Options** >

FIGURE 10.3 Safe Mode

Add-Ins section you can see in Figure 10.4. As I mentioned in the previous chapter, the Add-Ins tool can help you manage Word Add-Ins. Click the **Go** button at the bottom of the screen to get into the tool that lets you enable or disable Add-Ins.

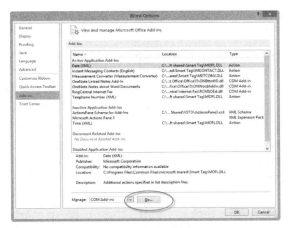

FIGURE 10.4 Managing Word Add-ins

Repair Installations

In Word 2007, one of the steps we'd take to diagnose issues was to run Office Diagnostics. Well . . . Office Diagnostics has been gone since Office 2010. Instead the recommendation is to do a Repair Installation of Office. It's really quite easy to do, though the exact steps vary slightly depending upon the operating system you're using.

In a nutshell . . . go to **Control Panel** > **Programs**. Find Office 2013 on the list of programs, select it, and click **Change** (or **Repair** if that's offered). The **Office Setup** program will start and present you with some options as you can see in Figure 10.5. Choose **Repair** and the Setup Wizard will take over, check all of your Office files for corrupted or missing files, and reinstall any that need it.

FIGURE 10.5 Repairing Microsoft Office

It's a fairly harmless thing to do; you won't lose any settings or data. At worst, you lose a few minutes of your time.

System Restore

If a Repair doesn't solve the problem, you might try running **System Restore** on your machine. System Restore will revert your drivers and settings back to the way they were at a previous date—but it doesn't touch your data so no worries about that. System Restore can be a little tricky to find, especially in Windows 8, but if you can't find it by tapping the **Windows Key** and typing *System Restore*, then the next way is to go to the **System Configuration** tool and on the **Tools** tab. All the way at the bottom is the **System Restore** tool. Launch it and it will offer to let you restore your system settings to a previous point in time.

Select a restore point that is before the problem started and let Windows try to restore. If you're not happy with the results of that restoral, you can always "un-restore" by having Windows restore you back to today. It's worth a try though; if a driver, update, or new program is causing your problems, this can help you resolve them.

Recovering from Word Crashes

If just starting Microsoft Word 2013 with a Blank Document causes it to crash or behave oddly, it could be that there is some corruption in your Normal.dotm, which is the standard Template Word 2013 loads when it first starts up. Luckily this is very easy to recover from. With Word 2013 closed, locate the Normal.dotm file, which should be located under *C:\Users\[your profile name]\AppData\Roaming\Microsoft\Templates* and rename it to something like *Normal.old*. Then start Word normally. Word will detect that it can't find the Normal.dotm file as it expected, and it will just automatically create a new one for you. If Word starts and runs normally, then you can be pretty sure that the problem was some kind of corruption in your old Normal.dotm file.

If that doesn't resolve the issue, then you may need to get down and dirty with your Registry. This is the time when I need to offer you the standard disclaimer that editing the Registry is really not something I encourage regular users to do. If you change the wrong thing in the Registry, you can do really bad things to your computer. So before you embark on this, you should make sure that you have a known good backup of your system and make sure you *really* want to do this yourself rather than asking a computer professional to take on this task for you. Assuming you really do want to proceed—and I have to make that assumption to continue this chapter—exit all Microsoft Office programs (including Outlook), then click **Start**, click **Run**, and type **REGEDIT** in the provided command box. Click **OK** or press **Enter**.

Within the registry find this subkey:

HKEY_CURRENT_USER\Software\Microsoft Office\15.0\Word\Data

Remember, at Microsoft, version 15 is the internal number of Office 2013.

With that subkey selected, click the **File** menu in **Regedit** and choose **Export**. Save the file to your desktop in a file named something like *Word Data Key.reg*. The reason we're doing this is because most of the Word customizations found Backstage are saved in the Data Key of the registry (and yes, that includes the Recently Used Files list). What we're about to do will wipe out those customizations, and if that doesn't fix the problem, you may want to be able to restore those customizations. Hence the exported .reg file.

Once you've exported your Data Key to the .reg file for safekeeping, delete the Data Key from the registry. Exit the Registry Editor and start Word. When Word 2013 starts up it will notice that the Data Key is gone and it will automatically create a new one for you using the factory default settings. If your problem is solved, then you're good to go from there. If not, either you can continue with this new setup or you can close Word, go to your Windows desktop, and double-click that *Word Data Key.reg* file we made, and it will put your customizations back in.

Corrupted Documents

Occasionally Word documents will get corrupted or otherwise damaged. That can happen for a number of reasons—**malware**, **hardware problems**, **power failures** . . . or just darned **bad luck**. Corruption in a document isn't always obvious either; it might be a document that won't load or text that is completely ruined (though both of those point to corruption). Sometimes it's more subtle like odd behavior in the document, such as page breaks moving around on their own, strange page renumbering, or other odd behaviors. If that happens, the first thing to do is confirm that the strange behavior is limited to that one document. Open another document and see if the problem exists there as well. If it does, then you have some other issue with your system that you need to address—the aforementioned Office Repair Installation or Safe Mode may come in handy.

If the problem is limited to the document, then the first thing to do is find out which Template is used by the document. With the document open in Word, click File and then Options. Click Add-Ins. Click the drop-down arrow on the Manage box (see Figure 10.6 below), and then click Templates from that list. Finally click **Go** to launch the **Templates and Add-Ins** dialog box you see in Figure 10.7 below.

From this dialog box you can quickly see what the Document Template is. In Figure 10.7, you can see that the current document template is Normal, which is the default Word Template. That's good news for your troubleshooting because you can rename the Normal.dotm global template (or delete it, if you're feeling brave), and the next time you start Word, it will automatically re-create it for you (hopefully without the

Note: If you have the **Developer** Tab showing on your **Ribbon**, you can also get to the **Templates and Add-Ins** dialog box by click the **Document Template** button on the **Developer** tab.

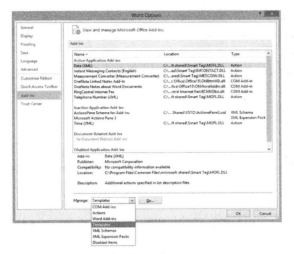

FIGURE 10.6 Managing Templates

FIGURE 10.7 The Templates and Add-Ins Dialog Box

corruption that caused your problems). The only downside to deleting Normal.dotm, honestly, is if you've customized the Normal template in some way and you don't want to lose those customizations. Chances are good that, like most lawyers, you haven't customized Normal.dotm (at least not intentionally), so deleting it is just fine. Again, Word will quietly re-create it for you the next time you start up.

You Can't Edit the Document

Sometimes you'll open a document and you won't be able to edit it. The Title Bar may even say Read-Only in it. Usually Word is pretty good about warning you about that in the Information Bar at the top of the screen, but in case you didn't notice that for some reason, it's possible that the document in question has been **Marked as Final**. Assuming you're the author you can turn that off again by going to **File** > **Protect Document** (on the **Information** group) and *un*selecting **Mark as Final**.

It's also possible that the file itself or the directory it resides in has been marked as Read-Only in Windows. Go to **File** > **Open**, find the file, right-click it, and choose **Properties** to see if Read-Only is checked. You can do the same for the directory it resides in.

Beyond that you're getting into territory that you may need your IT support people to help with . . .

Finding and Fixing Formatting Mysteries

One of the more perplexing issues lawyers and law firms have to deal with tends to be formatting problems. "Why the heck is that italicized?!" is a common refrain. In the good ol' days of Word Perfect we'd just open the **Reveal Codes** pane, track down the offending code, and remove it. But Word doesn't use codes that way, so tracking down an errant bit of formatting can be a little more challenging. (That's why you want to use Styles as often as possible and as little Direct Formatting as you can.)

There are two common scenarios where you may have to trouble-shoot some curious formatting . . .

Documents You Created

If it's a document that you created, the chances are good that you have an unfortunate combination of Direct and Indirect Formatting. You may want to reread Chapter 4 and pay particular attention to the information on Styles. The other thing you might want to do is go into **File** > **Options** > **Advanced** and make sure that **Keep Track of Formatting** and **Mark Formatting Inconsistencies** checkboxes are enabled (review Chapter 9). Then Word will help you to locate and fix places where you may have inconsistent use of Styles and Direct Formatting.

Generally when I see formatting issues in a document I created, I'll select the offending text and press **Control+Spacebar** to remove any Direct Formatting. Then ensure that I have the correct Style applied. That fixes it almost every time.

Documents from Somebody Else

Sometimes if you receive a document from somebody else, there may be formatting issues, especially if that person is using a different word processor or even a different version of Word. A common cause of formatting issues is that the fonts installed on the two machines are different. For example, the other person may be using Word for Mac and have older, non-Unicode fonts on their machine, and these fonts aren't installed on your machine. Generally if the differences are minor, you can solve it by just reformatting the text with your own font, creating minimal disruption. If, on the other hand, the differences are substantial and the formatting is unusable on your machine, you may have to go back to the originator of the document and ask that person to reformat the document using a more common, or updated, font and then resend the document to you.

Of course the originator of the document is just as likely (or more likely, if they haven't read this book!) to have made the mistake of using Direct Formatting instead of Indirect Formatting (Styles). If so, the same tactic of selecting the offending text, pressing **Control+Spacebar** to remove the Direct Formatting and then making sure the proper style is applied to the text may resolve the font issues.

If **Control+Spacebar** doesn't solve the problem, you might try using the **Clear Formatting** button on the Ribbon (see Figure 10.8), which will strip out all of the Direct Formatting and reset the applied style to "Normal." From there you can reapply the formatting you need, if Normal wasn't it.

FIGURE 10.8 The Clear Formatting Button

Printing Issues

There are two basic kinds of printing issues with Word: documents that don't print the way you expect them to and documents that don't print at all. The first kind is a little harder to troubleshoot because there are so many variables.

Document Doesn't Print as Expected

The first thing to check if a document doesn't print the way you expect it to is to run a **Print Preview** and see if it looks correct on the screen. If it looks fine on the screen but doesn't look the same when the print actually hits the paper, then the problem may be with your printer.

The next thing to check is the **Font** you've used in the document. If the text that doesn't print right is in an unusual font, it may be that you've chosen a font your printer doesn't support. In some cases you can add the font to the printer, but in most

Tricks of the Pros

Sometimes if I have a document-printer combination that just doesn't want to print correctly, I'll save the document as an Adobe PDF file. If it looks right there, then I can print the PDF file.

cases it's a lot easier to just select a more standard font. There are a lot of PostScript fonts available, and all modern printers should support PostScript fonts. In some really unusual cases, you may be able to have your printer print the font as an image instead of text, or download the font from the computer to use. You'll just have to decide how committed to that esoteric font you really are, I guess, to determine how much effort you want to go to in order to make it work.

The next thing to check is to make sure you have the latest and correct **print driver** installed for your printer. Especially if you've upgraded the computer to a new operating system, it's possible that the printer is still using drivers from the old operating system. Make sure you've got the right drivers for your printer and that they're up to date.

Document Doesn't Print at All

Not surprisingly most nonprinting issues are the result of problems with the printer. Before you get involved in any complex troubleshooting, try a few basics: make sure the printer has **paper** and **toner** (or ink as the case may be), is **turned on**, and is **connected to the computer** (or network) that it's supposed to be connected to.

▼▼▼▼▼

Tales from the Field

Client called and said one of their printers had stopped printing. They tried everything they could think of, but it just wouldn't print and hadn't worked in days. When I arrived, I started asking questions and discovered that it had stopped working when they had moved it to clean the area. They assumed they had broken something in the printer and were preparing to order a new printer to replace it. I pulled the printer out and discovered they'd forgotten to reconnect the network cable to the back. I plugged it in and all of the queued up print jobs immediately started printing.

If that all checks out OK, try **powering the printer off and back on**. That will clear the memory of the printer and cause it to try and reestablish connection with your computer and/or the network.

The final thing to try, before seeking professional assistance, is to **reboot your computer** in case your print queue is jammed up.

If none of those remedies get the printer to work, then your problem is more than casual, and you should contact your tech support person for further guidance.

▼▼▼▼▼
WARNING: GEEK CONTENT AHEAD

The Print Spooler. Put simply, the Print Spooler is a software process that resides on both the client computer (i.e., the workstation you're using) and the print server (which may also be the workstation you're using if the printer is directly attached), and it handles the processing of the print jobs. The spooler handles the final rendering of the print job. If the Print Spooler stops for any reason, your print jobs will back up and never make it to the printer. You can restart the service if you know how, but it's probably easier to just restart the computer. If the problem persists, then you should contact your tech support person—if it stops once, that could be a fluke. If it keeps stopping, that's a problem.

An Extra Page Prints at the End

Another common printing issue is that an extra blank page may print at the end of your document. Usually that's because you actually have a few extra lines at the end of the document you didn't know about and couldn't see. Go to the end of your document and turn on **Show Paragraph Marks** by clicking the **Show/Hide Paragraph Marks** button in the **Paragraph** group

▼
The ¶ symbol is called a Pilcrow. It is also sometimes referred to as the alinea from the Latin word meaning "off the line."

of the **Home** tab (it looks like this: ¶) or press **Control+Shift+8**. You'll probably discover a couple of extra paragraph marks at the end of your document. Delete them and then check Print Preview to make sure that your blank page is gone.

Word May Seem to Hang When You Try to Insert a Building Block

Sometimes when you go to insert a Building Block, Word might appear to freeze up, and the problem seems to get worse when you add more and more items to your Building Blocks list. That seems sort of obvious when you think about it, but the issue is really with how long it takes Word to build the Building Blocks Gallery. Word isn't really frozen; it's just struggling to get the galleries populated. The faster and more powerful your machine, the less problem you'll have with freezing when using Building Blocks. So there are two basic solutions: either upgrade your computer, or remove some unneeded Building Blocks from the Template, so that Word doesn't have to work so hard to get those galleries built.

Not surprisingly, this problem is less and less common as people upgrade to faster machines with more RAM and 64-bit Windows.

You're Seeing a Lot of Oddly Named Files

If your folders are filling up with files whose names start with a tilde (~) you may have a problem with Word not shutting down properly. Those files are temporary files that Word should clean up when it shuts down normally; while Word is running, you'll see those files from time to time, and that's fine. If Word is closed or if you're seeing growing numbers of those files, that may indicate a faulty Add-In or other problem that is preventing Word from shutting down normally. If you're sure Word is closed, and that all of the files you need are correctly saved, you can generally delete those files if you want to.

You See a Lot of Odd Text in Brackets

What you're seeing are field codes and they are often used in complex documents—especially documents that make use of document assembly. Word is supposed to substitute data for the field code, such as the **path name to the document**, **author name**, **current date or time**, **Merge data**, and so forth. If you're seeing the codes instead of the data, chances are you just have **Display Field Codes** turned on. To turn them off, press **Alt+F9**.

You See a Lot of Curious Marks in Your Document . . .

. . . like dots where the spaces should be and pilcrows at the end of every paragraph. You've just got the formatting marks displayed. You have several options to turn that off (and back on) but the easy ways are either to click the **Show/Hide** button (looks like a pilcrow) on the **Home** tab of the **Ribbon** or press **Control+Shift+8** on your keyboard. If you want to display some of the formatting marks but not all of them, you can configure that Backstage: **File** > **Options** > **Display**.

Performance Problems

If Word isn't performing very well, there are a few things you can do to improve it, other than adding more RAM to your system, which is almost always a good idea.

1. **Use fewer fonts in your document.** If you have a lot of fonts, that can suck up system resources.

2. **Store your documents on a local hard drive.** You may not be able to do this due to policy issues at your firm but if you *are* able to, you may find that Word operates faster on documents that are located on a local hard drive instead of a network drive. This is a good example of where enabling **Copy Remotely Stored Files onto Your Computer, and Update the Remote File When Saving** can really help. Go back to Chapter 9 if you don't recall how to enable it. Go ahead, we'll wait.

   > If you're one of that tiny percentage of folks who still has a floppy drive in your computer, *never* edit Word documents that are located on the floppy drive. Copy the document to the hard drive first, edit it there, and then copy it back. You're welcome.

3. **Disable the automatic spelling and grammar checks.** These features require a little bit of system attention to operate; turning them off can optimize Word performance a bit. See Chapter 9 for details on how to turn them off.

More Resources

- **Office for Lawyers** (http://www.officeforlawyers.com) A site I created to post supplementary information and articles for these books. It's free, no registration required.
- **Microsoft Support Forums** (http://social.answers.microsoft.com/forums) Free peer-support forums hosted by Microsoft and frequented by Microsoft MVPs. There are forums for Windows, Office, and other Microsoft products. Ask and answer questions for free.
- **Shauna Kelly's Word Site** (http://www.shaunakelly.com/word) Great site created by a Microsoft Word MVP with answers and information about Word.

- **Adriana Linares' Site for Word for Lawyers** (http://www. lawtechpartners.com/WordforLawyers.htm).

▼▼▼▼▼
What's a Microsoft MVP?

A Microsoft MVP or Most Valuable Professional is a volunteer who has been recognized by Microsoft as an expert in one or more particular products. Anybody who demonstrates a level of expertise and a willingness to help support that product can be an MVP. They are not Microsoft employees and aren't paid for their efforts. For more information visit http://support.microsoft.com/mvp.

Summary

Microsoft Word 2013 is the most robust and recoverable version of Microsoft Word yet. But that doesn't mean you'll never have problems with it. Office Repair installs will fix most things that go wrong with the program itself, but often the problem in Word may be a corrupted Template or a misbehaving Add-In. Be very reluctant to add even more Add-Ins to Word, especially if you're not sure what they are or why you need them. Having more Add-Ins is not better—the best installation of Word is tight and fast with only the Add-Ins you actually need and use.

Mistakes Lawyers Make with Microsoft Word 11

Over the last twenty-five years, I've seen lawyers make a lot of mistakes with word processors—as the systems have gotten more powerful and easier to use, the mistakes have become easier to make. Let's take a few minutes to look at some of the most common mistakes and how you can avoid them. Remember: the first step to recovery is admitting the problem!

Licensing

One big mistake firms make with Microsoft Office is they buy it from their hardware vendor with their computers. They just call Dell or HP, and as part of the spec for the machine, firms have the vendor include Microsoft Office—they think that they're saving money that way. They're not! The software version you get that way is called an **OEM Version**. The software itself is identical to the retail or volume license versions but the *license* is different. Specifically:

- OEM software is locked to the machine it came on. If you ever replace that machine, you cannot move the Microsoft Office license to the new machine. You have to buy a new license. Even if the machine dies in fifteen months and you have to replace it—you'll need to buy a new copy of Office too.
- OEM software can only be installed on that single machine. No additional machines.

The better play for almost any law office—certainly any office with five or more machines—is either to buy a **Volume License** of Microsoft Office or to get Office via **Office 365**.

The volume license can be installed on *any x* machines (where *x* = the number of licenses you buy) but additionally you can install the *same* license on a portable device. Let me explain that.

Let's say Joe Lawyer has a desktop computer. You install one of your Office 2013 licenses, obtained via volume license, on that desktop computer. But Joe also has a laptop that he uses when he travels or visits clients. You can install the *same* Office 2013 license that you used on Joe's desktop . . . on his laptop. The key is that the second machine has to be a portable machine with the *same* primary user (i.e., Joe).

But wait, there's more . . . volume licenses are extremely price competitive with retail and OEM licenses—and often cheaper.

The **Office 365** subscription gives you Office 2013 that you can install on up to five PCs or Macs, and the current price is $12 per month per user. The other advantage to the Office subscription plan is that you won't have to pay separately for upgrades again. When the new versions come out, you'll just get them as part of your subscription. Twelve dollars per month may sound like a lot, but especially if you have two or three computers (or more), the price per device per month becomes awfully good.

So why not just walk into Best Buy and pick up five Microsoft Office 2013 boxes? Those aren't tied to any specific machine, so you can move them when the machine gets replaced. And with the **Retail License** you *can* install on the desktop and a portable for the same primary user! But . . . with retail licenses, you have to keep track of the licenses. You have to know which license you installed on which machine, and if you ever have to reinstall . . . heaven help you if you got them mixed up.

With **Volume Licensing** you get *one* product key to keep track of and it's tied to *x* number of licenses that you've purchased. You just use that *one* product key for all of your installs. And if you later need to add additional licenses, you just call up your vendor and buy however many (or few) additional licenses you need. No need to keep track of multiple product keys. That will save you money in administration and management.

With Office 365 you don't even need to keep track of the product keys. You install from the web and they keep tracking the product keys for you.

If you want to keep up to date on Microsoft Office, you can purchase your **Volume License with Software Assurance**—that gives you free upgrades to the current version of Office within the period of the subscription. If you know a new version of Office is due within the next eighteen months and you're confident you'll want it, then it's probably cost effective to get your Volume License with two years of Software Assurance.

If you get the Office 365 version of Office 2013, you'll never have to worry about future versions; Microsoft will simply update your installed version of Office for you as new versions come out at no additional cost.

"But darn, we only have *four* users!" That's OK. The five-license minimum for Volume Licensing only has to be five licenses . . . it doesn't have to be five licenses of the same thing! You can buy four licenses of **Microsoft Office 2013 Professional Plus** and one license of something cheap like **Microsoft Math** or **Microsoft Streets and Trips**. That extra license is just a placeholder to fill out the five-license pack . . . but it counts.

For the Office 365 version there is no minimum quantity required— you can just buy one seat if you like.

Inconsistent Use of Styles

Styles are a powerful tool to standardize how paragraphs and text are formatted in Word. Sadly, most lawyers don't take advantage of their full potential. Too many lawyers rely on Direct Formatting instead of a well-thought out set of Styles. In Chapter 4, we explored Styles in more detail— if you only read one chapter in this book, well then you've spent a lot of money for just one chapter. If you want to get the most for your money, choose Chapter 4.

Document Naming

As discussed in Chapter 6, lawyers and staff are often in a hurry when they create documents—so much so that when it comes time to Save and Exit the document, they occasionally name the document *Memo* or *Letter* or some other quick thing they can type without thinking about it. The problem is that with a title like that, it's almost impossible to find this document later or figure out what it's supposed to be. Worse yet, if you don't have a good document management system, you could end up with a folder full of documents called *Memo.docx, Memo1.docx, Memo2.docx*, and so on, and that just doesn't help anybody. Word supports long file names like *Memo to Dr Sanders regarding Bruha claim.docx*. Take the time to really name your documents. You'll be a lot happier, and you'll save a lot of time in the long run.

Saving Over Old Documents

One thing most lawyers do is reuse old documents. The Smith will was so good that when Mr. Jones needs a will, you just open the Smith will, make the necessary changes, and save as Mr. Jones's will. One problem with that arises when you open the Smith will, make your changes, then just click **Save** . . . and you've just saved over Mr. Smith's will with Mr. Jones's will. Oops.

▼▼▼▼▼

We get two to four calls per month from law firms who need us to help them retrieve a previous version of a document because somebody saved over the old one with an incorrect version. Fortunately most of them have backup systems that allow us to retrieve the old version. In the case that happens to you, however, don't delay. Backups are in a constant state of change. Every night (hopefully) a new backup is done and in many cases it overwrites a previous backup. If you wait too long to request a restoral, the correct file may be overwritten by the erroneously edited one. Let your IT staff know as soon as you realize the error—that will maximize your chances to get it fixed.

There are a couple of ways to prevent saving over a document you want to keep. One is that when you open Mr. Smith's will, but before you make any changes to it, click **File** and do a **Save As** to save a copy of the document with a new filename (if you prefer the keyboard, press **F12**), Then you're working with that new document and Mr. Smith's original will is untouched.

A second way, and we'll talk about it in more detail a little later in this chapter, is that after you open Mr. Smith's will, select all of the text by pressing **Control+A**, Copy that text to the clipboard with a deft **Control+C**, then press **Control+N** to start a new blank document. **Control+V** pastes that text into the blank, new document, and **Control+S** lets you save that now not-so-blank new document with a new filename and location if desired. You may then tap the **Control** key however many times you like to make yourself grin at how clever you were not only to preserve Mr. Smith's will but probably to reduce significantly your metadata issues in one (well, four or five) swift strokes.

Not Saving Documents

Saving over old documents is one mistake with Save. Another mistake is not saving often enough. I can't tell you how many times I've gotten calls from folks who lost a document (or at least part of one) because something bad happened, and they'd forgotten to save during the last one or two hours.

▼▼▼▼▼
Tales from the Field . . .

A few years ago I got a call from a client late on a Thursday afternoon. She had spent the better part of the day working on a brief for a case she was involved in, and at the end of the day, she went to close her word processor (in fairness, it wasn't Microsoft Word, but for our purposes the story is the same). It asked her if she wanted to save the document. In her haste she accidentally clicked "No" and her word processor quickly and dutifully closed down . . . discarding hours of her work in the process. She immediately realized her mistake and grabbed her phone to call me. After she explained her predicament, the call went something like this:

Me: OK, well, how long ago did you last save the document?
Her: <long pause> I didn't.
Me: You didn't save it *at all* today?
Her: I know, I know. <sigh>
Me: OK, well, did you e-mail a copy of it to anybody?
Her: No.
Me: Did you print a copy?
Her: No. Is it gone?
Me: <long pause> Maybe not. I'll be there in ten minutes. *Don't touch anything!*

Pondering her problem, I remembered that her word processor, like Microsoft Word, makes automatic backup copies every few minutes in the background. Those are there in the event that your computer (or even just your word processor) has an unexpected shut down. These can be due to power failure, system error, foot/dog/cat/child/spouse brushing up against the power switch . . . you name it. If that kind of unexpected shutdown happens, the next time the word processor starts it detects that the backup files are there and offers to let you recover them. That can be quite a relief in those instances when you really need them.

However, when you close the document normally (such as by closing the word processor and answering "No" to the "Do you want to save?" question) the word processor is a good computer citizen and cleans up after itself, which includes deleting all of those apparently unnecessary backup copies. It occurred to me, in pondering her problem, that perhaps there was a way to recover one of those deleted files.

A computer deleting files is not really as thorough as you might imagine. All the computer really does in those instances is mark that space as available. It doesn't actually clean off the bits on the hard drive that previously stored that file. It leaves them as is, but it just indicates that the space is available to be used by the next piece of data that needs to be stored. If I could get to her computer before any further data was written to that space on the hard drive, I just might be able to get it back.

When I arrived at her office, she was in a bad way . . . she was sure that all was lost and she was going to have to spend all night recreating hours' worth of work. "It's impossible, isn't it?" she said with a pained voice. "It's unlikely," I responded. "But don't give up just yet."

I fired up my handy undelete program (there are a number of them available from various vendors) and set to work browsing to see if I could find the deleted backup files. Sure enough, I found several files that were of the type we were seeking, and by comparing the date and time stamps, I identified one or two likely suspects. I restored them to her hard drive and started her word processor, which correctly recognized the presence of the backup files, assumed it had crashed, and offered to recover them. She jumped up and down with glee when she recognized the first page of her lost document. Sure enough, she had lost only about the last five minutes of her work, which amounted to a couple of minor edits she was able to redo easily. To say she was happy is an understatement and our firm earned our unofficial slogan: We Make The Impossible Unlikely.

Fortunately modern technology has largely, but not entirely, minimized this problem. I have my computer plugged into an uninterruptible power supply, so that if my electricity blinks momentarily, my computer won't notice. **AutoRecover** means that Word has frequent backup files so that if Word happens to crash for some reason, I have a good shot to be presented with a recovery file the next time I start Word, and I'll only lose a couple of minutes worth of work.

And, now with Word 2013, you can recover an unsaved document—even if you closed without saving. Just open **Word**, click **File**, and click **Manage Versions**. There you'll find **Recover Unsaved Documents**. Click that and you'll see the **Saved Drafts** folder, which should contain your document.

Note . . . these documents are only saved for four days. If you've waited longer than that to recover them . . . you're probably out of luck.

But honestly, how hard is it to press **Control+S** to save your document? Watch, I'll do it right now. There, wasn't that satisfying? Even though I know intellectually that the odds of losing my document (currently well into the eleventh chapter) are increasingly slim, I've been in this business long enough to remember when it was a regular occurrence. And I'm in the good habit of frequently saving my work as I go, so that just in case the cat jumps on my keyboard at the wrong moment, I still have a recently saved copy I can reopen. Right after I figure out whose cat that is.

Is it annoying or difficult to press **Control+S** every few minutes? Not at all. Look, I'll do it again.

Metadata

Metadata is data about data. Simple as that. The text of your document is data. The *title* of your document is Metadata. The date the document was created, the name of the author, the number of words or characters within the document, any comments or tracked changes within the document . . . these are all Metadata.

It's a popular misconception that Metadata is strictly a Microsoft problem. In fact, virtually all office productivity applications, including Corel's WordPerfect, use Metadata and face potential issues with it. That's why Corel included a Metadata checker/cleaner in WordPerfect X3 and all subsequent versions.

What's the Matta with Metadata?

Other than being a sort of cheesy section heading, the "matta with metadata" is that there may very well be information contained therein that would be damaging to your case, your client, and perhaps your career if it should be leaked outside your firm.

For example: let's say you have a Word document and you have Track Changes turned on. (Go back to Chapter 6 if you're not sure what Track Changes does.) This Word document is going to be a settlement offer to opposing counsel. You decide that you will offer the other party $500,000 to settle the matter. Before sending the offer and after discussion with your client, you decide to reduce the offer to $350,000. So you open your Word document, change *$500,000* to *$350,000*, save the document, and promptly e-mail it to opposing counsel. Opposing counsel opens the document in Word, makes sure that they have Track Changes turned on as well, clicks the **Review** tab on the **Ribbon**, and changes their view to **Final Showing Markup**. At this point, they discover that you had originally intended to offer $500,000 but later revised that figure down. Do you suppose that might affect your negotiating position?

Does it make your situation better or worse if you and the client collaborated on the document and used the Comments feature of the document to discuss your settlement strategy as you prepared the offer letter?

Another scenario: you're assisting a client with a press release for a pending acquisition. It's all very hush-hush and not finalized yet, so you're just holding on to the draft of the release. In the meantime that client also wants your help with a press release for their new bond offer. Since you like the press release you did for the acquisition and it already has all of the client's contact information in it, you decide to reuse the pending acquisition release and just change the relevant bits. You've already read the bit I wrote about not saving over old documents, so you know that you should open your original document and do a Save As to save the new version with a new name. You change the names, dates, and amounts to reflect the bond offer, and once you're satisfied that's all done, you helpfully send it off to the local business press. The next day the front page of the local paper reads "BIGCO Inc. to Acquire SmallCo, LLC, for $50 million!" Oops.

How Do You Discover Metadata

There are a number of tools available to discover Metadata but the simplest is Word itself. With a Word document open and **Track Changes** turned on, go to the **Review** tab and make sure under **Tracking** that you have **Final Showing Markup** selected in the **Display for Review** field. Then you should be able to see the edits and changes made, if any were preserved in the document.

Alternatively, you can use third-party tools like **Metadata Assistant** or **Doc Scrubber** to analyze your document (and remove potentially damaging Metadata).

How Do You Clean/Prevent It

There are a number of methods available to clean Metadata out of a Word document and a few ways to prevent it in the first place. The method you use to clean it should depend upon what the document is ultimately intended to do.

If the intention is to print the document and provide it in hardcopy, then your Metadata worries are few. Very little Metadata would appear in a printout—in fact you would have to set the print options deliberately *to* print the metadata (such as Comments and other markup) for it to appear (see Figure 11.1). By default Print Markup is *not* checked in Word 2013.

FIGURE 11.1 Markup Is Not Included in Printouts by Default

So if your intent is to print the document and only provide it via hardcopy, then don't worry about the Metadata. Print your document, proofread it, and then rest assured that they aren't getting anything you didn't intend to give them (unless they're going to be testing your printout for incriminating fingerprints or DNA).

If the intent is to send the document electronically, as it so often is these days, then you have to make another determination before you proceed: do they need to edit it? If not, then the preferred way to send the document—and for them to receive it—is as an Adobe PDF file. PDF has a number of advantages.

First, the formatting is going to be consistent. The way the PDF looks on your computer is how it looks on their computer and how it looks on their printer. No questions about whether they have the right fonts or what version of WordPerfect they're using. A PDF is a PDF is a PDF. It's electronic paper. All they need is a compatible version of **Acrobat Reader** and they can get that from Adobe for free.

Second, it's portable. This relates a bit to the first advantage, but there are PDF readers for nearly every platform. So if you're dealing with a lawyer who is still running Windows 98 or a lawyer who has gone over to the Mac or a real propeller-head who insists that Linux is the only true operating system . . . it doesn't matter. They can read and print PDF files you send them. Heck most mobile devices like iPhones, Windows phones, and Android phones can read PDF files now too.

Third, and most importantly for the purposes of Chapter 11 in this book, almost no interesting Metadata goes with a PDF file. When you send a Word document to PDF, you're effectively printing it, and that means the same rules apply . . . unless you have explicitly told Word to include things like Comments, Tracked Changes, or other markup in the PDF file, it won't. The worst you're likely to see in a PDF file is the document title, author, and perhaps some keywords. You have to try pretty hard to get significant Metadata into a PDF file.

That said, Adobe does create just a little bit of its own Metadata, like all files on a computer it will have an associated creation date for example. But I'd suggest that if you're really concerned with the simple creation date of the document, you may want to reexamine the ethical issues of the matter.

So, let's examine the scenario where you need to send a document out that they *do* need to be able to edit or where you are, for some reason, required to send it in Microsoft Word format.

Document Reuse

One thing that lawyers *love* to do, as we've discussed a few times already, is reuse existing documents. It's a big time saver and can help to maintain a high standard of quality. If you already know a document is good, why not use it as the basis for a future document? Well, the answer to that question can be found in Chapter 8. You're really better off using Templates and/or document assembly software and building a fresh new document with those tools rather than using an existing, completed, work product as the basis for a new one. Unfortunately, the practice of document reuse is widespread, and old habits are hard to break. When you reuse that old document, you risk also reusing the Metadata from that document. So, in our scenario where you *have* to send a Word document and you've succumbed to the pressure to reuse an old document, then you want to try to minimize the chances that any Metadata is transferred from the original document.

To do that, open your old document, and the very first thing you want to do is make sure **Track Changes** is turned **ON** in that document. Then go to **File** and click **New** to start a new blank document. In that document make sure that **Track Changes** is turned **OFF**. (Yes, OFF.) Now go back to your original document (sometimes referred to as the

Donor Document) and press **Control+A** to select all of the text. Press **Control+C** to copy that text to the clipboard. Go to the new document (sometimes referred to as the Recipient Document) and press **Control+V** to paste that text in. Now **Save** that new document with a new file name. Close the old, or donor, document. Now you can go through and make any edits or changes you need to make to the new document. When you have it finished, go to **File**, click **Check for Issues**, then **Inspect Document**, and let Word's built-in **Metadata Inspector** take a look at your document.

If you haven't saved it lately, the Metadata Inspector will prompt you to save. That's a smart move. Then it will ask you what data to check for (see Figure 11.2). Generally speaking, I would just let it check for everything. Except perhaps for Headers, Footers, and Watermarks, there probably isn't any of that other data that your recipient should have. Besides, the Metadata Inspector will ask you before it removes anything, so I'd just leave them all checked.

FIGURE 11.2 Running the Document Inspector to Check for Metadata

After it's done inspecting, you'll get a report, like in Figure 11.3. You can see in our example that there were Comments, Personal Information, and Custom XML Data found. Word's tool is reasonably primitive in two respects:

1. It's not going to show you the specifics of what it found. It just tells you it exists; that's all.
2. It doesn't let you selectively remove it. If you have Word remove Comments, for example, it's going to remove all of them. If you want to selectively remove some, you'll have to go back through the document yourself and delete just those Comments you don't want to retain.

FIGURE 11.3 What the Document Inspector Found

Configure Word to Warn You

If you use Track Changes a lot, then you might want to have Word warn you if you go to save or send a file that has tracked changes in it—if nothing else, it's a good reminder to run the built-in Metadata Inspector. To enable that, just go to **File** > **Options** > **Trust Center** and click **Trust Center Settings**. In the **Privacy Settings** group, halfway down the page you'll see what I have in Figure 11.4.

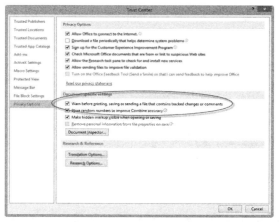

FIGURE 11.4 Be Warned If You Save or Send a File with Tracked Changes On

The very first option lets you turn on the warnings that you want, and I encourage you to enable it—again just to be on the safe side.

The third option is another one you'll want to enable—it makes sure that if you open a document that has tracked changes in it, the tracked

If you're collaborating on a document with others, you may not even realize that a document has Track Changes turned on. It's possible that somebody else has enabled Track Changes without your knowledge—or even theirs. Better safe than sorry.

changes are shown—even if you changed the **Display for Review** setting to **Final** the last time you worked on this document. It may seem like a nuisance, but it's a valuable reminder that the document has markup and tracked changes that you may need to deal with before passing it along.

The final option here, **Remove Personal Information from File Properties on Save**, will change the author, manager, and company names as well as dates and times associated with comments or tracked changes. That sounds really useful! But it's not available in Word 2013—it'll be grayed out unless you're working on a document that was created in an earlier version of Word and you had this option turned on in that earlier version of Word. Too bad.

Summary

Word seems like a pretty simple tool, but it's a powerful one as well. As any first semester law student can tell you, documents are a critical part of the practice of law, and the word processor is an important tool for the law firm. There are a number of mistakes that lawyers and staff can make with Word—some of them are merely efficiency issues, but others can be very serious. Leak the wrong Metadata to the wrong person, and the consequences could be as severe as disbarment. And that's really not the way to move your practice forward.

Tricks to Impress Your Law School Classmates | **12**

Word 2013 has a surprising number of great tricks that can be used to improve your productivity, and considering that law is such a document-intensive field, anything that helps improve your effectiveness in this product can directly translate into your practice. In this chapter we'll take a look at some of those nifty tricks you can use to get even more out of Word.

Mark as Final

Want to pass your document to somebody for review but want to discourage them from editing it? Mark it as Final. That will set the document to be Read-Only and marked for review only. Is it foolproof? No, not really. The other person can just click the Edit Anyway button that Word presents, but that's affirmatively defeating your clearly stated desire that the document be Final.

Mark as Final is just a handy way to flag a document so that others know that it *shouldn't* be edited any more. It doesn't prevent editing; there are other mechanisms for that if that's what you're after.

Note: I occasionally mark my own documents as Final as a reminder to myself that the document shouldn't need to be edited any further.

To mark a document as Final, go to **File** and click **Protect Document** on the **Information** page.

Restrict Editing

If you want to get a little more hardcore about it, you can Restrict Editing so that people can read or make limited changes to the document but have to enter a password to do more than that. Click **File** and on the **Information** page click **Protect Document** > **Restrict Editing**. You'll get the task pane you see in Figure 12.1. Set the permissions you want to grant and then click **Yes, Start Enforcing Protection**. Word will prompt you to **Enter a Password** (twice) that will be required to unlock the protections. Don't forget that password . . . you'll probably want it someday.

FIGURE 12.1 Restrict Editing

Encrypt Document

There may come times when you'll want to protect the content of your document—perhaps you're collaborating with co-counsel, and you want to control who can access your document and what they can do with it.

Encrypt with Password

If you just want to keep unauthorized eyes off the document, you can choose to encrypt the document with a password. Just go to **File** > **Protect Document** > **Encrypt with Password**. When you do that, Word will ask you to give the document a password or pass phrase. When somebody (including you) goes to open the document henceforth, they'll be asked to provide the password. Without it . . . no document.

Of course, if you're planning to share this document with somebody else, you'll need some way to safely get them the password. It's not really a good idea to e-mail them the document with the password in the e-mail. Anybody who intercepts the e-mail has the document and the password. Better to somehow get them the password through a different channel—phone call, face to face, SMS text message, perhaps? Or you just pick a password that has some shared meaning for both of you and give them a hint: *Name of the restaurant where we met.*

This is a good solution if you just want to protect the document at a basic level. Beyond that, though, once they're in the document, they're in. This method doesn't stop them from editing or printing or anything like that.

Digital Signatures

You can use a digital signature in much the same way you use a printed signature—to lend authenticity to your document. Digitally signing a document requires a digital certificate that verifies your identity. There are two basic classes of digital certificates:

1. **Third-Party Certificates.** These are certificates that you obtain from a trusted certificate authority like **Verisign**, **Thawte**, or others.
2. **Self-Signed Certificates.** These are certificates that you generate yourself.

The Self-Signed Certificate has several big advantages and only one real drawback. On the plus side, it's free, and you can generate one and use it immediately. You know who provided the certificate, you don't have to jump through many hoops to create one, you don't have to break out your credit card, and you can start to use your certificate right away. The only real downside is that it's almost useless.

Self-certifying a certificate is like letting people print their own driver's licenses. Without an independent authority, there's almost no way to confirm that a signature is authentic or that the sender is who they say they are. What stops me from creating a Self-Signed Certificate that claims that I'm you? Nothing.

The only thing self-signed digital signatures will do for you is confirm that the version of the document someone receives hasn't changed since it was signed. If a signed document is changed, the signature is invalidated. Of course, if somebody intercepts your document and changes it, there's nothing to stop them from *re*-signing your document with a forged digital signature. Again, if you're self-signing.

To do digital signatures correctly you need to get a real certificate from a third-party authority. It's not hard to do; when you go to sign your document digitally for the first time (**File** > **Protect Document** > **Add a Digital Signature**), you'll be offered a button that will take you to the **Office Marketplace** online where you can get a digital signature from one of a variety of digital signature providers. If you already have one, then you can just use that, of course.

Either way, if you're self-signing or using a third-party certificate, you'll get the **Sign** dialog box that you see in Figure 12.2. You have an optional field that asks for the reason you're choosing to sign the document, and you'll have a chance to choose which certificate (if you have more than one) to sign with. Assuming it's already signing with the certificate you want to use, you can just click the **Sign** button, and your digital signature will be affixed.

FIGURE 12.2 Digitally Signing Your Document

If you're using a third-party signature, then when you send this document to others and they open it in Word, Word will verify, in the background, that the signature is authentic by contacting the third-party provider—and yes, they will have to be connected to the Internet to do that verification. If you're using a Self-Signed Signature, then it will just tell them that there isn't any way to verify the signature.

Open Multiple Files

If you need to open two or more documents at once, you could open one, then open the next, and then open the next. Or . . . you could click **File** > **Open**, then hold down the **Control** key, and click on each of the documents you want to open. Once you have them all selected, let go of Control and click the Open button. All of the documents you selected will open in one step.

Note: the one catch is that all of the documents have to be in the same folder or library.

Collapse the Ribbon

One of the first comments folks have when they see the Ribbon is that it takes up a fair bit of screen real estate at the top of the screen. If you'd like to minimize it to give yourself more room to work, just right-click anywhere on the tab line and choose **Collapse the Ribbon**. To get it back . . . repeat that process. Alternatively you can double-click any of the Ribbon tab labels to collapse, and subsequently restore, the Ribbon.

Outlining

Outlines are a powerful way to create new documents (it's how I started this book for instance) as well as a handy way to organize your thoughts. Word is a very good **Outlining Tool**, even if you never take your outline all the way to a full document. Word is even smart enough to recognize an outline when you start one. Just type an *I* (like a roman numeral 1) followed by a period and then your first heading. Word will automatically jump into Outline Mode for the succeeding text.

Use **Tab** (and **Shift+Tab**) to move items up and down levels (left and right), or use your mouse to drag items up and down within your outline.

Generally I'll start with my major level items (*I.*, *II.*, etc.), then go back through and fill in the second-level items, then go back through and flesh those out with third- and fourth-level items and . . . next thing you know, I have a fairly detailed outline. From there, I can start writing the actual text to explain each of the items.

Word's **Outline View** is actually pretty nice and has some good outlining tools. If you're a hardcore outline user, you might want to give that a try. On the **View** tab of the **Ribbon**, click **Outline** to see your document in outline format.

As I mentioned in Chapter 7, I will often do my outlining in Microsoft OneNote and then send that nearly completed outline to Word to finish the document. If you haven't looked at OneNote yet, you really should check it out. Great stuff for lawyers; it does a lot more than just outlining and note taking.

AutoCorrect

AutoCorrect is great for correcting spelling errors but did you know you can also use it to speed up your typing? Create custom AutoCorrect entries that replace shorthand acronyms with full text. Great for firm names, people names, long titles of oft-referenced statutes, and so on. We talked about that a bit in Chapter 8 in the discussion of automating Word.

Navigation Pane

When you're creating a lengthy and extensive document, like a book on Microsoft Word 2013, for example, it can often be handy to be able to see all of your headings in the style of a Table of Contents, so that you can make sure that your content is complete and in a logical order (see Figure 12.3). The Navigation Pane shows you the headings in your document and provides for an easy way to navigate up and down in the document. This is especially important when your document is more than 200 pages long and your Page Up button is getting a bit worn down.

FIGURE 12.3 The Navigation Pane in Action

You can also use it to reorganize your content. Grab a header in the Navigation Pane and drag it up or down. Word will reorder your text accordingly. I've even used it to delete entire sections of text—just right-click the section on the Navigation Pane and select **Delete**.

Search

The Navigation Pane also includes a really good search capability. Click in the **Search Document** field at the top of the Navigation Pane and press

Enter. Word will find all of the instances of that search term, tell you how many there are, and give you a few of those search results, in context—as you see in Figure 12.4. Click any of the contextual results, and Word will take you to that place in the document and highlight your searched-for term in yellow.

FIGURE 12.4 Search Results in Context

The only bit of the Navigation Pane that I don't find wonderful is the Pages tab—which I think is moderately useless unless you're looking for something that you can't find with Search and that is plainly visible with the page four feet away.

Research Tools

Most people seem to think that the pinnacle of Word document creation assistance is the real-time Spell Checker that puts a red squiggly line under words it thinks you've misspelled. Actually Word offers a far richer set of tools than just that. If you're like me, you probably are used to having a dictionary and maybe a thesaurus close at hand when you work. You just may not have realized quite how close at hand. Select any word you've typed, right-click it and choose **Define**. The Research Pane will appear on the right side of your screen offering you dictionary, thesaurus, encyclopedia, and even a translator that will translate the word to and from about fourteen different languages (see Figure 12.5).

FIGURE 12.5 The Research Pane

Legal Research

The folks at **LexisNexis** have even gotten on the bandwagon. If you go to http://www.lexisnexis.com/msoffice, you get more information about their tool that connects to LexisNexis so you can Shepardize cases, access the LexisNexis Bookstore, and even LexisONE (if you're a LexisONE user).

> **Tip**
>
> Some of these features, like the Thesaurus, will work even when you're disconnected, but most of them will require you to be connected to the Internet.

Watermarks

One of those features that many users didn't realize Word has had for quite a while is the ability to add a watermark to your document. A watermark is a bit of text or image that is in the background, behind your text. It's a fairly subtle effect—subtle enough that I can't even screen capture it and have it look decent for this book. It can say or be just about anything you want, and it's a really handy way to mark a printed document with an indication of the document status—for instance *Draft* or *Confidential*, or *Client Copy*. To use the **Watermark** feature just go to the **Design** tab and click the **Watermark** tool (see Figure 12.6). You'll get the Watermark gallery, which has twelve sample watermarks you can use. If you don't like any of those, you can create your own by clicking the **Custom Watermark** command you see toward, the bottom of the gallery. Clicking that will get you the **Printed Watermark** dialog box that you see in Figure 12.7.

FIGURE 12.6 Inserting a Watermark

FIGURE 12.7 The Printed Watermark Dialog Box

In the Printed Watermark dialog box you can create a picture watermark by selecting that radio button, then selecting the image you want to use. Word will automatically scale the picture so that it aligns on the page properly, but you can customize that if you like.

If you don't want to use a picture watermark, you can type your own custom text, complete with custom layout, color, font, and everything. Watermarks can be a nice way to add a stylish and functional element to your printed or PDF'd documents.

Full Text Search

One of the big trends in desktop computing in recent years is the move toward powerful full text search engines. **Google Desktop**, **Copernic Desktop**, and, of course, **Windows Desktop Search** all let you index your workstation, server, and even external hard drives to make searching for files and documents faster and easier. If you're not using a Full Text

Search tool, you really should be. It can help you find documents and files, including documents and files you might not have thought about. The thing with full text search that makes it different from what you may be used to is that it searches the *content* of the document, not just the name. Any words or phrases you've got will be found. And the Full Text Search tool will not just search Word documents, but PowerPoint, Excel, Outlook e-mails . . . all sorts of documents.

Run a Full Text Search for a particular citation, and you may discover other documents in your document library that refer to it that you hadn't thought of. Doing conflict checks? How about a quick full text search on the name; who knows what you might discover?

Windows Desktop Search is built into Windows. Just hit the **Start** button and start typing in the search box and Windows Desktop Search will do the rest.

Note: If you're using Windows 8, you may have to click at the top of the Search Pane and change from **Everywhere** to **Files** to get the list of files containing your search term.

Redaction

Every now and then you may want to send out a document with parts of that document blacked out, to obscure particular facts the other party (or the public) shouldn't read. As you probably know that's called redaction, and there are a couple of ways to do that in Word.

First off, it once again comes back to knowing the medium in which your document is going to be transmitted. If it's going to be printed or sent as an image-only PDF file, then you could just select the text you want to redact and use the Highlighter tool in Word to redact those words you want hidden (see Figure 12.8) by highlighting the black text with black highlighter.

FIGURE 12.8 Using the Highlighter to Redact

That works fine if you're transmitting in a format where the end user can't access the actual document data. But you can't use that if you're going to be transmitting the document as a Word document—because the recipient could just turn off the highlighting. If you're PDFing the document as an *image* (not a searchable file), then all the recipient is going to get is a picture of the text and it will be obscured. If you're going to print the document, then the printer will just print your redactions and that will work OK.

There are some other creative ways to redact text but really . . . if it's text that needs to be redacted, then it's probably important that it be done right. If you go to http://www. codeplex.com/redaction, you can find the Word 2007/2010 Redaction tool. It's made by the team at Microsoft but not officially supported by Microsoft. Yes, I know . . . but it works in Word 2013 too.

When you install it—which can take quite a while, by the way, so be sure you don't wait until five minutes before the document is due—it adds a **Redact** group to the Review tab of the Ribbon as you see in Figure 12.9. To use the tool then you just go through your document marking text that you want redacted. When you've marked everything you want to redact, you can click the down arrow on the **Mark** button and have it redact the entire document. Figure 12.10 shows you that menu. The Redaction tool will then go thru your entire document and replace all marked text with black bars.

> As with any URL I give you in this book, I can only vouch for its accuracy as of this printing. The Internet is sort of like a river, you step in the river but the water has moved on. If you try one of the URLs I've posted and it doesn't work, then I would suggest Googling for the content . . . perhaps it has merely moved somewhere else.

FIGURE 12.9 The Redact Group on the Ribbon

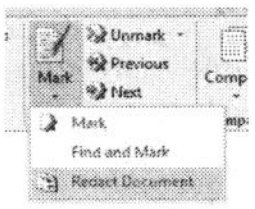

FIGURE 12.10 Redacting Text

CAUTION: *This can't be undone*. I strongly suggest that you save a copy of your document **un**redacted first, and then do your redaction. That way if it turns out that you inadvertently redacted something, you can go back to the pre-redaction copy. After you finish the redaction, the tool will suggest that you run Word's Metadata Inspector (remember Chapter 11?), which is a good idea.

One other thing you'll notice on the menu in Figure 12.10 is a **Find and Mark** command. That lets you search the document for all instances of a string (a client's name for example) and have all of those instances marked for redaction automatically . . . so you don't have to search it manually.

Publishing to Web

These days it's all about the web, of course. Microsoft Word has long been "capable" of generating web content, in that you could put together a basic web page and have it generate the HTML (HyperText Markup Language) for that page. Did it look OK? Sure. But there's a reason why professional web designers don't use Microsoft Word for that task. The HTML code it generates has been widely derided as being fairly sloppy. Still, if you just need a quick and simple page and Word is the tool that you're comfortable with . . . you can use it for that purpose. Just lay out your page, do a **File** > **Save As**, and choose **Web Page** to save your document in the right format. Upload it to your website and you've got a basic web document.

The more interesting new feature in Word, however, is the ability to use it as a blogging client. Blogging has really taken off in the last year or two not only as a way to get information but also as a marketing tool for lawyers. More lawyers have blogs today than ever before. Word is a powerful tool for creating text, so there's no reason why you shouldn't use it to author your blogs as well.

To get started, go ahead and create your first article. Go to **File**, click **New**, and one of the templates on the New Document dialog box is **Blog Post**.

The first time you select that template you will have to register your Blog with Word . . . which is to say tell Word where and how to send the content. You'll be prompted to register your blog, as in Figure 12.11. Click the down arrow next to **Blog** and choose your blog provider. Chances are pretty good that it's one of the ones listed there, but if it's not you may still have some hope.

Select your blog provider from the list and click **Next**. Word will then lead you though a short wizard that asks you to give it the URL, username (if applicable), and password for posting to your blog. Depending on your

FIGURE 12.11 Registering Your Blog with Word

provider, it may ask you for one or two other bits of information, or instruct you about one or two minor adjustments you have to make in your blog configuration (such as configuring **Live Spaces** to accept **Email Publishing**).

Once you have it set up though, posting new entries is as simple as starting a new Blog Post (**File** > **New** > **Blog Post**) and publishing it to your Blog (**File** > **Share** > **Post to Blog**).

▼

The best blogs are the ones that are updated regularly. If you only post to your blog a couple of times a year, then you won't get many readers. Try to post at least once a week. Consider repurposing some of your other writings for your blog—maybe that great article you wrote for the local bar journal three years ago could be updated and posted as a blog entry? Or maybe it could be broken up and posted as a series of blog entries?

Speech Recognition

For years lawyers have been asking for a good speech recognition application, and many lawyers have spent a lot of money over the years trying various products with varying degrees of success. Windows offers a free built-in speech recognition module that's really pretty good. In **Vista** it's called **Vista Voice** (you may find it in the **Programs** list as **Windows Speech Recognition**). In later versions of Windows, it's got the less fanciful (or at least less alliterative) moniker of Windows Speech Recognition. Can you use it to dictate text into Word 2013? Well I'm dictating this sentence right here. Is it perfect? No. But it's good. Really, I think it's better for voice control of your system. I can be working away and suddenly realize that I want to switch to another program on my system. I can just say, "Switch to Inbox," and Outlook pops up with my Inbox displayed.

It's just another way to interact with your system but I think it's worth a shot.

▼▼▼▼▼

TIP #1: Get a good headset if you're going to give it a try.

TIP #2: Like all speech recognition, it works best in a quiet environment. If you have the TV on in the background, you're likely to get a phrase like "Next week on *The Real Housewives of New Jersey* . . . " in the middle of your brief. And you really don't want to have to admit to that. Any background noise can affect the accuracy of speech recognition though, so if your neighbor is having fun with the leaf blower or your office is *right* next to the copier . . . you may not have that much success with speech recognition.

Calculate

One of the most surprising features of Microsoft Word 2013 is a feature most people have no idea even exists: **Calculate**. I'm not talking about your run-of-the-mill, add-a-column kind of calculate. That's just so 1993. I'm talking about calculating with numbers in sentence format. Yes, it's a little primitive, but it's still pretty cool.

To use it, first you have to configure access to it. This feature isn't on any of the Ribbon tabs, so you'll need to add it to the QAT. To do that, click the drop-down arrow to the right of the QAT and click **More Commands**. Set the list of commands on the left side to **All Commands**, and scroll down that list to find **Calculate**. Click **Add** and then **OK** to close the customize dialog. You'll now see a curious green sphere on your QAT—that's the button for Calculate.

So, now that you can access it, what can you do with it? Type a sentence that has some numbers in it, such as "Carrie has 5 apples and Emily has 3." Then click the Calculate button. Nothing happened? Look at the Status Bar at the bottom left. This feature is still fairly primitive and it tends to prefer addition, but if you use symbols such as 32,213-11,235, that will work for subtraction and other basic mathematical functions too.

Fancy Replacements

The Replace tool from the Editing group of the Home tab can do more than replace *Jerry* with *Gerry*. It can actually be used to make some more sophisticated replacements—of font elements, for example. Maybe you mistakenly used superscript throughout your document and you meant it to be subscript.

Click **Replace** and then the **Format** button. Choose **Font** from the list that appears and you'll get a dialog box that looks like Figure 12.12. Select

FIGURE 12.12 Replacing Font Elements

Superscript. Then click the **Replace With** field and go back to **Format** > **Font**. Select **Subscript**. Click **OK** and have it replace all.

Of course . . . it would have saved you the hassle if you'd just applied that superscript with a style like I told you to in Chapter 4. Then you'd just have to change the style from superscript to subscript and it would have been instantly fixed throughout the document. But some lessons have to be learned the hard way.

Collapsible Headings

One of the other nifty new features of Word 2013 is the ability to collapse headings. You might do this if you're writing a fairly extensive document and you find it a little overwhelming to have all of the sections displayed at once. You can collapse bits you're not actually working on right now to keep the view a bit tidier. If you've applied a heading, such as Heading 2 for example, and then created text beneath that heading, you can collapse that entire block (see Figure 12.13). Simply move your mouse to the left of the heading and click the arrow that appears. Click it again to re-expand.

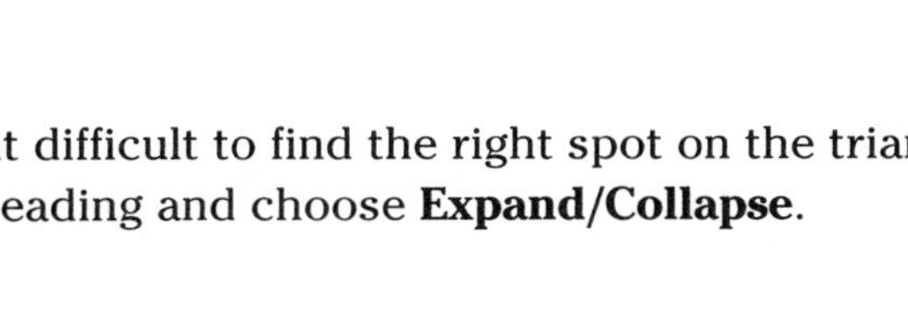

Collapsible Headings

Summary

Like any powerful program Word 2013 has a lot of potential for tricks to improve its utility and

efficiency. Heck, I have to admit at one point I had about 25 different sections in this chapter and I finally

had to whittle it down a bit (though some of those tips found their ways into other chapters of the

book).

FIGURE 12.13 Collapsed Headings

If you find it difficult to find the right spot on the triangle, you can right-click the heading and choose **Expand/Collapse**.

Summary

Like any powerful program, Word 2013 has a lot of potential for tricks to improve its utility and efficiency. Heck, I have to admit at one point I had about twenty-five different sections in this chapter, and I finally had to whittle it down a bit (though some of those tips found their ways into other chapters of the book).

Some of the tricks, like minimizing the Ribbon, using Speech Recognition, or using the Navigation Pane, are ways to make Word a more productive environment to work in. Others, like encryption or web publishing, are about new ways to produce content that you might not have thought of before.

Getting the most out of Word requires constantly learning—we've barely scratched the surface of what Word is capable of so far.

Keyboard Shortcuts

13

Like most of Office 2013, Word has a number of great and useful keyboard shortcuts that can really help the fast typist who resents having to use the mouse to get things done.

One important thing to remember is that, despite the Ribbon interface, the keyboard shortcuts that you learned for Word 2003 are still going to work in Word 2013. They may *look* a bit different, but they're still there.

Almost all of the commands on the Ribbon can be accessed via keyboard shortcuts; it's just that many of them are actually a sequence of keystrokes as opposed to a Hotkey.

To see the keyboard shortcuts to activate a command on the Ribbon, just press (and release) the **Alt** key.

In Figure 13.1, you can see that pressing the **F** will activate the File menu, pressing numbers **1** through **6** will activate the corresponding shortcut on the Quick Access Toolbar, and you can see

> A Hotkey is a single key or a combination of keys pressed at once to activate a command or feature. **Windows Key+S** is a Hotkey as opposed to a sequence of keys like **Windows Key, S,** which means to press and release the **Windows Key** and then press and release the **S** key. If you see me type the plus sign (+), that means press this key *and* that key at the same time by pressing the first key and holding it down while you press the next key. If I type a comma, that means press and release the first key, and then press the next key.

FIGURE 13.1 The File Menu Activates When Alt and then F Are Pressed

the letters that correspond to the tabs on the Ribbon. Pressing the **H** key to activate the Home tab gives you Figure 13.2.

FIGURE 13.2 Activate the Home Tab by Pressing Alt and Then H

If we were to press **Alt**, followed by **H** (to activate Home), and then the number **5,** that would set the font of the selected text to Subscript. Pressing **Alt**, **H**, **7** activates the Change Case feature. **Alt**, **H**, **A**, **R** sets the alignment of the current paragraph to the right. And so forth . . .

Hotkeys in Office are almost always either Function Keys (**F1** to **F12**) or combination keys where you press and hold the **Shift**, **Alt**, and/or **Control** (Control) keys in combination with one or more Function Keys or letter keys.

For example: pressing **F4** will repeat the last action. Need to type *I have no recollection of that a t all, Senator* over and over again? Just type it once, and then press **F4** as many times as you need to.

Pressing and holding the **Control+Alt+F1** (then you can let go of all of them) will launch a very handy tool most users never realized was there . . . **System Information**.

The two previous examples are both Hotkeys. The first keyboard sequence I'm going to teach you here is to press **F1** to launch the **Help** system, and then type **Keyboard Shortcuts** in the search window. That will get you a list of articles and resources on the subject right on your own screen, and you can readily find any shortcut in the program that way. In this chapter, I'm going to give you a few tricks to using keyboard shortcuts and highlight my favorite keyboard shortcuts and how you might use them. A full list of shortcuts would just be cheating on my page count, and since I don't get paid by the page, I think I'll just be a little green here and not waste the paper with a simple list of shortcuts you can readily get elsewhere.

Navigating and Managing Word

First of all, there are a few good shortcuts for getting around in Word that you may like. I juggle dual monitors in the course of my work, and for that reason, I frequently find myself minimizing and maximizing windows, so that I can move them around my screens and then work with them.

Alt+Tab is a well-known keyboard shortcut that isn't really a Word shortcut but rather a Windows shortcut that launches the Task Switcher. It can be a quick way to switch between running programs, including multiple Microsoft Word instances. Hold down **Alt**, and then press **Tab**. As long as you hold down the **Alt** key, the list of applications will be displayed on screen as a set of icons or thumbnails. Each time you press **Tab**, the focus will change to the next application on the list (clockwise). Let go of **Alt**, and Windows will switch system focus to that application (in other words, put it in the foreground so you can work with it). **Alt+Shift+Tab** does the same thing, but goes counterclockwise through the list. As long as you don't let go of the **Alt** key, the list will stay up, so if you're a little dexterous, you can go back and forth between **Alt+Tab** and **Alt+Shift+Tab** to move back and forth through the list without having to start over.

Windows 7 and 8 have a feature called **Snap**, which lets you dock your windows to the left or right side of the screen. This is pretty handy, especially with the newer wide-screen monitors, if you want to see two windows side by side. To snap a window to one side of the screen or the other, just select that window and press **Windows Key+←** or **Windows Key+→** to snap to either the left or right sides of the screen, respectively.

If you have multiple monitors, pressing **Windows Key+←** (or →) repeatedly will step the window across the screens. For example: if you have a Word document open on the right-hand monitor and you press **Windows Key+←**, the document will snap to the left side of the right-hand monitor. Press that combo again and it will snap to the right side of the left-hand monitor. Press it one more time and it will snap to the left side of the left-hand monitor.

These keyboard shortcuts for snap are handy because it can be tricky to snap a window to the side of multiple monitors.

If you want to close your current Word window, you can press **Control+W** or **Control+F4**. This is one of those curious instances where the same command can be accessed from two different key combinations.

Don't worry about hitting those keys accidentally and losing all of your data; if you press those keys while you have unsaved changes in your document, Word will pop up a dialog box prompting you to **Save**, **Discard**, or **Cancel** like you see in Figure 13.3.

It's handy to know what keyboard combinations are duplicates because it gives you an idea of a key combo you can remap to some other function if you want or need to. We talked about customizing the keyboard and third-party applications like AutoHotKey in Chapter 8.

FIGURE 13.3 Do You Want to Save This File?

If you accidentally hit the key combo for **Close**, just click **Cancel**, and Word will return you to your document without any ill effects.

You can quickly minimize or maximize the current Word window just by pressing **Alt+F5** (to window it) or **Control+F10** (to maximize it). **Windows Key+↑** also maximizes the current window. **Windows Key+↓** windows it again.

You probably already know that you can copy a picture of the screen to the Windows clipboard by pressing **Print Screen** (**PRTSCN** on many keyboards), but I'm going to show you two better ways to do it . . .

1. You usually don't want the *entire* screen, but rather a selected part of it. To capture just the active window to the clipboard, press **Alt+Print Screen**. That will crop off all of the other stuff on the screen and only grab the active window.

2. If you have Microsoft OneNote installed (and if you have Office 2013, you do), it has a terrific screen grab tool in it. Just press **Windows Key+S** (**Windows Key+Shift+S** in Windows 8.1), and you can select any part of your screen to copy to the clipboard, as big or small as you want. There are other third-party utilities that can do this as well, like **SnagIt**, but OneNote is one of the best I've seen.

Word 2013 has a built-in **Screenshot** feature as well, but in my experience it's a little flakey. You'll find it on the **Insert** menu in the **Illustrations** group if you want to try it out.

If you want to open an existing document, you can get to the **File > Open** dialog box by pressing **Control+F12** or **Control+O**. For a fast typist this is a lot faster than mousing up to **File**, clicking that, then choosing **Open** or pressing **Alt**, followed by **F**, followed by **O**. **Control+F12** has the added bonus of skipping the Backstage step.

If you want to create a new document, **Control+N** gets you started on that.

Pressing **F12** will display the Save As dialog box. That, along with **Control+S** to Save, is a Hotkey you definitely want to know about.

For printing documents, **Control+P** launches the print dialog. **Alt+Control+I** used to just give you a print preview of the current document—handy for seeing what you're going to get before you use the paper—but now it just does the same thing as **Control+P** . . . since Print Preview is built into the Print dialog box.

Control+Left Arrow or Control+Right Arrow will move you one word left or right. **Control+Up** or **Control+Down** moves one paragraph up or down. **Control+Home** or **Control+End** will take you to the beginning or the end of the document. **Home** and **End** go to the beginning or end of the current line. Use the **Shift** key in conjunction with any of those to select those things. **F8** is a handy tool for selecting as well. Pressing it twice selects a word, three times selects the current sentence, four times selects the current paragraph, and five times selects the entire document. (Easier to press **Control+A** to select the whole document, I think.)

Speaking of selecting—this is actually a mouse trick—if you click once, you put your cursor on that spot to type. If you click twice, you select that word. Click three times to select the entire paragraph. Didn't see "select the sentence" in there, did you? **Control+Click** does that.

▼▼▼▼▼
The Coolest Feature That Works AGAIN!

One of the niftier Word shortcut keys is one that was sort of broken in recent versions: **Shift+F5**. It returns you to the last place in the document you edited. In fact, it will step you back through the last three edit points if you continue pressing it. (Pressing it a fourth time will return you to where you started this exercise.) Unfortunately in Word 2007, that functionality was broken. So, while you could still use **Shift+F5** within an open document to go back to recent edit points, you couldn't use it on a freshly opened document to pick up where you left off. That bug was fixed in Word 2010!

BONUS TIP: If you occasionally find yourself accidentally skipping to another part of the document (as I occasionally do when I brush the wrong key on the keyboard), **Shift+F5** is an easy way to navigate back to where you were a moment ago.

The **F5** key will launch the GOTO dialog box—which you can then use to navigate to just about anywhere in the document. Handy if you want to go to a specific page number; or if you want to advance a certain number of pages. One feature of GOTO I also want to call to your attention (you have to scroll down to find it) is the **Table Option**. If you press **F5** and then pick **Table** in the left-hand pane, you can have Word automatically take you to the next Table in the document. Handy if you have quite a few, and you want to step from one to the next.

The last operational Hotkey I want to bring to your attention is one you may find yourself using a lot: **Control+Z**. Undo. It will undo whatever your last action was, at least within some reason. If you deleted some text and didn't mean to, **Control+Z** is your hero. If you lent your car to a teenager, though, **Control+Z** doesn't really help.

Working with Text

There are several Hotkeys available for setting the format of your text. Some of them you may be familiar with already, like **Control+B** to turn on boldface, **Control+I** for italics, or **Control+U** to underline. Others may be a pleasant surprise. Did you know that **Control+Shift+C** will copy the formatting from a piece of text and **Control+Shift+V** will paste it? Yes, just like the Format Painter. Of course, don't let the giddiness of these Hotkeys shake your resolve to make better use of Styles instead of Direct Formatting . . .

Maybe you need to select all of your text before applying (or removing) a particular bit of formatting. **Control+A** is your shortcut for that.

Want to increase the font size of your text? **Control+Shift+>** is the answer. (That's a "greater than" sign, probably on the same button with the period on your keyboard.) **Control+Shift+<** reduces the font size of the selected text. The increments are the same as the increments in the font size drop-down menu (12, 14, 16 . . . 28, 36, 48 . . .). Or you can go point by point . . . **Control+]** increases the font size by 1 point while **Control+[** reduces it by 1 point.

In Chapter 4, we talked about Direct and Indirect Formatting. There may be times when you want to strip the Direct Formatting off of a paragraph in an effort to clean it up or troubleshoot an issue. To reset the formatting to the underlying style, just select the affected paragraph and press **Control+Spacebar** to remove the Character Formatting. **Control+Q** removes any Paragraph Formatting. **Control+Shift+N** returns the current selection back to the Normal style.

Sometimes when I'm typing I create a section title but forget to capitalize the first letter of each word. Or maybe I was typing too fast to notice that I accidentally activated my **Caps Lock Key** for the last sentence. Either way, I may want to quickly change the case of my text. To do so I need only select the text, then press **Shift+F3** in order to toggle between the different Case settings in Word.

While I'm creating that section title, I almost always want to assign a heading style to it. **Control+Alt+1** will assign Heading 1 style. **Control+Alt+2** will assign Heading 2, and so forth. If I want to adjust after I've assigned the heading style, then **Control+Shift+Left Arrow** and **Control+Shift+Right Arrow** will promote or demote through the heading styles.

Summary

Fast typists often find the keyboard to be preferable to the mouse. Taking your hands off the keyboard to use the mouse can slow you down and break your train of thought. Learn the keyboard shortcuts for the five or ten most common commands you use, and you may find that you save quite a bit of time over the course of your day. Not to mention the value of a regular **Control+S**. There, I just pressed it again myself! Note that I've barely scratched the surface of what you can do with a keyboard in Microsoft Word in this chapter. Use the Help files and online resources, and you'll probably find a keyboard shortcut to do nearly anything you want.

Index